T5-CQH-809

AUGUSTINE

FROM RHETOR TO THEOLOGIAN

JOANNE MCWILLIAM, EDITOR

IN COLLABORATION WITH
TIMOTHY BARNES, MICHAEL FAHEY, AND PETER SLATER

Wilfrid Laurier University Press

WLU

CANADIAN CATALOGUING IN PUBLICATION DATA

Main entry under title:

Augustine : from rhetor to theologian

Includes bibliographical references.
ISBN 0-88920-203-6

1. Augustine, Saint, Bishop of Hippo. 2. Christian saints – Biography. 3. Theology, Doctrinal-History – Early church, ca. 30-600. I. McWilliam, Joanne, 1928-

BR65.A9A8 1992 230′.14 C91-094655-8

WILFRID LAURIER UNIVERSITY PRESS
Waterloo, Ontario, Canada N2L 3C5

Cover design by Connolly Design Inc.
after a likeness of Augustine on a fresco
of the Lateran Palace in Rome

Printed in Canada

CONTENTS

CONTRIBUTORS

William S. Babcock
Associate Professor of Church History
Perkins School of Theology
Southern Methodist University
Dallas, Texas, USA

T.D. Barnes
Professor of Classics
University of Toronto
Toronto, Ontario

J. Patout Burns
Thomas and Alberta White Professor of Christian Thought
Department of Classics
Washington University
St. Louis, Missouri, USA

Robert D. Crouse
Professor of Classics
Dalhousie and King's Universities
Halifax, Nova Scotia

Michael A. Fahey, S.J.
Professor of Theology
University of St. Michael's College
Toronto, Ontario

Leo C. Ferrari
Professor of Philosophy
Saint Thomas University
Fredericton, New Brunswick

Thomas Halton
Professor of Greek and Latin
Catholic University of America
Washington, DC, USA

Joanne McWilliam
Professor of Religious Studies
University of Toronto
Toronto, Ontario

J.J. O'Meara
Professor Emeritus
School of Classics
University of Dublin

Jamie S. Scott
Associate Professor of Humanities / Religious Studies
York University
Toronto, Ontario

C. Peter Slater
Professor of Divinity
Trinity College
Toronto, Ontario

Colin J. Starnes
Associate Professor of Classics
Dalhousie and King's Universities
Halifax, Nova Scotia

Kenneth B. Steinhauser
Associate Professor of Theological Studies
Saint Louis University
Saint Louis, Missouri, USA

Roland S. Teske, S.J.
Professor of Philosophy
Marquette University
Milwaukee, Wisconsin, USA

James Wetzel
Assistant Professor of Philosophy and Religion
Colgate University
Hamilton, New York, USA

ABBREVIATIONS

AUGUSTINE'S WRITINGS

Ad. Simp.	Ad Simplicianum
Agon.	De agone
Ann. Job	Annotationes in Job
Bapt.	De baptismo
Beat. vita	De beata vita
Civ. Dei	De civitate Dei
Con. Acad.	Contra Academicos
Con. Cres.	Contra Cresconium
Con. ep. Parm.	Contra epistulum Parmeniani
Con. Faust.	Contra Faustum
Con. Fort.	Contra Fortunatum
Cont. fund.	Contra epistulam quam vocant fundamenti
Con. litt. Pet.	Contra litteras Petiliani
Conf.	Confessiones
Doct.	De doctrina Christiana
Don. pers.	De dono perseverantiae
En.	Ennead
Enn. Ps.	Enarrationes in Psalmos
Ep.	Epistula
Ep. cath.	Epistula ad catholicos de secta Donatistarum
Exp. ep. Gal.	Expositio epistulae ad Galatas
Gen. litt.	De Genesi ad litteram
Lib. arb.	De libero arbitrio
Mend.	De mendacio
Mor. ecc.	De moribus ecclesiae catholicae et Manichaeorum I
Mor. Man.	De moribus ecclesiae catholicae et Manichaeorum II

Mus.	De musica
Nat. bon.	De natura boni
Nat. grat.	De natura et gratia
Praed.	De praedestinatione sanctorum
Qu. Ev.	Quaestiones Evangelicum
Ret.	Retractationes
Serm.	Sermones
Spir. litt.	De spiritu et littera
Tract.	Tractatus in Ioannis Evangelium
Trin.	De Trinitate
Util. cred.	De utilitate credendi
Vera rel.	De vera religione

OTHER

BA	Bibliothèque augustinienne
CCLS	Corpus Christianorum Latina
CSEL	Corpus Scriptorum Ecclesiasticorum Latinorum
ILS	H. Dessan. Inscriptiones Latinae Selectae
PIR	E. Groag, A. Stein and L. Peterson. Prosopographia Imperii Romani.
PL	Patrologia latina
PLRE	A.H.M. Jones, J. Martindale and J. Morris. The Prosopography of the Later Roman Empire

INTRODUCTION

The occasion for these papers was a conference held at Trinity College, Toronto, to celebrate the 1600th anniversary of the conversion to Catholic Christianity of Augustine of Hippo. The conference was both international in character and illustrated the growing strength of Canadian Augustinian scholarship. Thirty-one papers were read; of these twelve were by Canadians, the others by persons from Eire, France, Germany, Italy, the Netherlands, the United Kingdom, and the United States. Fifteen of those papers make up the present volume.

"Conversion," a phenomenon common to all major religions, is interesting in itself, and when the convert is of the stature of Augustine, momentous in its consequences. Augustine is one of a handful of converts (Paul, Origen, Luther) whose interpretations of the Christianity they espoused significantly shaped that tradition. He set his stamp on the Latin Church, yet only in this century of profound, even paradigmatic change have the descendants of that church – Anglican, Reformed, Roman Catholic – recognized the degree to which their inbred attitudes and theological positions are "Augustinian." It is, however, another measure of the importance of Augustine that many aspects of his life and meanings of his writings are still disputed. This continuing investigation and debate is evidenced in this volume.

Of the contributors, some are historians, some theologians, some bridge disciplines. Historian T.D. Barnes examines the possibility that Augustine's patron, Symmachus, was related to Ambrose, perhaps even his first cousin. Such a relationship would explain the tone of the confrontation between the two in 384 over the Altar of Victory. Barnes describes Symmachus's letters as formal, "verging on the querulous," yet presupposing "some tie of kinship or amity." Barnes speculates further that, rather than Augustine going to Milan as Symmachus's protégé, he was chosen "precisely because he was not a protégé," because Ambrose, "in an ambiguous political situation" after the Altar of Victory affair, "wished to preserve his distance from the court of Valentinian." If this were so, it was not Augustine's court appointment, but his conversion, "which brought [him] rapid social mobility in a Christian society."

The *Confessions,* the book in which Augustine reflects self-consciously on his conversion, still provokes controversy, and five of the contributors deal with that work directly. Some turn to its structure. Kenneth Steinhauser takes up and extends the question of unity and completeness, putting forward arguments in favour of both, based on the recognized criteria of external comparison (Augustine's own outlines in the *Retractions*), biographical context (his lifelong concern with aesthetics, which finds its goal in the divine beauty), and internal coherence (his search for identity, fulfilled in "Cognoscam te, cognitor meus, cognoscam, sicut cognitus sum"). While the *Confessions* are usually seen as "original and originary," Jamie Scott demonstrates that Augustine also had a rich inheritance upon which to draw. In an extended examination, he brings together the several meanings of *confessio* (juridical, liturgical, cultic) to present Augustine's work as "a literary self-sacrifice." In his analysis, books ten to thirteen (often seen as a poorly integrated afterthought) provide the context for this self-sacrifice – "the aetiology and implied eschatology of Genesis." Colin Starnes more particularly examines the reason for the inclusion of book nine, concluding that it is the literary expression of Augustine's recently acquired appreciation of "the objective requirements of the process of becoming Christian." Monica, in her faith and her temptations, in her vision of God and her need for grace, is the exemplar of that process.

Can there be anything left to say about the nature of Augustine's conversion in 386 and the relation of his Christian faith to his Neoplatonic philosophy? Starnes touches on this question as well, convinced that Augustine converted in 386 to a Christianity "absolutely distinguished from Platonism" because his "submission to Christ" replaced his confidence in an intellectual knowledge of God. But Roland Teske sees Augustine's view of Platonism as less an alternative to Christianity than a more privileged avenue within it. Augustine's Platonists (and the group, Teske argues, includes Paul and even Christ himself) are the "spirituals" in the church, but beyond that "able to conceive a spiritual substance, capable of intellectual knowledge of incorporeal realities."

The description in the *Confessions* of Augustine's conversion is, as always, a point of interest, and two of the essays examine again the historical facticity of that work. J.J. O'Meara suggests that Pierre Courcelle's important recognition of "elements of fiction" in the *Confessions* should be extended to see the work not as autobiographical, but as an example of the genre of the *vita* (or, more accurately, *vitae*), a tale with a moral. Augustine was concerned with states of soul (his own, Monica's, Alypius's) which can be described only "in terms of a subjective internal perception," and lack of strict historicity is not convertible to "untruth." Augustine, O'Meara continues, distanced himself from his text; its meaning was not necessarily what the author intended, but other meanings could be found with the help of the Holy Spirit. Today's increasingly sophisticated hermeneutical approach, which precludes a simple "yes" or "no" to the question, is illustrated again in Leo Ferrari's suggestion that the whole work, including the conversion scene, was written to be read aloud, "as a script for a dramatic performance."

Augustine, of course, left his powerful legacy to the medieval world, and R.D. Crouse, dealing with the influence of Augustine's "conversion of Platonic thought," focusses on its interpretation and development in Boethius and Eriugena. Because of the rapprochement of Augustinian and pagan Platonism (which also gives importance to "conversion"), it is difficult to evaluate "the relative weights of those influences," but Crouse maintains that Boethius, in the *Tractates,* was "explicitly Christian and Augustinian" and that Eriugena, too, was "fundamentally Augustinian." In both, he sees an interpretation, which is also development, consistent with Augustine's own development.

Athough the *Confessions* is the most widely read of Augustine's works, his theological influence flows from the treatises written in the contexts of controversy. The classic questions of evil, free will, and grace are not neglected in these essays. James Wetzel expresses the puzzlement of many over the importance Augustine gives to *Ad Simplicianum;* is it only "creative reinterpretation"? Not entirely. *Ad Simplicianum,* in moving away from Augustine's earlier notion of divine foreknowledge of the acceptance or rejection of grace, provides a significantly different interpretation of the divine gift and establishes "divine sovereignty over the human will." Wetzel suggests that Augustine's increasing emphasis on inward transformation in his anti-Pelagian theology of grace has less to do with how he understands God to dispense grace "than with how human beings are understood to receive it." The treatise of 396 does not stress the inward character of the working of grace (as does *De Spiritu et Littera,* with which Wetzel compares it), but it does mark an important shift in Augustine's thinking, and his recognition of that shift was "the hindsight of a genius [showing] us where his foresight had begun."

William Babcock looks at the coin from the other side. In *De Civitate Dei* it is clear that Augustine sees the evil will preceding the evil deed, in both angels and human persons, but how does the will become evil? He rejects any external force, any social pressure. There can be no efficient cause of the *first* evil will; it has its origin instead in a deficiency, an absence of divine activity. We are left with "the inexplicable mystery of a God who gives and withholds aid without apparent regard for consideration of justice," and the moral responsibility of the agent remains obscure.

Babcock notes that it is only this privative understanding of the origin of evil which keeps Augustine from Manichaeism, and Peter Slater concurs, pointing out that it was Augustine's conviction that God cannot be "compromised" that recommended this answer to him. The concept of evil as the absence of good is matched by that of an ascending order of good, but Slater argues that in *De Civitate Dei,* book nineteen, Augustine went beyond this notion of goodness as order to that of goodness as harmony of wills. Right willing is when individual persons and societies are at peace within themselves and with each other. If Augustine's notion of harmony had gone beyond that of proper order to a more dynamic understanding which sees humankind as able "to plan, experiment and become partner in the work of creation," his Christ, too, might have been the "transformer of culture."

J. Patout Burns turns to the Donatist controversy and traces the shift in Augustine's understanding of the relationship between the work of Christ and that of the Spirit in baptism. Augustine's well-known position is that it is Christ who, through the minister, confers the consecration of baptism, but, Burns points out, it is the Holy Spirit, through charity, who gives forgiveness of sins. Charity, in Augustine's thought (following Cyprian) is found only in ecclesial unity, and so, parallelling the human minister in the consecration, the unified church becomes the "middle term" in the forgiveness of sins.

Although all the papers reflect and depend on the strides made in Augustinian scholarship in the twentieth century, three focussed specifically on this topic. Michael Fahey, dealing with studies of Augustine's ecclesiology from 1861 to 1979, lauds the shift away from searching the writings in order to consecrate "one's contemporary confessional preoccupations" to serious textual study. He mentions as particularly significant Hofman's parallelling in 1933 of Augustine's spiritual development and his understanding of the church, Lamirande's three books (1963, 1969, 1973) which stress the pluralism and complexity of his thought on this subject, and Borgomeo's rich citations and insights (1972). Fahey concludes by stressing the importance to Augustine of the community of churches, particularly the North African community (evidenced in the eleven councils between 393 and 407). Joanne McWilliam, surveying the writing on Augustine's christology since the beginning of the century, offers reasons for its relative meagreness and lack of critical acuity. She argues that Augustine's christology was "occasional," developed in the context of other concerns, and not thought through as a piece. And finally, Thomas Halton gives an overview of English translations of Augustine's works, with a compendium that should prove invaluable to the reader.

All those who planned and attended the conference are greatly indebted to Kelley McCarthy-Spoerl, who took care of the myriad of organizational details with efficiency and graciousness. The Social Sciences and Humanities Research Council of Canada, the Toronto School of Theology, and Trinity College helped to fund the conference, and the editors and contributors wish to express their thanks to all three institutions. I also wish to thank my associate editors – Timothy Barnes, Michael Fahey, and Peter Slater – and the readers for Wilfrid Laurier University Press for working with me in selecting and preparing the conference papers for publication.

AUGUSTINE, SYMMACHUS, AND AMBROSE

T.D. BARNES

After teaching rhetoric in Carthage for several years, Augustine left Africa in 383, at the age of twenty-nine, and went to Rome. There he lodged with a Manichaean "hearer" and made the acquaintance of other Manichees in the city. He began to teach rhetoric in Rome and had completed the school year 383/4 when an imperial order came that the *praefectus urbi* Symmachus send someone to Milan to hold the official chair of rhetoric in that city. Augustine offered himself as a candidate through his Manichaean friends: Symmachus tested his skills in impromptu declamation and chose him. Augustine then went to Milan – and to Ambrose.[1]

The next three years (384-387) were the most momentous in the whole of Augustine's life and have been much studied from many different perspectives.[2] The present brief paper does not set out to describe yet again the turbulent political background to the conversion of Augustine, to investigate its precise intellectual context, or to follow Augustine's mental, moral, and spiritual development. It merely examines one aspect of the relationship between the young African rhetor, the *praefectus urbi* at Rome, and the bishop of Milan – for it is not always realized that Symmachus and Ambrose may have been first cousins.

The father of Ambrose the bishop was Ambrosius, praetorian prefect in Gaul at the time of his son's birth, i.e., in 339.[3] Since Ambrosius died soon after his son was born, it is an attractive conjecture that he perished in 340 when, as praetorian prefect of the emperor Constantinus, he would have accompanied his imperial master on his ill-fated invasion of Italy.[4] On the prevailing contemporary definition of *nobilis* as the descendant of prefects and consuls, therefore, Ambrose was a man of noble birth.[5] But his father was not the first holder of high office in the family. Ambrose observes that his sister Marcellina must have been inspired to her life of virginity by her ancestor Soteris, who endured martyrdom without flinching.[6] Presumably, Soteris was tortured and executed in the Diocletianic persecution.[7] Moreover, what Ambrose says about Soteris in his *Exhortatio Virginitatis* assumes that his forbears attained nobility through office-holding before the fourth century: "*nobilis virgo maiorum prosapia consulatus et praefecturas parentum sacra posthabuit fide, et immolare iussa non acquievit.*"[8]

These implied consuls and prefects of the third century cannot be identified with any confidence. Consideration should go, however, to the Marcellinus who was ordinary consul with Aurelian in 275. Nothing else is known for certain about him, but the consul has been attractively identified both with the Marcellinus whom Aurelian left in charge of the eastern frontier in 272 and also with the Aurelius Marcellinus attested as *dux ducenarius* at Verona in 265.[9] If the double identification is correct, then this Marcellinus made his family both senatorial and noble.

Ambrose discloses, though only on one occasion in his voluminous writings, that he was related to Symmachus. In the funeral lament for his brother he refers to Satyrus's insistence on coming to Milan despite the danger of a barbarian invasion: "*cum a viro nobili revocareris, Symmacho tuo parente, quod ardere bello Italia diceretur, quod in periculum tenderes, quod in hostem incurreres, respondisti hanc ipsam tibi causam esse veniendi, ne nostro deesses periculo, ut consortem te fraterni discriminis exhiberes.*"[10] In Ambrose's mouth, the term *tuus parens* used of another should imply kinship, not merely benevolent protection by an older friend, as the bare *parens* or the phrase *parens meus* so often does in writers of the late fourth century.[11] Ambrose and Satyrus, therefore, were related to the noble Symmachus. But to which Symmachus, the orator or his father? In theory, the Symmachus whom Ambrose names here could be either L. Aurelius Avianius Symmachus, *praefectus urbi* in 364-365, or his son Q. Aurelius Symmachus, who was *praefectus urbi* in 384-385, and modern scholars have espoused both identifications.[12] But there is a decisive argument in favour of the son. The elder Symmachus (it is attested) died as consul designate in late 376.[13] On the other hand, Ambrose refers to a barbarian peril beginning in the autumn before the winter during which Satyrus died, and it has now been proved beyond reasonable doubt that the winter in question is that of 377-378.[14] It follows that the Symmachus who communicated with Satyrus in the autumn of 377 must have been the younger Symmachus.

The relationship between Symmachus and Ambrose also surfaces in a letter of Symmachus to his brother Celsinus Titianus, which describes Satyrus as their *frater communis.*[15] Even though Symmachus uses the terms *frater noster* and *frater meus* somewhat freely, the explanation may be that Ambrose and Symmachus were first cousins. The grandfather of the orator Symmachus was Aurelius Valerius Tullianus Symmachus, ordinary consul in 330. He has sometimes been identified as one of the barbarians whom Constantine advanced to the consulate according to the emperor Julian.[16] That is doubly mistaken. First, Julian did not mean "barbarian" in the literal, racial sense, even though Ammianus interpreted him thus and criticized him for inconsistency in appointing the barbarian general Nevitta consul in 362. By "barbarian" Julian meant non-Hellene, i.e., Christian, and quite a few Christians can be identified among the consuls whom Constantine appointed.[17] Second, it seems probable that the Symmachi of the fourth century descended from a senatorial family of the third, among whose members was the Chrysaorius to whom Porphyry dedicated his *Isagoge* and who had an ancestor called Symmachus.[18] The consul of 330 had been proconsul of Achaea in 319,[19] and was born, therefore, no later than 290. His son, the father of Symmachus, was born c. 310, Symmachus himself c. 335.

Like Symmachus, Ambrose possessed the *nomen* Aurelius:[20] he may have derived it from his mother, who could be a daughter of the consul of 330, and thus the aunt of Symmachus. The praetorian prefect Ambrosius may, therefore, have been the son-in-law of the consul of 330, so that his son was a cousin of Symmachus. But if prosopography allows Symmachus and Ambrose to be cousins, by the same token it fails to provide positive confirmation for the precise inference drawn from Ambrose's speech and Symmachus's letter.

What then of the attested relations of the two men with each other? Their confrontation in 384 over the Altar of Victory was conducted with great elegance and a politeness on both sides which may seem surprising in the circumstances. Yet it is not remarkable for two aristocrats to treat each other with courtesy, especially if they were in fact cousins. The eight letters of Symmachus to Ambrose which survive have a cool and distant tone, a formality verging on the querulous. They do not bespeak any sort of warm friendship between the two men.[21] On the other hand, the letters appear to presuppose some tie of kinship or amity, since Symmachus writes as one who expects his addressee to accede to the requests made, even if they need to be repeated – though he never states precisely or alludes plainly to the nature of the obligation on which he obviously feels entitled to call.

All the eight letters of Symmachus to Ambrose are requests to help someone, and in one case Symmachus virtually warns Ambrose to avoid exercising his episcopal jurisdiction in a matter affecting one of the writer's clients. The circumstances of the majority of the letters remain somewhat obscure. But two request Ambrose to intervene at court on behalf of former magistrates. One of the men was Magnillus, who was attested as *vicarius* of Africa in 391, but was detained there after he left office for an investigation into his official conduct.[22] It would be worth knowing the precise date and with what emperor or high official Symmachus hoped Ambrose to intercede for Magnillus's return. It should be one of the legitimate emperors rather than the usurping regime of Eugenius in 392-393.

The other former magistrate was Marcianus, who was being dunned for repayment of the salary (*annonarum pretia*) which he had received under a usurper (*invidia tyrannici temporis involuti*).[23] It is hard to avoid identifying this Marcianus with the Marcianus whom the unnamed prefect of the anonymous *Carmen contra paganos* appointed proconsul. The letter has usually been dated to 394-395 and used to document Symmachus's political influence at court after the usurpation of Eugenius.[24] However, the date of 394-395 for the *Carmen contra paganos* seems now to have been disproved.[25] The poem is to be lodged, rather, in the later 380s, with Vettius Agorius Praetextatus (who died in December 384) as the prefect denounced. Marcianus could be the proconsul of Africa for 384-385 or else a proconsul of Campania.[26] More important, he was embroiled in the usurpation, not of Eugenius, but of Maximus, a more serious and more ambiguous affair.[27] Theodosius recognized Maximus as a legitimate emperor in 383 and was very slow to disown him – indeed there is much to be said for the discredited view that it was only after his interview with Valentinian, Justina, and Galla in 387 that he turned against his fellow catholic and kinsman. If that is so, then Symmachus's panegyric of Maximus on 1 January 387 need not have been, at the time, an act of open hostility or disobedience towards Theodosius. In 388 Theodosius took a lenient view of the conduct of men like Symmachus between 383 and 387: he had excused many magistrates of that period from repaying the proceeds of their employment under the tyrant before Symmachus wrote to Ambrose on behalf of Marcianus. Such clemency, it can be argued, does not so much attest the political power of the pagan nobility at Rome as reflect the real political ambiguities of the years which Augustine spent in Italy.

It has often been asserted that "Augustine went to Milan as the protégé of Symmachus" or that he "came to Milan under the highest pagan patronage ... to reap the rich rewards of a now established career" with a commendation to Bauto, who was "the most powerful man in the Empire," or, even more extravagantly, "the effective ruler of the Empire."[28] On Augustine's own showing, he had no prior acquaintance with Symmachus before the *praefectus urbi* chose him after testing him in an impromptu declamation. Would it be naïve or cynical to suggest that Symmachus chose Augustine precisely because he was not a protégé? In late 384, after the affair of the Altar of Victory and in an ambiguous political situation, Symmachus may have wished to preserve his distance from the court of Valentinian at Milan. Augustine's chair in Milan is sometimes presented as a "vital post," whose occupant "would have found himself, in many ways, a 'Minister of Propaganda.'"[29] That is a false perspective. In 384 Augustine was a bright young man from the provinces who had lived on the fringe of aristocratic society in Rome: he came to Milan with ambitions, but to a very modest place at the outer fringe of the imperial court. It was his conversion which brought Augustine rapid social mobility in a Christian society.

NOTES

1. *Conf.* 5.13.23.

2. Among classic modern treatments, note P. Courcelle, *Recherches sur les Confessions de Saint Augustin* (Paris: E. de Boccard, 1950), 78 ff.; *Les Confessions de Saint Augustin dans la tradition littéraire* (Paris: Etudes Augustiniennes, 1963), 17ff.; P. Brown, *Augustine of Hippo: A Biography* (London: Faber and Faber, 1967), 79ff.; R.J. O'Connell, *St. Augustine's Early Theory of Man, A.D. 386-391* (Cambridge, Mass.: Belknap Press of Harvard University Press, 1968).

3. Paulinus, *Vita Ambrosii* 2.3, cf. Ambrose, *Epp.* 59, the date of which was established by J.-R. Palanque, *Saint Ambrose et l'Empire Romain* (Paris: E. de Boccard, 1933), 480-82, 542-43.

4. *PLRE* 1 (1971), 51; T.D. Barnes, *Phoenix* 34 (1980), 161 n.5.

5. T.D. Barnes, "Who were the Nobility of the Later Roman Empire?" *Phoenix* 28 (1974), 444-49.

6. *De virginibus* 3.7.38 (*PL* 16.244): *qui enim fieri posset, ut sancta Soteris tibi non esset mentis auctor, cui auctor est generis?*

7. *PLRE* 1.850.

8. *Exhort. Virg.* 12.82 (*PL* 16.376).

9. Respectively, Zosimus 1.60-61 and *ILS* 544, cf. A. Stein, *PIR*^{2} A 1546; *PLRE* 1.544, 545, 549; *PIR*^{2} M 178.

10. *De excessu fratris* 1.32 (*CSEL* 73.227-28).

11. O. Faller, *CSEL* 73 (1955) 227. Symmachus's letters to Ambrose alone furnish several examples of the looser use of familial terms with *meus: fratres mei Dorotheus et Septimius* (3.32), *frater meus Marcianus* (33), *frater meus Magnillus* (34), *filius meus Caecilianus* (36). S. Roda, "Simmaco nel gioco politico del suo tempo," *Studia et Documenta Historiae et Iuris* 39 (1973) 53-114, at 68-69, denies kinship and uses the evidence adduced here as proof of a deep and longlasting friendship between Symmachus and the two brothers Satyrus and Ambrose.

12. F.H. Dudden, *The Life and Times of St. Ambrose* (Oxford: Clarendon Press, 1935), 176-77 (father); *PLRE* 1.886-87 (son).

13. Symmachus, *Orat.* 4; *ILS* 1257 (Rome), cf. A. Chastagnol, *Les fastes de la préfecture de Rome au Bas Empire* (Paris: Nouvelles Editions Latines, 1962), 163.

14. O. Faller, "Situation und Abfassungszeit der Reden des hl. Ambrosius auf den Tod seines Bruders Satyrus," *Wiener Studien* 44 (1924-25), 86-102; *CSEL* 73 (1955), 81*-89* – tying the allusion to and correctly dating Ammianus Marcellinus 31.10.1-5.

15. Symmachus, *Ep.* 1.63.

16. Ammianus 21.10.8, 12.25, cf. E.A. Thompson, *The Historical Work of Ammianus Marcellinus* (Cambridge: Cambridge University Press, 1947), 80.

17. T.D. Barnes, "Christians and Pagans in the Reign of Constantius," *L'Église et l'empire au IVe siècle (Entretiens sur l'Antiquité classique)* 34 (1989), 301-37.

18. Elias, *In Porphyrii Isagogen*, praef. 15, cf. T.D. Barnes, *The New Empire of Diocletian and Constantine* (Cambridge, Mass.: Harvard University Press, 1982), 103-4.

19. G. Polara, "Il nonno di Simmaco," *Parola del Passato* 29 (1974), 261-66.

20. *ILCV* 1800 (the manuscript report of an inscription from the church of St. Nazarius in Milan).

21. Symmachus, *Ep.* 3.30-37, cf. J.F. Matthews, *Colloque genevois sur Symmache* (Paris: Société d'édition Les Belles Lettres, 1986), 173-74. For a different assessment (and the details known about all the men named in these letters), see M. Forlin Patrucco and S. Roda, "Le lettere di simmaco ad Ambrogio. Vent'anni di rapporti amichevoli," *Ambrosius Episcopus* 2 (Milan: Universita Cattolica del Sacro Cuore, 1976), 284-97.

22. *CTh* 10.17.3 (19 June 391); Symmachus, *Ep.* 3.34; 9.122.

23. Symmachus, *Ep.* 3.33.

24. *Carmen contra paganos* 56, cf. S. Roda, "Simmaco" 112; J.F. Matthews, *Western Aristocracies and Imperial Court, A.D. 364-425* (Oxford: Clarendon Press, 1975), 245, 266.

25. D.R. Shanzer, "The Date and Identity of the Centonist Proba," *REAug* 32 (1986), 232-48.

26. The names of all the proconsuls of Africa between 363 and 386 appear to be known except for that of the proconsul of 384-385: see T.D. Barnes, "Proconsuls of Africa, 337-392," *Phoenix* 39 (1985), 144-53, 273-74. The rank of the governor of Campania was raised from *consularis* to proconsul in 378, and two proconsuls are attested before 382, but it is not known precisely when the governors again became *consulares* (*PLRE* 1.678, 152, 1093). It is not plausible to suppose that Praetextatus could secure the appointment of Marcianus as proconsul of Achaea – which was under the control of Theodosius.

27. For what follows, see the essay "Religion and Politics in the Age of Theodosius," in *Grace, Politics and Desire: Essays on Augustine,* ed. H.A. Meynell (Calgary: University of Calgary Press, 1990), 157-75.

28. P. Brown, *Augustine* (1967), 70; J.J. O'Meara, *The Young Augustine* (London: Longman, Green and Company, 1954), 115, 127.

29. P. Brown, *Augustine* (1967), 69.

THE LITERARY UNITY OF THE *CONFESSIONS*

KENNETH B. STEINHAUSER

The thirteen books of Augustine's *Confessions* frequently leave scholars perplexed because of apparent inconsistencies among these books and the various disjunct themes treated therein. The first nine books are autobiographical and end significantly, with Augustine grieving the death of his mother at Ostia. In book ten Augustine describes his present condition at the time of composing the *Confessions;* however, in this book he also dedicates a lengthy philosophical excursus to the nature of memory. The last three books constitute a commentary on the first chapter of Genesis, the creation narrative; book eleven also contains an excursus on the nature of time. In other words, in the *Confessions* one finds autobiography, philosophy, and exegesis. Who would attempt to treat such diverse topics in one literary work? And more importantly, why? This diversity within the *Confessions* has led some scholars to raise redaction critical questions. Is the work complete as it now stands or unfinished? Is the work logically consistent or a *mélange* of previously composed units? Or is the *Confessions* merely "a badly composed book?"[1]

STATEMENT OF THE PROBLEM

The problem of the unity or lack of unity among the thirteen books of the *Confessions* may be treated separately but not in total isolation from other questions frequently asked about the *Confessions.* What is the literary form of the *Confessions*? Are the events of Augustine's life presented with historical accuracy or does the *Confessions* contain elements of fiction?[2] On one hand, the answers to these questions will certainly affect how one attempts to solve the problem of the unity of the *Confessions* as a literary work. On the other hand, one could approach the subject from the opposite direction, stating that the solution to the problem of the unity or lack of unity among the thirteen books will affect one's answer to questions concerning the literary form and historical reliability of the work. In spite of this complexity of themes and the relationship of these various questions and their answers to one another, the present study will be limited to the problem of the unity and structure of the *Confessions.* Ultimately the question of unity does not merely seek to satisfy some idle curiosity because one's answer to this question will influence one's interpretation of the entire *Confessions.* The goal of the present study is to determine the unity of the *Confessions* or lack thereof. That determination will present a basis of interpretation. In any study the answer depends upon the question, and the question about unity and structure has traditionally been asked in two ways.

First, some scholars ask the question: "Why does Augustine present an exegesis of Genesis in the last books of his *Confessions*?" In fact K. Grotz makes this question the subtitle of his dissertation written at Tübingen and completed in 1970.[3] Phrased in this manner the question of the unity of the *Confessions* will revolve around the relationship of books eleven to thirteen to books one to ten. Focussing on books eleven to thirteen at the beginning of the study points the research in one direction and a priori excludes many possible solutions to the problem. A similar approach is found in the research of J.C. Cooper,[4] R. Herzog,[5] and E. Feldmann.[6]

Second, other scholars ask the question: "Why does Augustine insert a treatment of memory in the middle of his *Confessions*?" Here the emphasis falls upon book ten. In fact, A. Pincherle has expressed the opinion that the place of book ten has not been given sufficient consideration in many studies on the unity and structure of the *Confessions.*[7] Actually beginning with book ten opens two possible lines of investigation. The first approach, already indicated in the question about memory, begins with the assertion that Augustine needed to establish a philosophical basis for his inward inquiry. Thus, P.J. Archambault considers Augustine's treatment of memory a peak or a turning point in the *Confessions* because it justifies the entire endeavour.[8] The second approach, also based upon book ten, begins with Augustine's state of mind at the time when he composed the work. Thus, W.C. Spengemann finds book ten significant because it reveals Augustine's personal attitude at the time of composition and gives a basis for determining a motive why Augustine decided to write his *Confessions.*[9] The psychohistorical approach of R.

Brändle and W. Neidhart also begins with Augustine's mental state at the time of composition.[10]

CURRENT RESEARCH METHODS

In the vast ocean of Augustinian literature three research methods have been used by scholars in dealing with the problem of the unity and structure of the *Confessions.* Though distinct, these research methods are not mutually exclusive and may be applied simultaneously. Furthermore, each method may yield a positive or negative response to the question of unity. Let us now proceed to a description of each method and some examples of how it has been applied to the problem at hand.

First, a scholar applies the method of *external comparison* when he or she attempts to find a basis for the structure of the *Confessions* implied in some other writing of Augustine. In the application of this method the other Augustinian writing becomes a guide for the interpretation of the *Confessions.* M. Wundt, for example, comes to the conclusion that the thirteen books of the *Confessions* indeed do form a literary unity but the work is unfortunately incomplete as it now stands.[11] In *De catechizandis rudibus* Augustine points out that the catechist should first instruct the convert in God's providence which brought him to the faith and then proceed to instruct the convert in the scriptures, "starting out from the fact that God made all things very good."[12] This is the exact same procedure which Augustine follows in his *Confessions.* Thus, the commentary on Genesis represents only the beginning of Augustine's commentary on the entire Bible and a complete exposition of dogma which he never finished.

Second, the method of *biographical basis* comes into play when a scholar seeks to establish the unity of the *Confessions* on the basis of Augustine's personal life story. Significant biographical information need not be limited to the data given in books one to nine, the so-called autobiographical section of the *Confessions.* One may also look to the earlier philosophical works which Augustine composed during his retreat at Cassiciacum.[13] Theoretically, at least, these writings should present a more accurate picture of Augustine's state of mind at the time of his conversion because they were composed in close chronological proximity to the events themselves. In addition, both F. van der Meer[14] and P. Brown[15] have demonstrated in their renowned biographies that both the sermons and the letters of Augustine contain a wealth of biographical information. Finally, there is the reliable biography of Augustine's contemporary Possidius.[16] Attempts have been made to relate the *Confessions* to Augustine's early infatuation with Manichaeism,[17] his reading of Cicero,[18] his exposure to Neoplatonism,[19] his relationship to his mother,[20] and his response to Donatist critics.[21]

Third, a scholar applies the method of *internal coherence* when he or she attempts to analyze the thirteen books in relationship to one another and in the context of the entire *Confessions.* The literary form or genre is frequently used as the basis for investigating the literary unity of the *Confessions.* For example, M. Zepf analyzes the *Confessions* in terms of the form *confessio.*[22] For G. Misch the form is autobiography.[23] For E. Feldmann *protrepticus.*[24] For R. Herzog *Gespräch* or conversation.[25] In each case the method involves first determining the form either through literary or linguistic analysis or by comparison to classical or religious literature contemporary to Augustine. Then, once the literary form is established, the formal critical analysis becomes the basis for describing the unity or disunity of the *Confessions.*[26]

A NEW SOLUTION TO THE PROBLEM

The three research methods described above will now be applied to the problem of the literary unity of the *Confessions* and a new solution to the problem will be proposed. There are several significant pieces of evidence which have been overlooked or not seriously considered in previous studies. First, the method of external comparison will be applied using the *Retractationes* of Augustine. Second, the method of biographical basis will indicate Augustine's preoccupation with beauty and aesthetics in his early life. Third, the method of internal coherence will reveal Augustine's motive for writing his *Confessions* and its effect on the literary unity of the work.

EXTERNAL COMPARISON WITH THE "RETRACTATIONES"

One finds it astounding how infrequently scholars consider Augustine's own explanation of the structure of the *Confessions* documented in his *Retractationes.* Augustine explicitly mentions his *Confessions* only four times in all his writings.[27] In the *Retractationes* he writes: "The first ten books were written about myself; the last three about Holy Scripture."[28] Although the *Retractationes* was written some thirty years after the *Confessions,* Augustine's description and evaluation of his own work certainly cannot be ignored. Furthermore, there is no reason to consider the *Retractationes* unreliable. Augustine is always quite candid in his *Retractationes*. Let us take two examples. First, Augustine does not hesitate to state that a work is incomplete. He indicates that his commentary on Romans is incomplete and he adds what he would have done if he had had the time to finish it.[29] Second, Augustine also does not hesitate to indicate how a work was composed. He states that in writing *De doctrina christiana* he added the fourth book at a later date.[30] If the *Confessions* was incomplete or if it was a composite of units written earlier, why did he not state that fact? In other words, Augustine himself points to the integrity of the *Confessions*. Therefore, the burden of proof is incumbent upon those who wish to disprove the completeness or unity of the work.

The *Retractationes* also provides some insight into Augustine's motive for writing the *Confessions:* "The thirteen books of my *Confessions* praise the just and good God for my evil and good acts, and lift up the understanding and affection of men to him. At least, as far as I am concerned, they had this effect on me while I was writing them and they continue to have it when I am reading them."[31] Reading the *Confessions* inspired many people, including Augustine himself! Nowhere else in his *Retractationes* does Augustine mention reading one of his own books for personal inspiration. Furthermore, only here does he disclose his subjective feelings when composing a work. In addition to writing for others, quite clearly Augustine had written the *Confessions* for himself.

External comparison to the *Retractationes* yields three pieces of evidence. First, Augustine certainly considered the *Confessions* a unity. He makes no mention of incompleteness or unusual circumstances of composition. Since he frequently mentions such items in dealing with other works, absence of comment leads one to conclude that the work was complete as written and intended as such from the very beginning. Second, Augustine provides an outline – books one to ten are about himself and books eleven to thirteen about sacred scripture. Any analysis which does not respect this outline must be considered invalid. Third, Augustine indicates a unique and highly personal attachment to this work. He was inspired when writing and reading his *Confessions*.

BIOGRAPHICAL BASIS – AESTHETICS AND AUGUSTINE

When he was twenty-six or twenty-seven years old, according to his own testimony recorded in the *Confessions*, Augustine began his literary career with his first work entitled *De pulchro et apto.*[32] At the time of his writing the *Confessions* the work had already been lost and Augustine claims not to remember it well. Augustine's reference to *De pulchro et apto* is significant for two reasons. First, this is the only work of his own which he mentions in the entire *Confessions.* He mentions the Manichaeans and the Platonists. He also mentions Aristotle, Cicero, and Paul. Obviously all these represent significant influences in his life. However, in this one instance he also mentions his own literary activity. That fact alone would seem to indicate its importance. Second, the subject matter of this lost work is aesthetics. He mentions neither logic nor ethics but aesthetics. He is concerned with neither epistemology nor metaphysics, but with aesthetics. This would lead one to conclude that aesthetics had been the primary philosophical preoccupation of his youth. On the basis of these two observations one must read the *Confessions* anew in terms of aesthetics.[33]

Num amamus aliquid nisi pulchrum?

In the fourth book of his *Confessions* Augustine asks: "Do we love anything save what is beautiful?"[34] This statement is the guiding principle of Augustine's aesthetics. Although he is recalling his youth and indeed a time before his conversion, Augustine never denies this axiom, namely, that we love only what is beautiful. The principle is often repeated in his other writings. In *De musica* Augustine writes: *Dic, oro te, num possumus amare nisi pulchra?*[35] In his *Enarrationes in Psalmos* he writes again: *Quare autem amas nisi quia pulchra sunt?*[36] Thus, the axiom may be considered the basic principle of the aesthetical philosophy of Augustine: "Do we love anything save what is beautiful?"

Quid est ergo pulchrum? et quid est pulchritudo?

Earlier in his life when he was sixteen years old, Augustine had stolen some pears. What in today's society might be considered a teenage prank becomes the object of extensive analysis occupying over half of book two of the *Confessions.* Augustine questions why he stole the pears. Peer pressure definitely played a role. However, he offers no self-justification. His reason for stealing the pears was quite simple: *Pulchra erant poma illa.* "Those were beautiful pears."[37] At the time he wrote his *Confessions,* he could add that they were beautiful because they had been created by God.

Ten years later at age twenty-six he was much more speculative: *Quid est ergo pulchrum? Et quid est pulchritudo?* "What then is beautiful? and what is beauty?"[38] In book four Augustine states that as a young man he had discussed such questions with his friends. These thoughtful inquiries occasioned the writing of his work on beauty and proportion. The lost work was strongly Manichaean in content; and, on the basis of Augustine's description of the work, one can obtain an understanding of its major themes.

First, *De pulchro et apto* was based on a purely materialistic concept of reality: "But I had not yet seen that this great matter [of the Beautiful and the Fitting] turns upon your workmanship, O Almighty by whom alone things marvellous are done; and my mind considered only corporeal forms. I defined and distinguished the Beautiful as that which is so of itself, the Fitting as that which is excellent in its relation of fitness to some other thing; it was by corporeal examples that I supported my argument."[39] Augustine continues: "I turned my throbbing mind away from the incorporeal to line and colour and bulk, and because I did not see these things in my mind, I concluded that I could not see my mind."[40] Spiritual realities simply do not exist and indeed cannot exist in this early world view of Augustine. Citing Aristotle's *Categories,* which he calls the "ten categories,"[41] Augustine subsumes the other nine categories under the chief category of substance.

Second, dualism is also clearly evident: "Further, loving the peace I saw in virtue and hating the discord in vice, I noted the unity of the one and the dividedness of the other: and it seemed to me that in the unity lay the rational mind and the nature of truth and the supreme Good: but in the dividedness I thought I saw some substance of irrational life, and the nature of supreme Evil. This Evil I saw not only as substance but even as life...."[42] In other words, Augustine asserted the existence of two principles – one good and the other evil. Both are substances and both are living.

Tu ergo, domine ... pulcher es.

In books eleven through thirteen Augustine once again takes up these preoccupations of his youth responding to the questions raised in *De pulchro et apto.* However, this time Augustine is more concerned with the creator than creation. "It was you, Lord, who made them: for you are beautiful, and they are beautiful: you are good and they are good: you are and they are. But they neither are beautiful nor are good nor simply are as you their Creator: compared with you they are not beautiful and are not good and are not. These truths, thanks to you, we know; and our knowledge compared with your knowledge is ignorance."[43]

First, Augustine solves the materialism problem by seeing God as the creator of the universe: "Let your works praise you that we may love you, and let us love you that your works may praise you. For they have a beginning and an end in time, a rising and setting, growth and decay, beauty and defect." "They were made by you of nothing – not of yourself, not of some matter not made by you or of some matter previously existent...." "you made formless matter of absolutely nothing ..."[44]

Second, the ability to conceive of a spiritual reality solves the problem of dualism. God is the "one supreme good."[45] God is not substance and he is not corporeal. Rather he has created all spiritual and corporeal reality. He alone is the fountain of all life. He is beautiful and has made all beauty.

Intus haec ago, in aula ingenti memoriae meae[46]

Between his question in book four, "What is beautiful?", and his response in book eleven, "You, O God, are beautiful," Augustine discusses his present state in book ten. This being the case, book ten will manifest insights different from those of his youth.

First, Augustine returns to the question of matter. However, here he has obviously adopted a new and different approach.

> And what is this God? I asked the earth and it answered: "I am not he"; and all things that are in the earth made the same confession. I asked the sea and the deeps and the creeping things and they answered: "We are not your God; seek higher." I asked the winds that blow and the whole air with all that is in it answered: "Anaximenes was wrong: I am not God." I asked the heavens, the sun, the moon, the stars, and they answered: "Neither are we God whom you seek." And I said to all the things that throng about the gateways of the senses: "Tell me of my God, since you are not he. Tell me something of him." And they cried out in a great voice: "He made us." My question was my gazing upon them and their answer was their beauty. And I turned to myself and said: "And you, who are you?" And I answered: "A man." Now clearly there is a body and a soul in me,

> one exterior, one interior. From which of these two should I have inquired of my God?[47]

Augustine has radically changed his mode of inquiry. In his search for beauty he leaves the exterior man and turns inward. In *De vera religione* he mentions this same procedure specifically regarding the quest for beauty and truth, which appear almost synonymous: *Noli foras ire, in te ipsum redi. In interiore homine habitat veritas.*[48] The influence of Plotinus's tract of beauty is obvious: "How can you see the sort of beauty a good soul has? Go back into yourself and look."[49]

Second, book ten also deals extensively with memory because without memory none of this would be possible. All the images of the senses are stored in the memory. Augustine asks: "But where in my memory do you abide, Lord, where in memory do you abide?... You have paid this honour to my memory that you deign to abide in it."[50]

For Augustine *memoria* is not merely remembering. More importantly, *memoria* makes sense perception possible.[51] Thus, the communication which takes place between God and Augustine occurs within Augustine's memory. Augustine can also return to the memory to recall the images of things which have already happened. The *Confessions* is Augustine's prayer or hymn of praise to God. The *Confessions* is also a response to God's call, which had previously taken place in the memory of Augustine.

> Late have I loved thee, O Beauty so ancient and so new; late have I loved thee! For behold thou wert within me, and I outside; and I sought thee outside and in my unloveliness fell upon those lovely things that thou has made. Thou wert with me and I was not with thee. I was kept from thee by those things, yet had they not been in thee, they would not have been at all. Thou didst call and cry to me and break open my deafness: and thou didst send forth thy beams and shine upon me and chase away my blindness: thou didst breathe fragrance upon me, and I drew in my breath and do now pant for thee: I tasted thee, and now hunger and thirst for thee: thou didst touch me, and I have burned for thy peace.[52]

Therefore, book ten represents a turning point in the *Confessions*. Augustine still writes of himself. However, he writes of himself in his present condition. Books one to nine consider the exterior man while book ten considers the interior man. This inward turn enables him and God to communicate with one another and, indeed, makes his *Confessions* possible.

Internal Coherence – "cognoscam te ... sicut cognitus sum."

Why did Augustine write the *Confessions*? The answer to this question may be found in book ten. In this respect the analysis of W.C. Spengemann is quite convincing,[53] when he considers the cryptic words of Augustine: *Cognoscam te, cognitor meus, cognoscam, sicut cognitus sum.* "I would know you, my knower; I would know you as I am known."[54] For Spengemann these words indicate an association between God and Augustine's true self. Furthermore, Augustine implies that he knows neither God nor his true self. Thus, the thirteen books of the *Confessions* represent Augustine's search for identity. Augustine's writing was therapeutic. Caught between the *taedium vivendi* and the *moriendi metus* he turned inward to find himself and his God.[55] His quest for beauty became a quest for truth and both were woven together. Since beauty for Augustine had been natural beauty only, the *Confessions* reveals a movement from beauty to knowledge until book ten, where the two predicates are used interchangeably of God.

THE AESTHETICAL STRUCTURE OF THE "CONFESSIONS"

On the basis of the previous study one may draw three conclusions. First, Augustine's own description of the *Confessions* must be respected. Second, the thirteen books of the *Confessions* are complete as they now stand. Third the final structure of the *Confessions* does not represent an artificial rearrangement of previously composed pieces.

First, Augustine's own description of the structure of the work is accurate: "The first ten books were written about myself; the last three about holy scripture."[56] The present analysis respects Augustine's own explanation of his work. In books one to ten Augustine does consider himself, specifically the exterior man in books one to nine and the interior man in book ten. He absolutely needs to deal with his complete self for his praise of God to be complete; in book ten he does turn inward but he is still considering himself – his present condition, his memory, his capacity to grasp spiritual realties. In books eleven to thirteen Augustine does consider sacred scripture. However, he needs only to deal with creation to explain the origin of the material universe. An explanation of the creation narrative of Genesis solves all the problems which he had explicitly raised. Extended exegesis at this point would have been inappropriate and superfluous.

Second, the thirteen books of the *Confessions* are complete. Books eleven to thirteen containing the commentary on the creation narrative of Genesis are an integral part of the work and an appropriate ending. In *De pulchro et apto,* Augustine had affirmed Manichaean materialism and dualism. These principles guided his youth. Not by accident did Augustine choose to end his work with a description of the creative activity of God. In the last three books of his *Confessions* Augustine rejects his previous materialistic and dualistic assertions by stating that God is a spiritual being and the source of all beauty. These books represent a positive response to the questions raised earlier. Indeed, had Augustine not presented a clear explanation of the origin and nature of the material world, his *Confessions* would have been incomplete. However, there is no need to continue his commentary on Genesis. He needs only to deal with creation and to demonstrate the origin of the material universe. Once this question is answered, he can end his *Confessions,* and he does.

Third, the thirteen books of the *Confessions* are not a *mélange* of previously composed pieces. In his *Retractationes* Augustine states his reason for writing the *Confessions:* "The thirteen books of my *Confessions* praise the just and good God for my evil and good acts, and lift up the understanding and affection of men to Him."[57] In other words, Augustine is engaged in communication with God, with other persons, and with himself. For this reason he must deal in book ten with memory, which enables this communication. Thus, memory, described in book ten, unified Augustine's life experiences with God, whose beauty is manifested in the beauty of creation. An extensive treatment of memory is absolutely essential to maintain the integrity and continuity of the work. Without book ten the first nine books of the *Confessions* would constitute a description of the exterior man only. *In interiore homine habitat veritas.*[58] Book ten gives the work perspective not only by identifying the contemporary situation of the author but also by justifying the entire communicative process which takes place in the memory. The *memoria* is, of course, central to Augustine's theory of knowledge. In other words, for Augustine neither knowledge nor communication is possible without memory.

Comparison to the *Retractationes* and reading the *Confessions* in terms of aesthetics have been the basis of this particular analysis. Augustine's quest for beauty is a thread which runs through the entire work. As a sixteen-year-old he had stolen pears because those pears were beautiful. *Pulchra erant poma illa.* [59] From a Manichaean perspective ten years later the twenty-six-year-old Augustine posed the question: *Quid est pulchrum? Et quid est pulchritudo?* [60] And he wrote his first work, entitled *De pulchro et apto* attempting to answer that question. Later in his life Neoplatonism and, specifically, the writings of Plotinus led him to turn inward in his search for beauty. *Intus haec ago, in aula ingenti memoriae meae.* [61] Some thirty years after he had stolen those pears and some twenty years after he had written his first work on beauty, Augustine could look at the material world and proclaim God the source of all beauty: *Tu, domine, pulcher es.* [62] From this perspective, in order to come to terms with himself, he pondered his own life and confessed: *Sero te amaui, pulchritudo.* [63]

NOTES

1. John J. O'Meara, *The Young Augustine: The Growth of St. Augustine's Mind up to His Conversion* (London: Longmans, Green and Company, 1954; rpt. 1980), 13.

2. Leo C. Ferrari, "Saint Augustine on the Road to Damascus," *Augustinian Studies* 13 (1982), 151-79 argues convincingly for the fictional nature of the conversion scene; for further literature see 154, n. 13. However, some equally convincing arguments in favour of historical reliability may be found in Michele Pellegrino, *Le "Confessioni" de Sant'Agostino: Studio introduttivo, Cultura* 15 (Rome: Editrice Studium, 1972). See Franco Bolgiani, *La Conversione de s. Agostino e l'VIIIe libro delle "Confessioni,"* Università di Torino, Publicazioni della Facoltà di Lettere e Filosofia 8,4 (Turin: Università di Torino, 1956), 15-52; Christine Mohrmann, "The Confessions as a Literary Work of Art," *Etudes sur le Latin des Chrétiens,* vol. 1 (Rome: Edizioni di Storia e letteratura, 1961), 371-81.

3. Klaus Grotz, *Die Einheit der "Confessiones": Warum bringt Augustin in den letzten Büchern seiner "Confessiones" eine Auslegung der Genesis?,* Diss. Unpublished (Tübingen, 1970).

4. John C. Cooper, "Why did Augustine write Books 11-13 of the Confessions," *Augustinian Studies* 2 (1971), 37-46.

5. Reinhart Herzog, "Non in sua voce: Augustins Gespräch mit Gott in den *Confessiones* – Voraussetzungen und Folgen," *Das Gespräch,* Poetik und Hermeneutik 11 (-Munich: Wilhelm Fink Verlag, 1984), 213-50.

6. Erich Feldmann, "Las *Confessiones* de Agustín y su unidad: Reflexiones sobre composición," *Augustinus* 31 (1986), 113-22.

7. Alberto Pincherle, "The Confessions of St. Augustine: A Reappraisal," *Augustinian Studies* 7 (1976), 127.

8. Paul J. Archambault, "Augustine, Memory, and the Development of Autobiography," *Augustinian Studies* 13 (1982), 23-30.

9. William C. Spengemann, *The Forms of Autobiography: Episodes in the History of a Literary Genre* (New Haven: Yale University Press, 1980), 1-33; see Janet Varner Gunn, *Autobiography: Toward a Poetics of Experience* (Philadelphia: University of Pennsylvania Press, 1982), 118-47.

10. Rudolf Brändle and Walter Neidhart, "Lebensgeschichte und Theologie: Ein Beitrag zur psychohistorischen Interpretation Augustins," *Theologische Zeitschrift* 40 (1984), 157-80.

11. Max Wundt, "Augustins Konfessionen," *Zeitschrift für neutestamentliche Wissenschaft,* 22 (1923), 186. Others have applied the same method using either *Trin.* or *Civ. Dei* and have come to the opposite conclusion: Horst Kusch, "Studien über Augustinus," *Festschrift Franz Dornseiff zum 65. Geburtstag* (Leipzig: VEB Bibliographisches Institut, 1953), 124-83; Ulrich Duchrow, "Der Aufbau von Augustins Schriften Confessiones und De Trinitate," *Zeitschrift für Theologie und Kirche* 62 (1965), 338-67; Marjorie Suchocki, "The Symbolic structure of Augustine's *Confessions," Journal of American Academy of Religion* 50 (1982), 365-78; C.J. Starnes, "La unidad des las *Confesiones," Augustinus* 31 (1986), 275-84.

12. *De catechizandis rudibus* 6,10; trans. Joseph P. Christopher, ACW 2, 26-27.

13. For a recent study of these writings in the context of autobiography see J. McWilliam Dewart, "La autobiografía de Casiciaco," *Augustinus* 31 (1986), 41-78, who finds essential agreement between the *Confessions* and the early writings.

14. Frits van der Meer, *Augustine the Bishop: The Life and Work of a Father of the Church* (London: Steed and Ward, 1961).

15. Peter Brown, *Augustine of Hippo: A Biography* (Berkeley: University of California Press, 1967).

16. Possidius, *Vita sancti Augustini;* PL 32, 33-66.

17. Alfred Adam, "Der manichäische Ursprung der Lehre von den zwei Reichen bei Augustin," *Theologische Literaturzeitung* 77 (1952), 385-90; Alfred Adam, "Das Fortwirken des Manichäismus bei Augustin," *Zeitschrift für Kirchengeschichte,* 69 (1958), 1-25; cf. W.H.C. Frend, "The Gnostic-Manichaean Tradition in Roman North Africa," *Journal of Ecclesiastical History* 4 (1953), 13-26; W.H.C. Frend, "Manichaeism in the Struggle between Saint Augustine and Petilian of Constantine," *Augustinus Magister* II (Paris: Etudes Augustiniennes, 1954), 850-66.

18. Erich Feldmann, *Der Einfluß der "Hortensius" und des Manichäismus auf das Denken des jungen Augustinus von 373,* Diss. Unpublished (Münster, 1975), 239-357.

19. Prosper Alfaric, *L'Evolution intellectuelle de saint Augustin: Du Manichéisme au Néoplatonisme* (Paris: E. Nourry, 1918); Robert J. O'Connell, "The Riddle of Augustine's 'Confessions': a Plotinian Key," *International Philosophical Quarterly* 4 (1964), 327-72; Robert J. O'Connell, *Saint Augustine's Confessions: The Odyssey of a Soul* (Cambridge, Massachusetts: Harvard University Press, 1969); Eckard König, *Augustinus Philosophus:*

Christlicher Glaube und philosophisches Denken in den Frühschriften Augustins, Studia et Testimonia 11, Diss. Erlangen-Nürnbertg (Munich: Wilhelm Fink Verlag, 1970).

20. Brändle and Neidhard, 159-66; for further literature on similar approaches see p. 158, n.4.

21. Wundt, pp. 166-78; see Pierre Courcelle, *Recherches sur les Confessions de saint Augustin* (Paris: Editions E. de Boccard, 1968), 26.

22. Max Zepf, *Augustins Confessiones,* Heidelberger Abhandlungen zur Philosophie und ihrer Geschichte 9 (Tübingen: Mohr, 1926), 63-112; see Ilse Freyer, *Erlebte und systematische Gestaltung in Augustins Konfessionen: Versuch einer Analyse ihrer inneren Form,* Neue deutsche Forschungen, Abteilung Religions – und Kirchengeschichte 4 (Berlin: Junker und Dünnhaupt, 1937); G. Pfligersdorffer, "Das Bauprinzip von Augustins Confessiones", *Festschrift K. Vretska* (Heidelberg: Karl Winter Universitätsverlag, 1970), 124-47.

23. Georg Misch, *A History of Autobiography in Antiquity,* vol. 2 (Cambridge, Massachusetts: Harvard University Press, 1951), 625-68; see A. Sizoo, "Autobiographie," RAC 1, 1050-55.

24. Feldmann, "Las *Confessiones* de Agustín y su unidad," 121.

25. Herzog, p. 215; see Walter Magaß, "Die Konfessorische Rede in den 'Confessiones' Augustins," *Linguistica Biblica* 55 (1984), 35-46.

26. A literary approach is also used by E. Williger, "Der Aufbau der Konfessionen Augustins," *Zeitschrift für neutestamentliche Wissenschaft* 28 (1929), 81-106; Georg Nicolaus Knauer, *Die Psalmenzitate in den Konfessionen Augustins* (Göttingen: Vandenhoeck und Ruprecht, 1955); Georg Nicolaus Knauer, "Peregrinatio animae: Zur Frage nach der Einheit der augustinischen Konfessionen," *Hermes* 85 (1957), 216-48; David J. Leigh, "Augustine's *Confessions* as Circular Journey," *Thought* 60 (1985), 73-88; Carl Avren Levenson, "Distance and Presence in Augustine's *Confessions,*" *The Journal of Religion* 65 (1985), 500-12. Others seek a philosophical coherence: Wilhelm Thimme, *Augustins Selbstbildnis in den Konfessionen: Eine religionspsychologische Studie,* Beihefte zur Zeitschrift für Religionspsychologie 2 (Gütersloh: Bertelsmann, 1929); Peter Schäfer, *Das Schuldbewußtsein in den Confessiones des heiligen Augustinus: Eine religionspsychologische Studie,* Abhanglungen zur Philosophie und Psychologie der Religion 25, Diss. (Würzburg: C.J. Becker Universitäts-Druckerei, 1930); Ephraem Hendrikx, *Augustins Verhältnis zur Mystik: Eine patristische Untersuchung,* Cassiciacum 1 (Würzburg: Rita-Verlag, 1936), 132-49; Cornelius Petrus Mayer, *Die Zeichen in der geistigen Entwicklung und in der Theologie des jungen Augustinus,* Cassiciacum 24,1, Diss. Würzburg (Würzburg: Augustinus-Verlag, 1969), 160-68; Eugen Dönt, "Zur Frage der Einheit von Augustins Konfessionen," *Hermes* 99 (1971), 350-61; Hans Robert Jauß, "Gottesprädikate und Identitätsvorgaben in der Augustinischen Tradition der Autobiographie", *Identität,* Poetik und Hermeneutik 8 (Munich: Wilhelm Fink Verlag, 1979), 708-17; Manfred Sommer, "Zur Formierung der Autobiographie aus Selbstverteidigung und Selbstsuche: Stoa und Augustinus," *Identität,* Poetik und Hermeneutik 8 (Munich: Wilhelm Fink Verlag, 1979), 699-702; Donald Capps, "Parabolic Events in Augustine's Autobiography," *Theology Today* 40 (1983),

260-72. Still others seek a thological coherence: p. Ramiro Flórez, "Apuntes sobre el libro X de las 'Confessiones' de San Agustín," *La Ciudad de Dios* 169 (1956), 5-34; Grotz, pp. 104-16; A. Holl, *Die Welt der Zeichen bei Augustin: Religionsphänomenologische Analyse des 13. Buches der Confessiones,* Wiener Beiträge zur Theologie 2 (Vienna: Herder, 1963); Henrique de Noronha Galvão, *Die existentielle Gotteserkenntnis bei Augustin: Eine hermeneutische Lektüre der Confessiones,* Sammlung Horizonte NF 21 (Einsiedeln: Johannes Verlag, 1981).

27. *Ret.* 2.6 (32); *Ep.* 231.6; *Gen. litt.* 2.9.22; *Don. pers* 20.53; Verheijen has thoughtfully provided the text of these passages in his edition of the *Conf., CCSL* 27, lxxxv-lxxxvi.

28. *Ret.* 2.6 (32); ed. Almut Mutzenbecher, *CCSL* 57; trans. Mary Inez Bogan, FC 60, 130.

29. *Ret.* 1.25 (24).

30. *Ret.* 2.4 (30).

31. *Ret.* 2.6 (32); trans. Bogan, FC 60, 130.

32. *Conf.* 4.13.20; cf. Takeshi Kato, "Melodia interior: Sur le traité *De pulchro et apto,*" *Revue des Etudes Augustiniennes* 12 (1966), 229-40.

33. Of the many studies on the aesthetics of Augustine, I have relied primarily upon Josef Tscholl, "Augustins Interesse für das körperliche Schöne," *Augustiniana* 14 (1964), 72-104; id., "Vom Wesen der körperlichen Schönheit zu Gott," *Augustiniana* 15 (1965), 32-53; id., "Augustins Aufmerksamkeit am Makrokosmos," *Augustiniana* 15 (1965), 389-413; id., "Augustins Beachtung der geistigen Schönheit," *Augustiniana* 16 (1966), 11-53; id., "Dreifaltigkeit und dreifache Vollendung des Schönen nach Augustinus," *Augustiniana* 16 (1966), 330-70; see K. Svoboda, *L'ésthétique de s. Augustin et ses sources,* Diss. Bruenn (Paris: Société d'édition les 'Belles Lettres', 1933); Luis Rey Altuna, *Qué es lo bello? Introdución a la estética de San Agustín* (Madrid: Consejo Superior de investigaciones Cientificas, Instituto 'Luis Vives' de Filosofia, 1945); Luis Rey Altuna, "La forma estética del universo agustiniano," *Augustinus* 1 (1956), 235-47); Luis Rey Altuna, "La actitud estimativa de lo bello en San Agustín," *Augustinus* 3 (1958), 351-58; Walter Magaß, "Die Kritik der Künste in den Confessiones des Augustin," *Kairos* 22 (1980), 122-28.

34. *Conf.* 4.13.20; trans. F.J. Sheed, 74.

35. *Mus.* 6.13.38; PL 32.

36. *En. Ps.* 79.14; ed. E. Dekkers and J. Fraipont, *CCSL* 39.

37. *Conf.* 2.6.12; my translation. For some fascinating observations on the pear theft see Leo C. Ferrari, "The Pear Theft in Augustine's Confessions," *Revue des Etudes Augustiniennes* 16 (1970), 233-42; id., "The Arboreal Polarisation in Augustine's Confessions", *Revue des Etudes Augustiniennes* 25 (1979), 35-46.

38. *Conf.* 4.13.20; trans. Sheed, 74.

39. *Conf.* 4.15.24; trans. Sheed, 76.

40. *Conf.* 4.15.24; trans. Sheed, 76.

41. *Conf.* 4.16.28; trans. Sheed, 78.

42. *Conf.* 4.15.24; trans. Sheed, 76-77.

43. *Conf.* 11.4.6; trans. Sheed, 264.

44. *Conf.* 13.33.48; trans. Sheed, 352.

45. *Conf.* 13.2.2; trans. Sheed, 322.

46. *Conf.* 16.8.14; on the interior space see Pierre Blanchard, "L'espace intérieur chez saint Augustin d'après le livre X des 'Confessions,'" *Augustinus Magister,* I (Paris: Etudes Augustiniennes, 1954), 535-42; W.G. Schmidt-Dengler, "Die 'aula memoriae' in den Konfessionen des heiligen Augustinus," *Revue des Etues Augustiniennes* 14 (1968), 68-89.

47. *Conf.* 10.6.9; trans. Sheed, 216.

48. *Vera Rel.* 39.72; ed. Klaus-Detlef Daur, *CCSL* 22.

49. *En.* 1.6.9; ed. P. Henry and H.R. Schwyzer and trans. A.H. Armstrong, Loeb 440, 259.

50. *Conf.* 10.25.36; trans. Sheed, 235.

51. For a clear explanation of Augustine's epistemology see Ronald H. Nash, *The Light of the Mind: Augustine's Theory of Knowledge* (Lexington, Kentucky: University Press of Kentucky, 1969); see Hermann-Josef Kaiser, Augustinus: Zeit und "Memoria," Abhandlungen zur Philosophie, Psychologie und Pädagogik 67, Diss. (Bonn: H. Bouvier U. Co., 1969).

52. *Conf.* 10.27.38; trans. Sheed, 236.

53. *Spengemann,* 16-17.

54. *Conf.* 10.1.1; my translation.

55. See *Conf.* 4.6.11.

56. *Ret.* 2.6 (32); trans. Bogan, FC 60, 130.

57. *Ret.* 2.6 (32); trans. Bogan, FC 60, 130.

58. *Ver. Rel.* 39.72.

59. *Conf.* 2.6.12.

60. *Conf.* 4.13.20.

61. *Conf.* 10.8.14.

62. *Conf.* 11.4.6.

63. *Conf.* 10.27.38.

FROM LITERAL SELF-SACRIFICE TO LITERARY SELF-SACRIFICE: AUGUSTINE'S *CONFESSIONS* AND THE RHETORIC OF TESTIMONY

JAMIE SCOTT

For the modern reader, the *Confessions* pose immediate problems above and beyond those of simple historical distance and secular detachment. These issues confront us when we come to almost any early Christian text. But it is a literary critical commonplace that so pervasive is the originary influence of the *Confessions* that to read it is *not* to know what kind of writing one is experiencing. Is it an autobiography? If so, how so, since it is scarcely historical, as Peter Brown's definitive biography of Augustine makes clear? If not an autobiography – if we take Augustine at his word and call the book "confessions" – what does this mean? Or then again, perhaps the *Confessions* are something quite unique, something too elusive to place within a literary critical history, perhaps, the *Confessions* are a work only generally indirectly knowable in and through the rhetorical traces it has left among the myriad of literary kinds it has generated.

THE "CONFESSIONS" AND THE PROBLEM OF GENRE

If the modern literary critic wishes to classify Augustine's *Confessions* generically, a likely place to look first is Northrop Frye's compendious work of modern formal analysis, *Anatomy of Criticism: Four Essays.* Such a move does not go unrewarded, for in "Rhetorical Criticism: Theory of Genre," the fourth of the four essays, Frye argues that prose fiction examined "from the point of view of form" may be analyzed in terms of the interweaving of "four chief strands ... novel, confession, anatomy and romance."[1] Two things should be noted here. The first is, as it were, extrinsic. For Frye, the term "fiction" is clearly not equivalent to the term "novel," for his three other categories for prose – confession, romance and anatomy – are also fictional. Rather, "the word fiction, like poetry, means etymologically something made for its own sake."[2] And secondly and, as it were, intrinsically, Frye stresses that "exclusive concentration of one form is rare."[3] Thus any given text might be a mix of characteristics from all four kinds of prose fiction, with those of one so predominating as to permit that text's classification.

This said, however, what are the predominating characteristics of confession for Frye? In the "Glossary" to the *Anatomy,* it is defined as "autobiography regarded as a form of prose fiction, or prose fiction cast in the form of autobiography."[4] But given that the fourth essay invites us to speak of "autobiography" as "the confession form," Frye seems here to give us everything and nothing.[5] In fact, as with many a formalism, what we have here is the problem of the chicken and the egg. Frye seems to be talking Platonically about the idea of confession as autobiography as well as in an Aristotelian way about different kinds of confessional writing, of which autobiography is but one variety. Other readers of Frye have noticed this too. Philippe Lejeune, for example, whose own theory of autobiography is based on the functionalist idea of "le pacte autobiographique" between author and audience, finds Frye's formalist approach "irritante et fascinante" – irritating because it builds "sur une sorte de logique qui appartient moins au domaine de la pensée scientifique qu'à cela de la pensée sauvage," yet fascinating because it does contain "l'idée très juste d'une combinatoire empirique."[6] As a result, Lejeune writes, "on ne saura jamais auquel des traits distinctif du genre [autobiographique] renvoie l'emploi du mot 'confession': s'agit-il du pacte autobiographique, du discours du narrateur, du récit retrospectif à la première personne, de l'emploi d'une focalisation interne, du choix d'un contenu (récit de ou vie privée *ou* de vie intérieure), on d'une attitude (construction d'un modele structure)?"[7] Put another way, we might ask whether Frye's association of confession with autobiography is not too easy an isomorphism.

This ambiguity originates in the fact that Frye does not simply equate confession with autobiography, but with the specific historical instance of Augustine's *Confessions.* Of the confessional form, Frye writes, Augustine "appears to have invented it."[8] This implies that confession, or autobiography, or both, begin with this one text. To be sure, there is such an animal as confessional autobiography, and critics other than Frye are generally agreed that Augustine is its progenitor. Georges Gusdorf, for instance, links confession, autobiography, and Augustine in a similar way to Frye.[9] And more recently, Avrom Fleishman has talked about the distinctly Augustinian pattern of confessional autobiography – a pattern of typological "figures" embracing natural childhood, a fall or exile, wandering or pilgrimage, a crisis, an epiphany or conversion, and final renewal or return – and about its recurrence in a variety of Victorian and twentieth-century autobiographies.[10] Moreover, even when Frye himself mentions other forms of confession, it is always with a reference to the Augustinian model. Rousseau's *Confessions,* for example, are "a modern type of it," even though, as Karl Weintraub has noted, Rousseau himself "seems to deny the validity of any comparison."[11] What is more, "after Rousseau – in fact in Rousseau – the confession flows into the novel, and the mixture produces the fictional autobiography, the *Künstler-roman,* and kindred types," and Frye sees "no literary reason why the subject of a confession should always be the author himself, and dramatic confessions have been used in the novel at least since *Moll Flanders.*"[12] Thus he derives a host of other confessional forms from Augustine's autobiography. But in all this, tracing the ways in which the matter and method of Augustine's *Confessions* have percolated down through the centuries into different kinds of confessional autobiography is not the same as identifying the distinctive characteristics of confessional literature.

This leaves us with two further sets of significant remarks from Frye, both having as much to do with the matter as with the method of confessional writing. In the first, he justifies his distinguishing confession from other kinds of prose fiction: "It gives several of our best prose works a definable place in fiction instead of keeping them in a vague limbo of books which are not quite literature because they are 'thought,' and not quite religion or philosophy because they are Examples of Prose Style."[13] Or, as he puts it further on in the essay, "nearly always some theoretical and intellectual interest in religion, politics or art plays a leading role in the confession."[14] That is to say, however much of a novel, an anatomy, or a romance a confession might be, it is in and of itself an implicitly reflective form, with as much emphasis on ideas themselves as on articulating them in and through character and plot. Secondly, Frye reminds us how much more than other forms of prose fiction confessional writing arises out of and is concerned with what we might call the problem of personal identity. If in the novel there are characters, in the anatomy caricatures, and in the romance allegorical figures, confessional literature offers individuals working out what it means to be a person. In this regard, confessional writing is certainly reflective, but in the sense that ideas inspire and contextualize an author's efforts to locate individual human personality within a broad matrix of religious, political, or aesthetic interests, he is both a "who" and a "what," to borrow Robert Sayre's locution.[15] For as Frye himself explains, "It is his success in integrating his mind on such subjects that makes the author of a confession feel that his life is worth writing about."[16]

For Frye, then, confessional writing constitutes a major form of prose fiction. But even if confessional autobiography, as Frye understands it, does begin with Augustine's autobiography, that is not the same thing as identifying the peculiar characteristics of confessional writing in itself. And conversely, though Augustine's *Confessions* are clearly autobiographical, that is not to say that all confessional writing need always take the form of an autobiography, whether historical or fictional, in verse or in prose, even if, as is likely, it does contain autobiographical elements or an autobiographical dimension. Frye sums up his easy association of confession and autobiography with the observation that all writing of this sort is at once "introverted" and "intellectualized in content."[17]

THE "CONFESSIONS" AND THE ORIGINS OF THE IDEA OF CONFESSION

We have seen that contemporary literary criticism values the *Confessions* as an original and originary work, but at the same time tends to too simple an isomorphism between autobiography and confessional writing. What, then, is distinctive about the idea of confession Augustine inherits? The word "autobiography," of course, is relatively modern, though not first coined by Robert Southey in 1809, as the Oxford English Dictionary has it, but, it seems, by one William Taylor in 1796, as James M. Good has shown.[18] Etymologically, it breaks down as, "a life of a person written by himself or herself."[19] This is the rationale behind Frye's calling confession autobiographical and his tracing its origins to Augustine's *Confessions.* The idea of confession, on the other hand, is not only a lot older than the word autobiography, but also predates Augustine. Western literature possesses any number of pre-Augustinian texts which might rightly be called confessional, many of which are not only not autobiographies, but not even autobiographical in any save the loosest of senses.[20] It is, therefore, to the etymological, historical, and theological origins of the idea of confession in those pre-Augustinian texts that we must turn if we are to discern more clearly what is distinctly confessional about the *Confessions.*

Georg Misch has illustrated that "the channel for all the essential tendencies of autobiography was cut in the ancient world, and Augustine's work is not a beginning but a completion."[21] If the idea of confession represents one of these essential tendencies, however, Misch does not pursue it in detail. Etymologically, the word "confession" is rooted in the Latin *confiteri,* meaning basically "to acknowledge" or "to agree."[22] *Confiteri* itself is an exact synonym for the earlier Greek ὁμολογεῖν. This is not an uncommon term in classical Greek literature, in Judeo-Christian scriptural usage, and in post-Biblical Jewish and Christian writings.[23] As Otto Michel has shown, ancient Hebrew understandings of confession pass into the Graeco-Roman world via the *Septuagint*'s rendering of *hodaah* and related words in terms of ὁμολογεῖν and its derivatives, a process further accelerated as writers like Philo and Josephus, and the Jewish authors of certain New Testament writings consistently use ὁμολογεῖν and related words where some sense of confession is required.[24] Conversely, classical Greek uses of ὁμολογεῖν and its derivatives enter the Judeo-Christian lexicon by the same means, while authors from the late first century onwards – pagan, Jewish, and Christian – draw variously upon these inter-related understandings of confession, as Latin replaces Greek as the *lingua franca* of the ancient world, and *confiteri* replaces ὁμολογεῖν.

Clearly the key term here is ὁμολογεῖν,, since it is the linguistic link among classical Greek, ancient Hebrew, and early Christian understandings of confession. What does it mean? Apart from the everyday sense of simple acknowledgement or agreement, it has specific philosophical, forensic, and religious implications. In Plato's *Crito,* for example, it denotes rational acceptance of a debated issue, and in the passive in Aristotle's *Politics,* unity between one thing and another.[25] Forensic contexts, which often involve political attitudes, include Thucydides' *History of the Pelopponesian War,* where ὁμολογία has to do with terms of surrender in war, and Xenophon's *Symposium,* where it denotes a majority decision.[26] And thirdly, there are the more familiar religious uses, both pagan and in the *Septuagint.* Certain Greek mystery religions seem to have included a kind of confession of sin, though according to H. Grimm, it is in the ancient Hebrew cultus and liturgy that we find for the first time two senses of confession quite clearly distinguished – confession as admission of sin and confession as profession of faith.[27]

All these connotations make their way into the broader arena of first- and second-century literature, whether Graeco-Roman, Jewish, or Christian. Cicero and Quintilian use *confiteri* and related words to mean both simple, personal acknowledgement and in more technical rhetorical and political contexts.[28] Similarly, as Gunther Bornkamm has shown, Philo takes advantage of the rich complexities of ὁμολογεῖν from its usage in Stoic philosophy to the more strictly religious sense of the *Septuagint.*[29] Of these religious senses Josephus, too, is aware, especially when they carry political implications, as in his account of the way in which six hundred Jews refused to confess "Caesar as their master" over against the God of Israel, even under torture.[30] And the Jewish authors of various New Testament writings, some more exposed than others to the wide range of pagan literature, draw upon both classical Greek and ancient Hebrew understandings of confession. In the New Testament, as Michel has demonstrated, ὁμολογεῖν and its derivatives assume the double religious sense – *confessio peccati* and *confessio laudis* – found in the literature of the Hebrew cultus and liturgy, but often with decidedly Greek rhetorical, forensic, and even political overtones.[31] In fact, Michel goes so far as to say that "the legal sense of ὁμολογεῖν is perhaps the most important in the New Testament tradition."[32] Whether the confession is simply christological or binitarian or trinitarian, it involves at least an implicit condemnation of one's own sinfulness and public witness to the lordship of Christ, to his sonship, or to the eternal presence of Father and Son in the Holy Spirit, couched in the forensic rhetoric of eschatological judgement.[33]

Citing a number of New Testament texts, Michel stresses three aspects of Christian confession as particularly important: "It is public, it is absolutely binding, and it is definitive."[34] This is the case whether confession is of sin or of praise, and nowhere do these characteristics assume greater clarity than in the experience of those whom the early churches honoured with the title, *confessor.* Though the legal and political, ramifications of Nero's attack on the Christians at Rome in 64 are unclear, it becomes evident as we move from Pliny's indictment of Bithynian Christians through the persecutions of Decius and Valerius to those of Diocletian and Maximian that, like the Jews whom Josephus describes refusing to confess Caesar as lord, Christians were viewed more and more as a political and religious threat to Roman *pax et ordo.* As such, they were subject to the full weight of Roman law. From several points of view, we find the rhetoric of legal, political, and religious confession bound up together here.[35] For professing Christians, being brought before the Roman authorities in a court of law was the ultimate test of faith: confess Christ or deny him. Not to confess Christ in response to the magistrate's questions – or worse, to confess the divinity of the Emperor or obeisance to the gods of Rome – risked excommunication from the church – or, at best, readmission only after a humiliating public avowal of sin and an even more rigorous series of public penitential exercises. Confession of sin and confession of faith thus overlap in the face of persecution.[36] Because of this, *confessor* became an honorary title bestowed only upon "Christians who had been imprisoned for their faith." In particular and of greatest significance, those Christians who were not only imprisoned, but were even willing to make the final self-sacrifice for their faith in acts of martyrdom were given the most elevated status of all.[37] As H. Strathmann has put it, as early as the Johannine writings, "all μαρτυρεῖν is a ὁμολογεῖν."[38] What is more, even if in this earlier period not all ὁμολογεῖν is μαρτυρεῖν, by the end of the second century, "the distinction between ὁμολογεῖν and μαρτυρεῖν disappears, as may be seen especially in the accounts of the South Gaul martyrdoms in Eus. Hist. Eccl. V. I, where the two terms are fully interchangeable."[39] The martyr is the *confessor in extremis.*

Much of the literature of the early churches came to be identified with the experiences of these persecuted Christians. Whatever importance one attaches to the ambiguous role of oppression in the formulation of the earliest extra-testamental confessions of faith originate at least in part as responses to persecution.[40] From the church's inception, it is true, preaching, teaching, worship, baptism, exorcism and polemics also called for some sort of statement of faith.[41] But in many early Christian communities, as Daniélou has remarked, *confessores* "had attained the dignity of the priesthood," and whatever the ecclesiastical context, the legal and political associations so long implicated in the rhetoric of confession and so forcefully realized in the experience of the *confessores* remain part of that rhetoric and constant reminder of that experience.[42] Among the written confessions arising out of persecution may be counted certain passages from the letters of Ignatius of Antioch, for example, and Polycarp's celebrated profession of faith before those who cast him alive into a martyr's pyre.[43]

Similarly, whether or not one finds evidence for private penance in the New Testament, the early churches certainly demanded public confession of sin – especially of apostasy. To quote Thomas Tentler, "A formal system of forgiveness of serious sins and reconciliation with the body of the faithful began to emerge in the middle of the second century and developed into 'canonical' penance, which ruled until the middle of the seventh."[44] From the various *acta martyrum* and the exhortations to martyrdom of Origen and Tertullian to Cyprian's writings on the problem of the lapsed and Justin's *First Apology*, then, a good deal of the more influential literature circulating among Christians of the first three centuries and more is preoccupied with one aspect or another of this legal, political, and religious conundrum which is the idea of confession – whether it is Roman law or canon law, imperial politics or ecclesiastical politics, Augustan divinity or that of Christ.

In brief, Michel has summed up the several senses of confession current in the early churches:

> This confession of Christ, which is judicially pronounced before the authorities, is the model of forensic confession to which the Christian is called in discipleship (Mt. 10.32; Lk. 12.8), the example of public declaration which the one who bears witness knows he is obliged to make (Jn. 1.20; 9.22; 12.42), and also the basic constituent in the liturgical and cultic baptismal confession which is solemnly recited at reception of the sacrament and ordination.[45]

What is more, these several inter-related senses of confession are very much a matter of public ecclesiastical record. By the time the Council of Nicaea of 325 is over, for example, Christians have not only a working system of graded penance for readmitting the lapsed – including a provision for giving the *viaticum* to death-bed confessors – but also, as John H. Leith has remarked, "a creed that was to be a test for orthodoxy and was to be authoritative for the whole church."[46] Such are the complexities of the idea of confession inherited by Augustine at the end of the fourth century.

CONFESSIONS IN THE "CONFESSIONS"

To be sure, at the time Augustine's *Confessions* were written, ferocious persecution of Christians was a thing of the past. But the rhetoric of confession still carries a complex etymological, historical, and theological mix of legal, political, and religious ingredients. To begin with, the memory of those who had suffered so cruelly for the faith was everywhere preserved. In Frend's words, "Each of the great provincial sees had its list of martyrs who were honoured by a eucharist and sermon which recorded for edification the circumstances of their deaths."[47] Augustine himself seems to have been particularly moved by stories of the martyrdom of Perpetua and Felicitas, to whose memory several of his sermons are dedicated.[48] More to the point, however, the faith was still being put to the test, even if now its foes struck from within. By Augustine's time, the temptation to apostasy suggested by literal trial at the hands of the Roman magistracy assumes the form of an inner trial – whether of Donatists and Pelagians within the body of the church, or of personal sins and doubts within the hearts and minds of individual believers.

As Peter Brown and others have noticed, "the *Confessions* are one of the few books of Augustine's, where the title is significant."[49] Augustine himself says elsewhere that confession involves "accusation of self; praise of God," and few commentators would disagree with Weintraub that however much Augustine proclaims *confessio peccati* in his autobiography, he intends *confessio laudis* all the more so.[50] More importantly, however, this trial of the self before God is not a matter only of words. Augustine's sermon on penance makes it clear, to quote Tentler, that "the sinner must change his life while he lives, while he is healthy."[51] There is thus a strongly didactic intent to the *Confessions,* and this leads J.J. O'Meara to argue that it is a mistake to omit a third sense of confession – *confessio fidei* – from any consideration of the confessions of sin and praise in Augustine's self-writing.[52] The Christian faith is a way of life, and though the Christian is not of the world, he is certainly in it. As Joseph Ratzinger has remarked, Augustine thus locates his own life's story within the sacrificial context of a long Judeo-Christian *Heilsgeschichte,* and, after the manner of the exodus from Egypt, his conversion to Christ from the presumptuous ways of pagan philosophy focusses a series of saving events, at once instructive and archetypal.[53] From a religious point of view, these are the things which make Augustine's autobiography *confessiones,* not *res gestae* or *memoriae* or another of the many pagan *vitae philosophorum.*[54] Insofar as Augustine felt himself "sick" and his "life on earth a period of trial," confessional writing is a practical form of self-therapy and self-judgement; and insofar as the *Confessions* relate Augustine's experience of the world at large, they are at once publicly instructive and a living judgement on that world.[55] When, for instance, he sends a requested copy of the *Confessions* to his friend, Comitus, Augustine is careful both to credit God for what is good in life and to present the book as an edifying lesson on "Him who should be praised concerning me."[56] Or as he puts it in the *Confessions,* "I wish *to act in truth* making my confession both in my heart before you *and in this book* before the many who will read it."[57]

This, surely, is how we must understand the *Confessions,* not so much as a literary autobiography or any other kind of literary object, but more as an action intending ultimate significance for the self and for others because it is performed before the judicial bench of indubitable truth. To begin with, in Weintraub's words, "The sheer act of writing is ... an act of self-orientation."[58] More specifically, it is essential to see that the first nine books of the *Confessions* are written from the standpoint of Augustine's conversion to Christianity. The critical moment of *tolle et lege* in the backyard in Milan functions at once as the chronological outcome of Augustine's life to that instant and as a meaningful centre of reference from which the past takes on the character of a series of revelatory events. This is especially so of Augustine's intellectual journey from dissolute youth through Cicero's *Hortensius,* various forms of philosophical dualism, including Manichaeism, and academic scepticism, to an embryonic Neoplatonic insight into the philosophical truth at the heart of Christianity, as "in an instant of awe" Augustine "attained to the sight of the God who IS."[59]

Slowly, this vision permeates through to the habitual details of everyday life. Now, Augustine begins to read the work of Paul in earnest, and he is struck not only by its intellectual rigour, but also by the appropriateness of Paul's doctrine of grace to his own experience. It does no good to try to will oneself into an attitude of life, Christian or otherwise, since it is clear that the act of willing in and of itself betrays an "inner self divided against itself."[60] A whole-hearted change of will involves the unquestioning acceptance into one's innermost being of an external authority, and for the Christian, this means the authority of "the Lord Jesus Christ."[61] In Augustine's case, this final breakthrough, the tipping of the scales of the heart from habitual profanity to habitual sacrality, happens in that backyard in Milan, where he hears the voice of the child urging him, or so it seems, to take up the Bible and read. Augustine does so, and with that the *Confessions* turn from images of sickness to those of health, from images of bondage to those of freedom, from images of darkness to those of eternal light, in a variety of metaphorical transformations reflecting Augustine's present understanding of the transformation of his own self.

But – and this is the crucial point – the *Confessions* are more than a narcissistic act of self-orientation through writing. Beyond the first nine books there are the last four books. Certainly, some sense of continuity and wholeness of identity distinguishes the *Confessions* as religious autobiography from *res gestae* or *memoriae* or the other sorts of pagan *vitae philosophorum.* But Augustine does not stop here; in fact, in a way, Augustine only starts here. From the time of his conversion forward, Augustine recognizes that life on earth involves a self-conscious participation in "the eternal Jerusalem for which," as he confesses to God, "your people sigh throughout their pilgrimage, from the time they set out until the time when they return to you."[62] In other words, even as he writes the *Confessions,* Augustine understands that conversion renders all subsequent human being a series of transformations of the Christian self in its state of incarnate ultimacy. As Weintraub puts it, "The searching goes on in the present, as in the past, as it will in the future, until the soul, lifted into eternity, will no longer face the problems which exist merely in the passing of time."[63]

In this sense, it is only in the final four books of the *Confessions* that Augustine really begins to fathom the full implications of his own guiding questions: "What do I do when I love my God?" and "What do I love when I love God?"[64] First, he scrutinizes the process of memory itself. "Memory ... is like ... a storehouse for countless images ... which I can fit into the general picture of the past," Augustine writes; "from them I can make a surmise of actions and events and hope for the future; and I can contemplate them all over again as if they were present."[65] For Augustine, it is the power of memory which makes it possible for someone to realise what Weintraub calls "the unification of the personality."[66] But reflection carries Augustine beyond a psychology of memory into a philosophy of time rooted in the first words of the Bible, "In the beginning you made heaven and earth."[67] Dwelling upon this leads Augustine to consider the question, "What was God doing before he made heaven and earth?"[68] It is not that such a question is unanswerable, Augustine claims, but that "People who speak in this way have not learnt to understand you, Wisdom of God, Light of our minds."[69] Rather, reflection reveals that philosophically "neither the future nor the past exist, and therefore it is not strictly correct to say that there are three times, past, present, and future."[70] Instead, "It might be correct to say that there are three times, a present of past things, a present of present things, and a present of future things."[71] We speak now in terms of past, present, and future because, as created beings, we necessarily live in time. For God the Creator, on the other hand, there is only the eternal present. To those who ask, "What was God doing before he made heaven and earth?" therefore, Augustine replies *in nomine dei,* "Let them see ... that there cannot possibly be time without creation.... Let them understand that before all time began you are the eternal Creator of all time, and that no time and no created thing is co-eternal with you, even if any created thing is outside time."[72] Then, having crossed thus from philosophy into theology, Augustine ends the *Confessions* with two books directly exegetical of the first chapter of Genesis. These books amount to a prolonged *exercitatio* in the aetiology and implied eschatology of all individual Christian being, for here, at the deepest level of self-reflection, Augustine gives us "a jubilant acknowledgement of the goodness of all creation."[73] In this respect, along with Max Wundt, we may regard the final four books of the *Confessions* as catechetical in character and reminiscent of the liturgical confession made by the new Christian convert at baptism.[74] But beyond this, these final four books transcend the confines of autobiography established in the first nine books to locate all individual Christian being – Augustine's and that of any one of his readers – in a context of ultimate significance in and through the confessional act of writing itself.

How best may we come to grips with what Augustine is doing in the *Confessions*? For him there is no clear-cut *imitatio Christi in extremis;* the days of persecution and martyrdom are long gone. Augustine's witness must assume another form – a written form. Augustine cannot offer himself physically to the fire, so he offers a written self to his fellow Christians as exhortation, and a statement of Christian fellowship, and of course, as a sacrifice to the Christian God himself. A confession of sin at once private and public; a confession of faith at once literary and liturgical; a confession of praise addressed both to God and to other human beings – these are the various aspects of confession Augustine's *Confessions* involve. In turn, these various kinds of confession take a number of forms, from self-therapy to catechetical edification, from self-judgement to a judgement upon the world, from self-exemplification to public witness. Here, in different degrees are all those senses of confession whose origins lie in the two literatures of the Graeco-Roman and Judeo-Christian worlds Augustine inherited.

AUGUSTINE'S "CONFESSIONS" AS TESTIMONY

Though in part he may be reading a later Judeo-Christian view back into the pagan world, Michel expresses what we may now call the structure of testimony at the heart of the act of confession:

> The noun ὁμολογία, as agreement through a common logos, is especially significant in the Platonic Socratic dialogue, and is the opposite of the average opinion adopted uncritically (δόξᾰ). ὁμολογία implies consent to something felt to be valid, and in such a way that it is followed by definite resolve and action, by ready attachment to a cause. The aim in ὁμολογία is not a theoretical agreement which does not commit us, but acceptance of a common cause.[75]

It is this structure of testimony – this "consent to something felt to be valid, and in such a way that it is followed by definite resolve and action, by ready attachment to a cause" – which links what Augustine is doing when he writes the *Confessions* to the actions of the confessors and martyrs of old, and which binds together the several senses of confession operative in Augustine's self-writing, at once informing and sustaining what Pierre Courcelle has called "une unité de ton" among the many uses of *confiteri* and its derivatives in the *Confessions.*[76] In turn, it is this structure of testimony that makes Augustine's self-writing confessional, not the fact that it is an autobiography, as Frye and several other literary critics and historians would have us believe. True, the *Confessions* are autobiographical, but this is not the primary intention informing Augustine's self-writing. Unlike other forms of autobiography – apology, for instance, which for Francis Hart is primarily ethical, or memoir, which is primarily historical or cultural – confession is primarily ontological; it is, in Frank McConnell's words, "*bene dicere* leading to and constituting *bene esse.*"[77] Occasionally, as Elizabeth Bruss has pointed out, this focus on the self deteriorates into "the delusions of sincerity and narcissistic indulgence of the confessional tradition" so brilliantly parodied in Vladimir Nabokov's *Lolita.*[78] But this need not be so. In Gusdorf's words, the more admirable confession – Augustine's, for instance, or Rousseau's – "takes on the character of an avowal of values and a recognition of self by the self – a choice carried out at the level of essential being"; or, as Hart has it, "Confession is personal history that seeks to communicate or express the essential nature, or truth, of the self."[79]

In contemporary philosophical terms, Augustine's reflections on the course his life has taken and will take are not just fond observations. As Gabriel Marcel has noted of the metaphysical structure of testimony as distinct from that of mere observation, testimony testifies to something absolutely and objectively other, yet involves the willed, inward commitment of the individual's "entire being as a person who is answerable for my assertions and for myself."[80] There is nothing here of narcissistic self-expression. Rather, Augustine's self-writing constitutes – in both active and passive senses of the word "constitutes" – what Jean Nabert has referred to as "le désir de Dieu," with all the wonderfully ambiguous overtones of the "de."[81] The *Confessions* act out Augustine's answer to the question at the heart of all testimony – the question which characterizes most clearly the martyr's literal self-sacrifice: "Do we have the right to invest a moment of history with an absolute character?"[82] To do so involves a kind of dialectic, a double "dépoillement" – literally, "divestment" – and a double judgement. The testimony of the witness at once purifies and puts on trial the individuals' self-understanding as well as their understanding of the nature of that to which they testify. And it is this structure of testimony – this "desire to bear witness" to what has absolutely moved him – that makes what looks like an autobiography really a confession.[83] To indulge in an anachronism, Augustine is fulfilling Sören Kierkegaard's call to Christian witness many centuries later. Kierkegaard writes in his *Journal:* "A witness is a man who immediately supplies proof of the truth of the doctrine he is proclaiming – immediately, well, partly by there being truth in him and blessedness, partly by at once offering himself and saying: see now, whether you can compel me to deny this doctrine."[84]

NOTES

1. Northrop Frye, *Anatomy of Criticism: Four Essays* (Princeton: Princeton University Press, 1957), 312.
2. Frye, *Anatomy,* 303.
3. Ibid., 312.
4. Ibid., 365.
5. Ibid., 307.
6. Philippe Lejeune, *Le Pacte Autobiographique* (Paris: Editions du Seuil, 1975), 332.

7. Lejeune, *Pacte Autobiographique*, 331.

8. Frye, *Anatomy*, 307.

9. Georges Gusdorf, "Conditions and Limits of Autobiography," trans. James Olney, in James Olney, ed., *Autobiography: Essays Theoretical and Critical* (Princeton: Princeton University Press, 1980), 28-48.

10. Avrom Fleishman, *Figures of Autobiography* (Berkeley: University of California Press, 1983), 55-69.

11. Frye, *Anatomy*, 307; and Karl J. Weintraub, *The Value of the Individual: Self and Circumstance in Autobiography* (Chicago: University of Chicago Press, 1978), 299.

12. Frye, *Anatomy*, 307.

13. Ibid.

14. Ibid., 308.

15. Robert F. Sayre, "Autobiography and the Making of America," in Olney, ed., *Autobiography*, 150.

16. Frye, *Anatomy*, 308.

17. Ibid., 307.

18. James M. Good, "William Taylor, Robert Southey, and the Word Autobiography," *The Wordsworth Circle* 12.2 (Spring, 1981), 125-27.

19. Walter W. Skeat, *An Etymological Dictionary of the English Language* (Oxford, 1882), 39.

20. There is no need here to go into detail about the phenomena of autobiography and confession in Eastern cultures. Suffice it to say that if, as Gusdorf asserts, "when Gandhi tells his own story, he is using Western means to defend the East" ("Conditions and Limits," in Olney, ed., *Autobiography*, p. 29), there is certainly no evidence to suggest that any of the authors of neo-Confucian self-writings went to Oxford University to study law, and there were exposed to the autobiographical form. On the contrary, as Rodney L. Taylor's "The Centred Self: Religious Autobiography in the Neo-Confucian Tradition," *History of Religions* 17.3 and 4 (1978), 266-83 has shown, theirs is their own form. Similarly, as far as confession is concerned, Pei-yi We seems not to think that he is carrying Augustinian or any other Western criteria to his analysis of certain kinds of sixteenth- and seventeenth-century Chinese literature when he discusses "Self-Examination and the Confession of Sins in Traditional China," *Harvard Journal of Asiatic Studies*, 39.1 (1979), 5-38. Their "self-stricture," as he calls it, is altogether their own (5). In fact, for a comprehensive study of confession of sin in literatures other than the Western Judeo-Christian from an historian of religion's point of view, see Raffaele Pettazzoni, *La confessione dei peccati*, 3 vols. (Bologna, 1929-36), as well as his shorter pieces, "The Confession of Sins: An Attempted General Interpretation," and "Confession of Sins and the Classics," in *Essays on the History of Religions*, trans. H.J. Ross (Leiden: Brill, 1954), 44-45, 55-67.

21. Georg Misch, *A History of Autobiography in Antiquity*, trans. E.W. Dickes, 2 vols. (London: Longmans, Green and Company, 1950), 1. 17.

22. Skeat, *An Etymological Dictionary*, 44.

23. For classical Greek uses, see H.G. Liddell and R. Scott, *A Greek-English Lexicon* (Oxford, 1843), p. 1226; and for biblical and post-biblical uses, see Walter Bauer, *A Greek-English Lexicon of the New Testament and Other Early Christian Literature* (Chicago, 1979), 568.

24. These and following remarks on the uses of ὁμολογεῖν and related words derive mainly from Otto Michel's word study in Gerhard Kittel, ed., *Theological Dictionary of the New Testament*, trans. and ed. G.W. Bromiley, 10 vols. (Grand Rapids: Erdmans, 1964-76), 5. 199-220. Michel schematizes his study into five areas – secular Greek uses of ὁμολογεῖν; Old Testament-Oriental and Hellenistic-Gnostic liturgical uses; the *Septuagint* and post-biblical Jewish uses; the New Testament; and post-apostolic uses. Other than Liddell and Scott, *A Greek-English Lexicon*, particularly important among Michel's sources are Gunther Bornkamm, "Ὁμολογία, zur Geschichte eines politischen Begriffes, *Hermes: Zeitschrift fur klassiche Philologie* 71 (1936), 239-62; Hermann Gunkel, *The Psalms: A Form-Critical Introduction*, intro. James Muilenburg, trans. T.M. Horner (Philadelphia, 1967); Richard Reitzenstein, *Das iranisches Erlösungsmysterium* (Bonn, 1924), especially p. 258, where the synonymity between *hodaah* and ὁμολογεῖν is argued; Oscar Cullman, *The Earliest Christian Confessions*, trans. J.K.S. Reid (Chicago, 1949); and Hans Rheinfelder, "*Confiteri, confessio, confessor* im Kirchenlatein und in den romanischen Sprachen," *Die Sprache* 1 (1949), 56-67.

25. Plato, *Crito*, 52b; and Aristotle, *Politics*, II. 9. p. 1270b. 31. Michel cites both in Kittel, ed., *Theological Dictionary*, 5. 200.

26. Thucydides, *History of the Pelopponesian War*, III. 90; and Xenophone, *Symposium*, VIII. 36.

27. Pettazzoni, "Confession of Sin and the Classics," analyzes texts in Ovid's *Metamorphoses*, Juvenal's *Satires*, and Plutarch's *On Superstition* which report confession of sin in Greek mystery religions. For the double meaning of confession in ancient Hebrew religion, see H. Grimm, "Der Begriff von hebraischen *hodaah* und *lehodah*," *Zeitschrift für die alttestamentliche Wissenschaft* 58 (1940-41), 234-40, especially 235.

28. See, for example, Cicero, *Oratio pro Caecina*, 9.24, and *De Deorum Natura*, 2.4.11; and Quintilian, *Institutiones Oratoriae*, 1.6.15 and 9.2.64.

29. Gunther Bornkamm, "Die Offenbarung des Zornes Gottes," *Zeitschrift für die neutestamentliche Wissenschaft und die kunde des Urchristentums* 34 (1935), 239-62, studies the several senses of confession in Philo.

30. Josephus, *De Bello Judaico*, 7.418.

31. See Michel's word study of ὁμολογεῖν in Kittel, ed., *Theological Dictionary*, 5. 207-17.

32. Ibid., 207.

33. For the different kinds of confessional statements in the New Testament, see Cullman, *Earliest Christian Confessions;* and more recently, J.N.D. Kelly, *Early Christian Creeds*, 3rd. ed. (London: Adam and Charles Black, 1972), especially Chapter 1.

34. Michel, in Kittel, ed., *Theological Dictionary*, 5. 221.

35. For general accounts of this period of church history, see Jean Daniélou and Henri Marrou, *The Christian Centuries,* Vol. I, *The First Six Hundred Years,* trans. Vincent Cronin (New York, 1964), 81-90, 205-8, 231-35; and more recently, Robert M. Grant, *Augustus to Constantine* (New York, 1970), 78-100, 165-72, 226-34. The most detailed account of the persecutions is W.H.C. Frend, *Martyrdom and Persecution in the Early Church* (Oxford, 1965). Three recent studies of the legal and political ramifications of early Christian conflicts with the Roman imperium are: A.N. Sherwin-White, "The Early Persecutions and Roman Law Again," *Journal of Theological Studies* 3 (1952), 199-213; G.E.M. de Ste. Croix, "Why Were the Early Christians Persecuted?" *Past and Present* 26 (1963), 6-38; and Herbert Musurillo, *The Acts of the Christian Martyrs* (Oxford, 1972), lvii-lxii.

36. See Eusebius, *History of the Church,* V.i. For a careful reconstruction of this sad chapter of religious history, see Frend, *Martyrdom,* 1-31.

37. Daniélou and Marrou, *First Six Hundred Years,* 163.

38. See H. Strathmann's word study of μαρτυρειν and related words in Kittel, ed. *Theological Dictionary,* 4. 497 n. 63, 505.

39. Ibid., 505.

40. Cullman, *Earliest Christian Confessions,* and Kelly, *Early Christian Creeds,* represent differing views on the nature of intra-testamental confession. Both agree that various circumstances demanded various kinds of confession, but there they part company. Cullman emphasizes persecution as a major influence on the development of creedal formulae: they were sound theological responses to the demands of Roman officials in a court of law. Kelly disputes this emphasis, finding Cullman's thesis too evolutionary and monolithic, and preferring to allow the various kinds of confession more or less independent development in various times and places. Even Kelly, however, admits the important role of persecution in his more relativized scenario (15).

41. Cullman, *Earliest Christian Confessions,* 18-24, and Kelly, *Early Christian Creeds,* 1-29, run through these several occasions for confession.

42. Daniélou and Marrou, *First Six Hundred Years,* 163.

43. For the creedal statements of Ignatius of Antioch, see John H. Leith, *Creeds of the Churches,* rev. ed. (Richmond, VA, 1973), 16; for Polycarp's, see Musurillo, *Acts of the Christian Martyrs,* 12-15.

44. Thomas Tentler, *Sin and Confession on the Eve of the Reformation* (Princeton, 1977), 4. For the view that some kind of private penance always existed in the churches, see Paul Galtier, *L'Eglise et la rémission des péchés* (Paris, 1932); and for a less sanguine analysis, see R.C. Mortimer, *The Origins of Private Penance in the Western Church* (Oxford, 1939).

45. Michel, in Kittel, ed., *Theological Dictionary,* 5. 211

46. Leith, *Creeds,* 28. For a thorough analysis of ecclesiastical penance, see Oscar D. Watkins, *A History of Penance,* 2 vols. (London, 1920).

47. Frend, *Martyrdom,* xi.

48. See, for example, Augustine, *Serm.,* 280.

49. Peter Brown, *Augustine of Hippo* (Berkeley, 1967), 175.

50. Augustine, *Serm.*, 67.2; and Weintraub, *Value of the Individual*, 22.

51. Tentler, *Sin and Confession*, 8. For the full sermon, see Augustine, *Serm.*, 393.

52. J.J. O'Meara, *The Young Augustine* (London: Longmans, Green and Company, 1954), 2-5.

53. Joseph Ratzinger, "Originalität und Uberlieferung in Augustins Begriff der Confessio," *Revue des Études Augustiniennes*, 3 (1951), 375-92.

54. For these generic distinctions, see Weintraub, *Value of the Individual*, 1-17.

55. Augustine, *Conf.*, trans. R.S. Pine-Coffin (Baltimore: Penguin, 1961), 232.

56. Augustine, *Letters*, 231.

57. Augustine, *Conf.*, 207. The emphasis is mine.

58. Weintraub, *Value of the Individual*, 24.

59. Augustine, *Conf.*, 151.

60. Ibid., 170.

61. Ibid., 178.

62. Ibid., 205.

63. Weintraub, *Value of the Individual*, 26.

64. Augustine, *Conf.*, 211, 213.

65. Ibid., 214, 215-16.

66. Weintraub, *Value of the Individual*, 40.

67. Augustine, *Conf.*, 256.

68. Ibid., 161.

69. Ibid.

70. Ibid., 269.

71. Ibid.

72. Ibid., 279.

73. Weintraub, *Value of the Individual*, 41.

74. Max Wundt, "Augustins Konfessionen," *Zeitschrift für neutestamentliche Wissenschaft und die Kunde des Urchristentums* 29 (1923), 161-206.

75. Michel, in Kittel, ed., *Theological Dictionary*, 5, 200.

76. Pierre Courcelle, *Recherches sur des Confessions de Saint Augustin* (Paris: E. de Boccard, 1950), 50.

77. Francis R. Hart, "Notes for an Anatomy of Modern Autobiography," *New Literary History* 1 (1970), 491; and Frank D. McConnell, *The Confessional Imagination: A Reading of Wordsworth's Prelude* (Baltimore: Johns Hopkins University Press, 1974), 9.

78. Elizabeth Bruss, *Autobiographical Acts: The Changing Situation of a Literary Genre* (Baltimore: Johns Hopkins University Press, 1976), 18.

79. Gusdorf, "Conditions and Limits," in Olney, ed., *Autobiography*, 44; and Hart, "Notes," 501.

80. Gabriel Marcel, *The Philosophy of Existence*, trans. Manya Harari (London: Harvill Press, 1948), 70.

81. Jean Nabert, *Le désir de Dieu* (Paris: Aubier-Montaigne, 1966).

82. Paul Ricoeur, "The Hermeneutics of Testimony," in *Essays on Biblical Interpretation,* ed. and intro. Lewis S. Mudge (Philadelphia: Fortress Press, 1980), 142. It should be noted that Ricoeur here depends heavily on Nabert, *Le désir de Dieu* and upon another of Nabert's works, *L'essai sur le mal* (Paris: Presses Universitaires de France, 1955).

83. Wesley A. Kort, *Narrative Elements and Religious Meanings* (Philadelphia: Fortress Press, 1975), 90.

84. Soren Kierkegaard, *The Journals,* ed. and trans. Alexander Dru (New York: Oxford University Press, 1938), 389.

AUGUSTINE'S CONVERSION AND THE NINTH BOOK OF THE *CONFESSIONS*

COLIN STARNES

Augustine ends his first confession in the ninth book, which brings to a close the account of how he moved from his birth in nature to his rebirth in the church. At the same time it prepares the transition to his second confession in book ten. The ninth book covers the period from his conversion in the garden in Milan, sometime in the first week of August 386, to the day of his mother's burial at Ostia in the fall of 387.[1] There are four points about this book which I want to discuss in relation to Augustine's conversion. The first is to ask why he bothered to include it at all and what its content is about. The second concerns the *Dialogues* which he wrote in the winter at Cassiciacum before returning to Milan to be baptized at Easter in 387. The third has to do with the famous vision at Ostia, and the fourth with the reason why he ended his first confession at this point – only to begin another in book ten. The first and the last of these questions have received almost no attention, and the second and third almost too much.

If Augustine's purpose in writing his autobiography was to provide a full explanation of the steps that led him to Christianity, then the question arises, why did he not end this first confession with his conversion – i.e., at the end of book eight? After all, that was the point at which he freely willed to become a Christian to the exclusion of all other beliefs – so what more was there to add? The obvious answer is that in a formal sense one only becomes a Christian through baptism. Augustine makes this clear in the *Confessions* by recounting the story which Simplicianus had told him about Victorinus, who finally saw that, however much he liked to think of himself as a Christian, he could not be counted such in this world until he entered the walls of a church and was baptized.[2] With this in mind we can say that Augustine did not think he had given a complete account of the steps that led him to the church until he had taken it up to the time of his baptism.

But if this is the purpose of the ninth book, it does not explain why the second half contains a brief *vita* of Monica from her early childhood through to her burial. Why does he take the account beyond his baptism, and why only so far as to include the few months between that event and his mother's death and burial? Augustine makes it clear that this "life" is not an accidental addendum – as if the mention of Monica at the end of the account of his baptism (chapter seven) had led him to ramble on beyond his original purpose. He tells us (chapter eight) that he has had to skip over many things, because he is only confessing the essential features in his conversion, yet insists that what he has to say here is essential to his purpose. But what do the details of *Monica*'s early life, and the vision at Ostia *after* his baptism, have to do with *his* conversion to the church? We must answer this or abandon our assumption that the content of the first nine books is the confession of how he became a Christian.

The answer lies at hand if we think of the differences between conversion itself – which Augustine describes as an inward unification of the will[3] – and the objective nature of the life thus willed. It is true that inwardly one becomes a Christian in the moment of conversion, but unless we die in the very next instant, the process is not complete until the objective and external aspects of one's life are brought into conformity with this inner will. There are two moments in this process. The first is Christ's requirement that those who live beyond their conversion must be baptized. Yet even when baptized, the process of *becoming a Christian* is not complete, for every act throughout the rest of one's life has still to be informed by the will to obey Christ in all things. This is clearly a process that can only end at death.

The content of the ninth book is thus about the *objective* requirements of the process of becoming a Christian. Augustine could deal with his own case between conversion and baptism. Yet, without a statement of the further requirements, between baptism and death, his account of the process in which he was involved would be incomplete. He could not illustrate these things out of his own life because it had not reached its end. He therefore concludes by showing the objective character of the life he had willed – between baptism and death – through the example of his mother. Understood in this sense, the life of Monica is an integral part of his first confession and its proper conclusion, since he uses it to show the final steps that are objectively necessary to becoming a Christian in this world.

My second point concerns one of the things Augustine tells us in the *Confessions* about the period between his conversion and baptism. He mentions the works which he wrote at Cassiciacum where he spent the fall and winter waiting until it was time to be baptized. The so-called *Dialogues* which he wrote at this time, the *Contra Academicos, De beata vita, De ordine* (all in November), and the *Sololoquia* (written in the winter) have been the cause of a great controversy that began a century ago. In 1888, Adolf Harnack noted that in the *Confessions,* written ten years after the event, Augustine presents his conversion as a sudden break – vividly distinguishing between his past life as a natural man and the new life of grace.[4] On the other hand, if one looks to the evidence of the *Dialogues,* written only a few months after his conversion, Augustine appears to be still contentedly immersed in the culture of late pagan antiquity. In these works he is only concerned with philosophical questions; there is scarcely anything that is identifiably Christian, and nothing of the tone of repentance and praise that so distinguishes the *Confessions.* If Augustine really was suddenly and completely converted in August of 386 and if this was a real revolution in his life, how then can we explain the fact that the works which he wrote right afterward show almost no perceptible Christian content or interest? Because of this discrepancy Harnack and others found themselves forced to call into question the historical accuracy of the *Confessions.* The *Dialogues,* they said, because closer to the event, should be relied upon in preference to the *Confessions* as witness to the true state of Augustine's soul at the time – and what *they* reveal is a man converted to ancient philosophy rather than to Christianity.

Harnack concluded that Augustine had altered the facts of his conversion in the account of the *Confessions* because he never intended it as a history in the strict sense. Loosely based on his life, it was organized on a theological principle that made it convenient for him to alter the facts and present his conversion as a sudden break – with his past life painted in exaggeratedly dark colours in contrast to the shining light of grace that attends those who have come to the church. At the time he was merely "converted" to philosophy; his conversion to Christianity came more slowly and was only completed years later.

The strength of this position found many advocates in the early part of this century. However, its shocking conclusion that for fifteen hundred years the world had blithely assumed the *Confessions* to be a true and historical account of Augustine's conversion when it was nothing of the sort soon galvanized others to attempt a defence of its historical accuracy. This effort gained strength through the first half of the century, culminating in Pierre Courcelle's magisterial work, *Recherches sur les Confessions de Saint Augustin* (1950).

Spurred by the critics to explain the apparent contradiction between the *Dialogues* and the *Confessions,* these scholars went to the heart of the problem as they saw it, and have shown how, on theological considerations, the *Dialogues* are really Christian. From the first they have attacked the critics at their weakest point – in the assumption that Christianity and Neoplatonism are poles apart. They insist, on perfectly sound theological grounds, that there is more that joins these two than separates them. Already in 1903, Portalie had argued that what seems in the *Dialogues* to be Neoplatonism is simply the philosophical expression of a truth which derives from Scripture.[5] This position lies behind all subsequent arguments for the historical value of the *Confessions.* The line of defence is clear. By showing that Christianity and Neoplatonism are not two different things, as argued by the critics, the apparent contradiction between the evidence of the *Dialogues* and the *Confessions* dissolves and the historical value of the latter is re-established.

This defence has won the day. But a problem still remains, for the defenders seem to have confirmed the substantial historical validity of the text by means of an interpretation which does not do justice to the theology of the *Confessions* itself. We can see this most clearly in Courcelle, who has given the most highly developed treatment of the position. He argues that Augustine was converted to Christianity when and as he says he was. The reason why the *Dialogues* are purely philosophical is that the Christianity which he had learned from Ambrose, the bishop of Milan, was already assimilated to Neoplatonism.[6] But if Augustine was converted to Christianity through his intellectual awakening to the truths of Neoplatonic philosophy, then what is the difference between the two positions?

Having made an essential identification between Christianity and Neoplatonism, Courcelle and his followers are forced to look for the differences in a secondary and peripheral realm – centring on such practical questions as the reform of conduct and the acceptance of uniquely Christian rites and doctrines which are assumed to follow the "intellectual" conversion as a matter of course. But this does not seem to be adequate to what Augustine says in the *Confessions.* He insists that while Platonism teaches truths that Christianity also teaches, nevertheless the difference between them is absolute and complete. On the one hand is the presumptuous philosopher, who has a true knowledge of God, yet willingly transmutes this wisdom into folly by refusing to accept the mediation of Christ. Without any concrete link between himself and God, he is likened, in Augustine's image, to one who knows the goal but not the way to it. His choice therefore is not for God and his city but for himself in the city of man. On the other hand there are the Christians who, believing in the Word made flesh, have humbly submitted to God's authority and placed their confidence in His power to unite them to Himself. These, says Augustine, not only see the heavenly city, but are also on the way to it (7.20.26). The absolute and uncompromising nature of this difference is lost in Courcelle's defence of the historicity of the *Confessions.*

The original difficulty about the historical accuracy of the text and the newer problem of the defenders would both evaporate if we could explain why Augustine, though truly converted to a Christianity which was poles apart from Neoplatonism, nevertheless wrote the philosophical *Dialogues* right after his conversion. From what we have already established about the purpose of the ninth book, I think this can be understood in the following way.

I take it for granted that Augustine was converted, in August of 386, to a Christianity which was absolutely distinguished from Platonism in the sense I have indicated. This is the point of book eight, where Augustine insists that he was not converted until his will had been brought to submit wholly and entirely to Christ and to accept his authority in all things. But if he had done this in August, why do the *Dialogues* of November make almost no mention of Christ? The answer lies in Augustine's peculiar status between the time of his conversion in the late summer and his baptism the following spring.

Before his conversion there would have been no problem in writing about Christianity from the position of an outsider. Nor would there have been any problem in writing about it from the standpoint of an insider once he had been baptized. But, in the period between August and April, Augustine was in neither position. His conversion ruled out any treatment of these matters from a profane and external viewpoint.

On the other hand, as he had neither been instructed in an authorized manner in the belief of the church nor was yet a member of it, it would have been presumptuous for Augustine to speak out as a Christian on Christian matters during this period. It does not matter that there can have been little, if anything, in the formal catechism that he had not already learned from Monica, Ambrose, or the Scriptures. What matters is that regardless of how much one knows of the doctrine of the church, no one, not even a Victorinus or an Augustine, can become a member until these things have been given authoritatively and received as such.[7] Until this had happened, at his baptism, Augustine, with the humility belonging to his status as a converted catechumen, did not attempt to speak as a Christian on Christian matters.

But this did not mean that he could not use the time to serve the church in another capacity. In the *Confessions* he deprecates the *Dialogues* as "panting" too much of the old air of "the school of pride" (i.e., ancient philosophy), from which he had only just been converted, yet he insists that in spite of this failing they were written in the service of God.[8] And for the converted Augustine this meant that they were written in the service of Christ. Indeed, he reports that he had to convince his friend and fellow convert Alypius – ever in awe of Augustine's philosophical learning – that the name of Christ should appear in them at all. "For he preferred that they should reek of the *cedars* of the schools which *the Lord had* already *broken* (Ps. 28.5) rather than the health-giving herbs of the church which are effective against serpents."[9] That is, Alypius, "panting" after his own fashion from his former worldliness, wanted Augustine to include only the high and noble concepts of human philosophy rather than have them point to the lowly and humble herbs of the field (the sacraments of the church) by which man's sin is cured.

But all of the *Dialogues* and the letters to Nebridius have this latter as their one aim. Each intends to show, by reason alone, how nature, according to its own logic, leads inexorably to the door of the church and to the recognition of the need for the mediation of Christ. This is what Augustine had found from his own experience. In his works at Cassiciacum he presents this argument in a number of ways for the benefit of others.[10] This is philosophy given over to the service of Christ while preserving an absolute difference between itself and the matters of faith about which he did not presume to speak. In this view we can see how Augustine was converted to a Christianity which he understood to be absolutely different from philosophy and yet wrote the philosophical *Dialogues* right after his conversion. From this standpoint there is no contradiction between the evidence of the *Dialogues* and the *Confessions,* and the original problem of the critics, as well as the newer one generated by the defence, both simply disappear.

My third point concerns the vision at Ostia. This chapter (ten) has been the subject of extensive studies by modern scholars. Of these, the most fundamental is Paul Henry's little book of 1938, *La Vision d'Ostie.* His great knowledge of Plotinus made the work of primary importance in "... the solution of the problem of the Christian/Plotinian opposition."[11] Coming in the midst of the historicity debate, with which however it is not explicitly concerned, his was one of the strongest voices to be raised against the view of the critics that Plotinianism and Christianity were merely antithetical opposites. Henry's work was used by Courcelle, who saw chiefly that Henry had shown how the vision at Ostia has Plotinian sources. But this is only one side of the matter, and Solignac can write with justice that "all interpreters agree in recognizing that a Plotinian expression does not prejudice the authentically *Christian* character of the experience described."[12] Yet if it is recognized by all that there are both Plotinian and Christian elements in Augustine's account of the vision at Ostia, it has not been possible to show clearly and exactly how these are related to, and distinguished from one another.

Let me illustrate briefly by showing how both Henry and Courcelle handle the question. Henry's position is far from simplistic. Throughout his book he deals with three strands which he distinguishes in the *Confessions* – philosophy, authority, life. He knows they are somehow one, yet he never manages to hold them together in anything more than a loose braid which easily falls apart in the hands of another. Thus Courcelle will say that, "One cannot doubt, since the work of P. Henry, that the plot of the story is constituted by the Plotinian treatises *On the Beautiful* and *On the Three Hypostases which are Principles.*"[13] For Courcelle, the vision at Ostia is basically Plotinian, though "transcribed into the Biblical style."[14] This is not Henry's position, for whom the Christian element is not simply a scriptural formulation of Plotinian thought. What Courcelle chooses not to see is where Henry also quotes Augustine at length to the effect that while Neoplatonists and Christians share the same notion of the blessed life, they differ completely in the estimate of how man can achieve it – the Platonists rejecting the incarnation and the resurrection and the Christians accepting both. Where Courcelle sees only Plotinianism in Christian clothing, Henry, with better justice, sees both Plotinianism and Christianity side by side. Yet Henry does not show exactly how they are related and how distinguished in Augustine's thought, and unless this can be done it is impossible to prevent their conflation.

I suggest that we will find a satisfactory answer if we consider the question in its context in the ninth book. If, as I argue, Augustine included the little *vita* of Monica to show the character of the Christian life after baptism, then it follows that he intended the vision at Ostia to be understood as specifically Christian – in contrast to the earlier vision at Milan. The vision at Milan was a Platonist vision. It is the knowledge of the invisible God which all men can achieve by their own natural powers through the consideration of creation. If Augustine expresses the content of the vision in book seven largely in scriptural terms drawn from the prologue to John's gospel, it is because he is writing for a Christian audience in whom he did not expect to find any philosophical culture. It did not matter whether his readers knew anything of Plato or Plotinus, or exactly which of their books had led him to the vision, and he does not trouble to specify the ones he read by anything more than a vague *quosdam libri Platonicorum* – "certain books of the Platonists."[15] His point is that Christians share with the Platonists the same notion of God the Father and the same notion of his eternally begotten Son – the Word in whom all things are made. He testifies, as one of the few who have risen to the actual vision of God, that the God of the Christians and the God of the Platonists is one and the same. Furthermore, the conception of the proper end of the human soul, of its perfect bliss, as consisting in this vision, is common both to Platonism and Christianity. The *City of God* is full of passages which say this unequivocally.[16]

I therefore take it for granted that the vision at Milan and the vision at Ostia are both the direct, though momentary, grasp of one and the same God, seen "in himself" – arrived at in both cases through the consideration of creation, and known in both cases to be the true goal and bliss of the soul. But here all similarity ends. Augustine's purpose in his discussion of the vision at Ostia is to show the absolute difference between the vision of God as experienced by the philosopher on the one hand and by the Christian on the other. He had known the same vision from both positions and could speak with authority. What he emphasizes, and what we are supposed to attend to, are the differences between the two –

differences explicable solely in terms of Christianity – which give to the vision at Ostia a character that lies altogether beyond the province and possibilities of human philosophy. The following nine points give an idea of what can be found once we know what we are looking for.

1) Although Augustine shares in the vision we should not forget that the description occurs in the little life of *Monica.* This *vita,* I argue, is included to show the objective nature of the Christian life. In the two previous chapters (eight and nine) Augustine had described how Monica fulfilled the duties of that calling. In the chapter on her vision and the subsequent one on her death he shows its earthly rewards.

2) In the vision of book seven we know, by implication only, that it took place in Milan – Augustine tells us nothing about its physical setting. The character of the Plotinian ascent – its ecstatic union of the mind and God by abstraction from all worldly conditions – makes physical details of no importance. In the vision at Ostia, on the other hand, these are carefully described. He and Monica were "standing leaning" against a window that looked out over an "inner garden of the house," "far from the turmoil" (of the world), enjoying a moment in which they could "renew," "repair," "celebrate," and "refresh themselves" (*instaurabamus*).[17] Here is an earthly anticipation of heaven which is the very opposite of Plotinus's "flight [from the world] of the alone to the alone."[18]

3) Both accounts also have spiritual setting and both are attributed to divine providence, but there is a great difference. The vision at Milan, in bringing Augustine to the true knowledge of God, is spoken of as curing the tumour which had prevented him from seeing the truth, and yet the whole thing is placed squarely in the economy of pride – the pride of the man from whom Augustine got the books of the Platonists, the pride of the Platonists in their knowledge of God, and the presumption which, for a while, this vision generated in Augustine.[19] There is none of this at Ostia. Augustine begins the account with the statement: "The day however was soon to come when [Monica] would quit this life – what day it was you knew, though we did not...."[20] Here there are no tumours to be cured and so far as anyone was to be cured of anything, Monica was going to be "cured" of this life, where we can see only in part – but only to go to another, better life, where she could perpetually enjoy the vision of God, face to face.

4) The whole account of the vision at Ostia is told in the first person

plural. This is true not only of the external narrative, as when Augustine says *we* were standing at the window and *we* talked together, but also of the vision itself – *we* strove towards that [goal] and *we* attained to it.[21] Of course, both *were* there. But what can this mean? We are not simply dealing with the extraordinary circumstance of two people coming to the vision of God in the same instant, but of a union or community in that vision. Their shared vision was not only simultaneous, but *mutual* – that is, each knew the other was there. But this is theoretically impossible according to Plotinus. It must be so for him, because in the One all the distinctions of finitude are lost – including the distinction between "you" and "me," between Monica and Augustine. The philosophical vision is essentially solitary, and those who come to it must do so alone – as was the case with Augustine at Milan. What then explains the difference between Milan and Ostia such that Augustine and Monica can now have the vision together? It only becomes possible if finite distinctions are themselves present in God. Plotinus knows nothing of this, but it is the meaning of the incarnation.

5) At Ostia, the discussion which led to the vision was about the nature of the life of the saints – that is, about their life in the world to come. They were inquiring after something which had been promised to them as their own and not, as with Augustine in Milan, after what was other than himself. The basis of this confidence was their belief in the promises of Christ. The suggestion that mutable man can be with the immutable God is, for Plotinus, the sign of an outrageous ignorance or arrogance.[22]

6) Henry insists that the object of the vision at Milan and Ostia is God Himself, *in id ipsum,*[23] seen "without any intermediary" – which is "identically that [object] of the highest Plotinian contemplation."[24] This is true as far as it goes, but it does not go far enough. The *id ipsum* towards which Augustine and Monica rose at Ostia is not simply the eternal Word of God in whom all things were made – which *was* the object of the Platonist vision of book seven. Their vision is the vision of the same Word, but seen here as incarnate and made available to humankind. In Milan he said, "I sensed the fragrance of the fare but was not yet able to eat it";[25] here they came to "that place of unending plenty where You feed Israel forever with the food of truth."[26] This is only possible because God, *in id ipsum,* is not simply known here in his otherness from the conditions of finitude but also in his (revealed) identity with it. But this is to say that the

vision at Ostia is the vision of the true church, the heavenly Jerusalem, which sees God face to face because it is held to him by the God who is God and man. Henry is wrong then when he says they came to the knowledge of God "without any intermediary" because theirs was rather the vision of the Mediator.[27]

7) The whole testimony of ancient philosophy, and of Augustine's own experience, is that it took years of training and considerable philosophical culture to escape the bonds of the sensible and rise to the vision of the intelligible God. Monica had none of this and yet she came to this vision as easily as Augustine. She could pass beyond the sensible in this way because the sensible to which she held in faith (Christ) was also the Eternal Word of God.

8) Augustine says "We sighed and we left there *the first fruits of the spirit* attached to it"[28] – that is, to the heavenly Jerusalem. This means that what they had glimpsed in the vision they understood to be a foretaste of what would be theirs forever on the resurrection of the body. This is what Paul teaches in the passage from which the phrase *primitias spiritus* is taken (Rom. 8.22-25),[29] and Augustine explicitly points to the resurrection when he asks in a rhetorical question, "But when will this be? *Will it be when we all rise...?* (1 Cor. 15.51)."[30] In Milan the body, the *consuetudo carnalis,* the "habit of the flesh,"[31] had been the inevitable and insurmountable obstacle to the continued enjoyment of God unless an adequate mediator could be found.[32] At Ostia it is the necessary condition of its fulfillment. That this is so depends entirely on the mediation of Christ.

9) Finally, in the vision of God at Milan, Augustine discovered himself to be in a *regione dissimilitudinis,*[33] a place of utter unlikeness to God – from which he had no hope of escape except in a temporal sense through repeated ecstatic visions. At Ostia, Monica and Augustine easily agree that where they had been, the *regionem ubertatis indeficientis*[34] – the place of unfailing plentiousness – it was possible to be forever and that this was the condition of the saints – Christian men and women who had died in the faith. Nowhere does Plotinus teach that temporal man can enjoy this vision eternally.[35] Without a true mediator, without Christ, the vision of God merely separates. With him it beckons man to his true and proper home in the heavenly city "which is meant to be no mere vision but our home,"[36] and Monica's response was to answer this call – which she could do because she believed there was no further work for her to do in this.[37]

Finally, for my fourth point, let me suggest in a few words why Augustine concludes with the *vita* of Monica and begins the second of his three confessions in book ten.[38] If, as I maintain, Monica's life is included in the first confession to show the objective character of the Christian life to which he had been converted and baptized, it is nevertheless clear that this is not the only, nor the most important, thing for a Christian. Augustine shows this in the last chapter of the ninth book. There, he sets aside his praise of Monica's good works – those that had an objective, visible character such as he has been speaking about – and he petitions Christ who is the "true medicine for our wound" (i.e., original sin), to cover and remit any sinful action which she may have done from her baptism.

> For I do not dare to say that from the moment she was regenerated through baptism no word ever left her mouth which went against your precept. For it is said by the Truth, Your Son: "*If anyone says to his brother, 'You fool,' he will have to answer for it in the fires of hell*" (5.22).

This is the standard to which Christians are held by Christ. It is a standard which goes far behind any embodiment in good works or any participation in the rites and sacraments of the church. Even when this objective side of things was fulfilled as well as it was with Monica, Augustine could still not be certain that she had perfectly fulfilled the law nor that she was a complete Christian. The tenth commandment – "Thou shalt not *covet* thy neighbour's house, nor his wife, nor his ox, nor his ass, nor anything that is his" (Ex. 20.17) – can have no objective embodiment. Christ not only echoed this commandment – which requires the same freedom from contradiction inwardly as the others demand outwardly – but insisted upon it as, for example, where he says that the man who merely looks at a woman lustfully has already committed adultery with her in his heart (Mt. 5.28). This last of the commandments which, alone, was of no concern to the ordering of human society because it could have no objective embodiment, was, so to speak, the main concern of the new society of Christians for whom, as in Augustine and Monica's case, objective compliance with the law was given in their baptism. He could not speak for Monica on these matters. Indeed no one can answer for another. All he could do was to offer up his prayers on her behalf and invite those of his readers. But about himself he could speak. The need for his second confession, about how he stood inwardly in relation to these subjective demands, arises in this way out of the conclusion of the first.

NOTES

1. See Solignac's chronology, *Les Confessions BA,* vol. 13, (Paris: Etudes Augustiniennes, 1962), 206.

2. See 8.2.3-5.

3. See 8.8.19-20, 24.

4. *Augustins Confessionen,* Giessen, Ricker. A brief account of the historicity debate may be found in Solignac's introduction to the *BA* edition, vol. 13, 55-84. Augustine speaks of the works he wrote at Cassiciacum in *Confessions* 9.4.7, without mentioning them by name. *On the Good Life, On Order,* and *Against the Academics* are the discussions he had "with those present." They were taken down by a shorthand writer: de Labriolle (*BA,* vol. 5, 9) notes that the transcriptions were "... revised and retouched by Augustine who adapted them to the Ciceronian manner...." The "discussion" Augustine had "with myself alone before you" refers to the fourth of the Cassiciacum works, the *Soliloquies.* In the *Ret.* (1.ii) Augustine says that *On the Good Life* was written at the same time as *Against the Academics* and was begun on his birthday (13 Nov. 387): in 1.3 he tells us that *On Order* was written at the same time as *Against the Academics.* On the date of the *Soliloquies,* see Bardy (*BA,* vol. 12, 565). The discussion of *On the Good Life* was accomplished in three days – *Ret.,* 1.2: see also *On the Good Life,* 1.6.

5. See E. Portalie, art. "Augustin," in *Dictionnaire de théologie catholique,* 1, 2273. Tr. R. Bastian and repr. as *A Guide to the Thought of Saint Augustine,* (Chicago: Henry Regnery, 1960), 16-17.

6. P. Courcelle in his *Recherches sur les Confessions de Saint Augustin,* (Paris: de Boccard, n.e. 1968), 179-81, understands Augustine's conversion in book eight simply as the decision to give up women and live a life of celibacy on the model of "... Plotinus and his friends [who], a little after 253, intended to found a Platonopolis in the countryside ..." (179). This plan is mentioned in Porphyry's *Life of Plotinus,* 12. Courcelle understands the retreat to Cassiciacum as Augustine's first concrete realization of the idea of such a philosophical community – which he had entertained from the time of his sceptical period (see 6.14.24) – and a stepping-stone to the monastic community he finally managed to found in Thagaste (*Recherches,* 181, n. 1).

7. Augustine specifies clearly that even the learned Victorinus – who had studied Holy Scripture and all the Christian books most thoroughly – could not be baptized until he had been formally and authoritatively instructed (*imbutus est*) in the *primis instructionis sacramentis* (8.2.4). The point is that the doctrines of the church – those things it holds which cannot be known by reason – have to be formally received, as from the authority of the church, just because they cannot be grasped by reason *and* to insure that one receives the orthodox doctrine rather than some other version.

8. See 9.4.7: *Ibi quid egerim in litteris iam quidem servientibus tibi....*

9. 9.4.7.

10. See, for example, *Against the Academics*, 3.20.43.

11. Solignac, *BA*, vol. 13, p. 191.

12. Ibid. Courcelle's treatment of the vision at Ostia can be found in *Recherches*, 222-26. He gives references (222, n. 3) to a number of other studies besides that of Henri; by Boyer, Hendrikx, Lebreton, Huby, Cavallera, Heim, and Marrou. A. Mandouze, " 'L'extase d'Ostie,' possibilités et limites de la methode des paralleles textuels," in *Augustinus Magister* (Paris: Etudes Augustiniennes, 1954), vol. 1, 67ff. was among the first to issue a caution about the philological method which Courcelle championed. See also J. Kevin Coyle's "In Praise of Monica: a Note on the Ostia Experience of Confessions IX," *Augustinian Studies* 13 (1982), 87-96.

13. *Recherches*, 222.

14. Ibid, 224, 226.

15. 7.9.13.

16. Henry himself makes this point (*Vision*, 115-20). He compares especially the *City of God*, 10.16 and *En.*, 1.6.7.

17. 9.10.23. Lewis and Short, *A Latin Dictionary* (Oxford: Clarendon Press, 1969) list all these as meanings of *instauro*.

18. *En.* 6.9.11.

19. See 7.9.13-15, 7.20.26.

20. 9.10.23.

21. See 9.10.24.

22. See, for example, the real outrage of Plotinus at such a suggestion on the part of the Gnostics – which, on this question, they shared with the Catholics (*En.* 1.9.46-60).

23. 9.10.24.

24. Henry, *Vision*, 114, 118.

25. 8.17.23.

26. 9.10.24.

27. See especially 9.10.25 read in this light.

28. 9.10.24.

29. Courcelle sees in the phrase *primitias spiritus*, "... nothing but a transcription into biblical style of Plotinus [signifying] that Augustine remains attached, by the best in himself, to the Intelligence glimpsed fleetingly." (*Recherches*, 224 – following Henry, *Vision*, 39.) It is not clear what sense Courcelle, and the others who agree with him, attach to this teaching. Do they mean that Augustine's soul is divided after Ostia, with the best part in heaven and the rest down on earth, or that he is simply repeating Plotinus's teaching about the undescended soul (*En.* 4.8.8)? Nothing much is said beyond the comparison of texts, and none of the supporters of this interpretation maintain that *primitias spiritus* is in any sense a literal translation of something from Plotinus – which it most certainly is not. If it is not a translation, but only a "transcription," then we are simply operating with a subjective

judgement: some will see it as such where others will not, and there is no way of settling the question. With this the Plotinian interpretation becomes unfounded, and we are left with the explicit Pauline quotation which is all Augustine actually puts before us. The text of Plotinus which Courcelle maintains Augustine "transcribed" is *En.* 5.1.1. A review of this question is found in J. Pepin, "*Primitiae spiritus.* Remarques sur un citation paulinienne des *Confessions* de saint Augustin," *Revue de l'Histoire des Religions* 140 (1951), 155-201. See also the article by A. Mandouze, "L'extase d'Ostie, possibilités et limites de la methode des paralleles textuels," and Solignac's note in *BA,* vol. 14, 552-55.

30. 9.10.25.

31. 7.17.23.

32. This is the teaching of 7.18.24 and the remainder of that book.

33. 7.10.16.

34. 9.10.24.

35. Courcelle is wrong to suggest that Plotinus teaches that the natural man can enjoy the vision of God "indéfiniment prolongée" (*Recherches,* 224). He implies that Plotinus does so in a text which he quotes from *En.* 1.6.7 (Ibid., n. 6), but this is to read far too much into the word. As long as Neoplatonism stays simply and exclusively with its own logic, and is not converted to Christianity, such a union of God and the world is impossible. This was well recognized by Plotinus – see, for example, the passage from the *En.* 1.9.46-60, referred to in n. 22.

36. 7.20.26.

37. See 9.19.26, 9.11.28.

38. My account of the argument of book ten is stated briefly in, "The Place and Purpose of the Tenth Book of the *Confessions,*" *Studia ephemeridis "Augustiniarum"* 25 (1987), 95-103.

"HOMO SPIRITUALIS" IN THE *CONFESSIONS* OF ST. AUGUSTINE

ROLAND J. TESKE

In book thirteen of the *Confessions* Saint Augustine says, "Thus man is renewed 'in the knowledge of God according to the image of the one who created him,' and having become 'spiritual, he judges all things,' those things, of course, which should be judged; 'he himself is judged by no one' " (Col. 3.10,12; 1 Cor. 2. 15). What I want to do in this paper is to attempt to describe or identify as far as one can the spiritual person of whom Augustine is speaking.[1] For the purposes of this paper I shall limit my consideration principally to the texts on "*homo spiritualis*" in the *Confessions,* along with a few from elsewhere. Though Augustine is obviously indebted to Saint Paul for much of what he says about the spiritual being as well as the animal and carnal being, he understands the Pauline expression in ways that Paul would, I suggest, never have dreamed of.[2]

It is possible, of course, to clarify the term to some extent by simply paraphrasing it in other scriptural expressions.[3] Thus the spiritual being is the perfect being, the adult able to take the solid food of wisdom, unlike the carnals or animals in the church, that is, the little ones who still require milk.[4] Others may well disagree with this move, but I think that it is both possible and necessary to spell out some characteristics of the spirituals in a way that breaks out of the circle of scriptural language and brings to light more sharply what Augustine had in mind.

The above text occurs within a prophetic interpretation of Genesis, that is, the first creation of humankind is seen as foreshadowing the second creation, or the renewal of humankind in Christ.[5] That the spiritual person judges all things means, Augustine tells us, that he or she has power over the fish of the sea, the birds of the air, the cattle and wild beasts, the earth and the reptiles. Each one has this power through the intelligence of mind (*per mentis intellectum*), by which are perceived those things which are of the Spirit of God (1 Cor. 2.14).

Augustine begins to unpack this by pointing out that the judgement of the spirituals is limited. First, they do not judge the spiritual knowledges shining in the firmament. These *cognitiones* are the eternal ideas in God's mind that one does not examine to correct, but rejoices to discover, if I may borrow a phrase from *De libero arbitrio.*[6] They do not, secondly, judge God's Book. Rather, they submit their intellect to it and hold as certain that things that they do not understand in it are nonetheless correctly and truly said. Thirdly, even those who are renewed and spiritual are not the judge of the law. Each should rather act according to the law, that is, be a doer of the law.[7] Fourth, the spirituals also do not judge the distinction between spirituals and carnals; such knowledge is known to God alone who called them in secret. Finally, the spirituals do not judge those peoples outside (1 Cor. 5.12) for they do not know who will enter into the sweetness of God's grace and who will not. The spirituals, in other words, judge nothing superior to them: God, the Book, the Law, and what God alone knows or does.

To what then does the power of the spirituals extend? Here Augustine interprets the fish of the sea as referring to the administration of baptism and the eucharist, the birds of the air as referring to spoken words, the fruitful earth as the faithful bringing forth good deeds. The spirituals judge and approve what they find correctly done and blame what they find wrongly done in the reception of the sacraments of initiation and in the eucharist and in the externally uttered words which are used in interpretations, explanations, discussions, disputations, blessings, and invocations.[8] The spirituals also judge the works and morals of the faithful, their alms, and the living soul – all those things insofar as they are perceived by the bodily senses. To sum up, in the words of R.J. O'Connell, the spirituals judge "all those features of the salvation-economy that belong to the sensible, corporeal order."[9]

What, then, are the characteristics of the spiritual person? A first condition for being a spiritual is quite clear: A spiritual must be in the church. They are in God's church (*in ecclesia tua, deus noster*), whether they preside spiritually (*spiritualiter praesunt*) or are spiritually subject (*subduntur*) to those who preside. For God has in this way made humankind male and female in his spiritual grace, where according to bodily sex there is neither male nor female (Gal. 3.28). The spirituals are by no means to be identified with those who preside, the hierarchy, or the males of the spiritual creation. There are spirituals among those who are subject as well as among those who preside. And a spiritual among the faithful judges the administration of the sacraments and preaching of one who presides. Moreover, the spiritual person is judged by no one – not even by one who presides. Augustine's cautious use of "we" in the passage in question would seem at least to suggest that one could know that he himself was a spiritual, even if others could not.[10] In any case the hierarchical aspect of the church would seem to be strangely irrelevant to the spirituals. And a bishop would surely have felt quite uncomfortable with such spirituals in his flock.[11]

Besides being in the Church, what further characterizes a spiritual? *Confessions* 5.10.20 offers a clue. There Augustine writes, "Now will your spiritual ones gently and lovingly laugh at me if they should read these confessions of mine. But such was I at that time." Courcelle has argued that Augustine is here thinking of Paulinus of Nola as one of those for whom the *Confessions* were written.[12] However, if one looks at the string of errors to which Augustine confesses, one finds that they are all rooted in his inability to conceive a spiritual substance, whereas there is no reason to suppose, as far as I know, that Paulinus of Nola was sufficiently adept at a spiritualist philosophy to be amused by such intellectual errors.

Let us look at these errors Augustine confessed to. He tells us of his despair of finding the truth in the church, for he thought that the church was committed to an anthropomorphism. "To me it seemed shameful to believe that you have the shape of our human flesh and are bounded by the outward lines of our bodily members."[13] Though he wanted to meditate on his God, he tells us,

> I did not know how to think of him except as a vast corporeal mass, for I thought that anything not a body was nothing whatsoever. This was the greatest and almost the sole cause of my inevitable error. As a result, I believed that evil was some such substance...." (5.10.19-20).

Thus with two masses, one of good and the other of evil, Augustine thought he was being more religious if he held that God, the good mass, was infinite on all sides except "where the evil mass stands in opposition to you, than if I thought that in all your parts you were bounded by the form of a human body" (5.10.20). He did not believe that God created evil; yet he thought of evil as corporeal, for he "could not think of mind except as a subtle body diffused throughout space." So too he thought of the Only-Begotten Saviour "as something extruded out of the mass of [God's] bright substance for our salvation," for he "could believe nothing of him except what [he] could picture (*imaginari*) by [his] vain powers." Even his rejection of the Saviour's being born of the Virgin Mary rested upon his picturing (*figurabam*) him being mixed with (*concerni*) and thus defiled by the flesh. For all of these errors, he says, God's "spirituals" will gently laugh at him. They will laugh at him, I suggest, precisely because these spirituals know better, for they are persons capable of rising to spiritual understanding (*se possunt ad spiritualem intellectum erigere*), that is, to an intellectual knowledge of incorporeal realities.[14] For "spiritual" is precisely the inspired or scriptural term for one who understands well, "*bonus intellector,*" as Augustine puts it in *De duabus animabus.*[15] But those who can rise to a spiritual understanding of this sort are precisely the Neoplatonists and only the Neoplatonists.[16] For apart from the Neoplatonists there was no one in the whole western church with a concept of incorporeal or spiritual realities. Hence, the second condition for being a spiritual is that one is a Neoplatonist. And since a spiritual must also be in the church, "*spirituales tui*" has to refer to people like Ambrose, Simplicianus and Theodorus and others Augustine met in the church of Milan.[17]

This identification is confirmed, I believe, by *Confessions* 6.3.4, where Augustine tells us that he heard Ambrose every Sunday. He says,

> But when I discovered that man's being made to your image was not understood by your spiritual sons, whom you regenerated by your grace from our Catholic mother, so that they believed and thought that you were limited by the shape of the human body – although what a spiritual substance would be like I did not surmise even in a weak and obscure manner – I blushed joyfully, because I had barked for so many years, not against the Catholic faith, but against the fantasies of a carnal imagination.

It is not *all* who have been regenerated by baptism, but the spiritual children of the *Catholica* who are discovered to be free from anthropomorphism. There are, after all, also in the Church the little ones, the carnal or animal Christians, who think of God in bodily form, whether in a human shape or as a power diffused throughout a mass. They think of God's having created a world outside of himself and in distant places by a new decision and of his speaking in words that sound and pass away. And unlike Augustine at that point and these little ones that he mentions in the *Confessions* 12.27.37, the spiritual children of the *Catholica* can grasp what a spiritual substance is.[18] Thus, in *De beata vita* 1.4, while speaking of Ambrose, but addressing Theodorus, Augustine tells of his amazement, "I noticed often in the talks of our priest and at times in yours that, when one thinks of God, nothing at all bodily should be thought of, and the same is true of the soul, for it is the one thing in reality closest to God." So too, it is the learned (the *docti*) of the Catholic faith who "hold it blasphemy to believe that God is limited by the shape of the human body" (*Conf.* 7.11.18).[19] For such reasons I believe that to be a spiritual in Augustine's sense involves at least two necessary conditions: first, that one is in the church and, second, that one is adept at Neoplatonic spiritualism.

There is at least one serious objection to my thesis, namely, that Augustine speaks of the apostles and even of the prophets as spiritual men; in the very passage of the *Confessions* with which we began Augustine clearly views Paul as a spiritual who did not want those he begot through the gospel to remain infants whom he would have to nourish with milk. Rather, Paul wanted them to be renewed in mind so that they could prove for themselves "what is the will of God, what is the good and the acceptable, and the perfect thing" (Rom. 12.2). God made human beings, Augustine insists, in his image, not after his own kind, so that the person renewed in mind perceives the Truth and does not need a creature to point the way. That is, the spiritual being renewed in mind has no need even for the humanity of Christ, the *via* and the *lac parvulorum*. Rather the spiritual sees "the Trinity of unity and the unity of the Trinity."[20] There are many problems in what Augustine is saying in this passage – not the least of which is how Augustine could possibly think of Paul of Tarsus as possessing the central insight of Neoplatonism. In response, I suggest that this anachronism should not come as a complete surprise to anyone who has read his history of philosophy in *Contra academicos* and has heard him have Christ explain to Pilate that his kingdom was not of this world, thus implying that there is that other intelligible world Plato had spoken of.[21] Recall, too, that immediately after his encounter with the *Platonicorum libri* he took up Paul, convinced that the apostles "would never have been able to do such great things, nor would they have lived as they evidently did live, if their writings and doctrines were opposed to this so great a good" (*Con. Acad.* 2.2.5).

There remain two questions I would like to address. First, what gives the spiritual person this power of judgement? I shall here merely appeal to a conclusion I drew in another paper, dealing with *De libero aribitrio,* namely, that one judges correctly in virtue of being in contact with the divine ideas.[22] Perhaps this is how Augustine understood Paul's claim that the spiritual person perceives those things which are of the Spirit of God (1 Cor. 2.14). If that conclusion is correct, then we have another reason for supposing that the spirituals are adepts at Neoplatonic spiritualism. Secondly, why is the spiritual judged by no one? We can get an answer to this question from an examination of Augustine's use of 1 Cor 2.15 in *De vera religione.* His use of the text occurs in an ascent to God parallel to that found in the second book of *De libero arbitrio.* In the course of the latter ascent to God as an eternal and spiritual substance, Augustine uses – in order to rise above the human mind – the principle: "He who judges is superior to that which he judges." It is precisely because one cannot judge the truths of mathematics and of wisdom, but rather judges in accord with them, that one has to admit that they are superior to one's mind. For, as he puts it in *De vera religione,* 31.57,

> And so when the soul realizes that it does not judge the form or motion of bodies according to itself, it ought at the same time to recognize that its nature is superior to the nature it judges and that the nature according to which it judges and which it can in no way judge is superior to it.

Nonetheless, it would seem that the spiritual person is judged at least by God. And that is what Augustine goes on to say, "As we and all rational souls correctly judge inferior things according to the Truth, so only the Truth itself judges us when we cling to it" (31.58). Not even the Father judges the Truth, for the Truth is his equal. The Truth is the Son, and the Father has given all judgement to the Son, as Saint John says (Jn. 5.22). Then Augustine cites Saint Paul (1 Cor. 2.15), "The spiritual man judges all things, but is himself judged by no one," that is, he adds, "by no man, but only by the law according to which he judges all things.... 'For we must appear before the tribunal of Christ' " (2 Cor. 5.10).

The spiritual person, he explains, "judges all things, because he is over all things, when he is with God. And he is with God when he has pure intellectual knowledge (*purissime intelligit*) and loves with whole charity (*tota charitate*) what he knows. Thus he becomes as far as possible the Law according to which he judges and which no one can judge" (31.58). The Law to which he becomes conformed would seem to be Christ, the Truth.[23] Hence, the spiritual is judged by no one, that is, no person, because the spiritual has by this knowledge become identified with the Law, Christ, in accord with which all things are judged. But having become Christ as far as possible, and thus being with God (the Father), each loves what is known with whole charity (*tota charitate*) – an odd expression, but surely one that refers to the Holy Spirit.[24] For having become as far as possible the Law, that is, Christ, and having come to pure intellectual knowledge – having become *nous* or *bonus intellector* as far as possible, each loves the One with the Charity poured out in the heart. Hence, the spiritual person – the one regenerated in the church, with the Neoplatonic spiritual knowledge of God – is caught up into the life of Trinity. This may seem terribly philosophical to some, but Augustine was early convinced that there was in his day but one genuine philosophy, not the philosophy of this world, but of another, intelligible world, the true homeland, to which God calls souls to return by his divine intellect's having assumed a body.[25]

NOTES

1. The task is, of course, far too extensive for a short paper. For another approach to the same subject, see my "Spirituals and Spiritual Interpretation in St. Augustine," *Augustinian Studies* 15 (1984), 65-81. I hope to come to a description of the spirituals that will permit one to identify those Augustine had in mind.

2. The chief scriptural texts for the spiritual and animal and carnal beings are the following: 1 Cor. 2 and 3, along with Heb. 5.12-13.

3. This is basically what A. Solignac does in his "Note complémentaire," on the spirituals and carnals, in the *BA* edition of the *Confessions,* vol. 2, 629-34. In dealing with the identity of "les spirituels," he concludes that they "sont donc les parfaits, adultes dans le Christ, capables d'assimiler la nourriture solide des écritures et de la distribuer à ceux qui leurs sont inférieurs." Similarly in a note to the BA edition of *Homélies sur L'Évangile de saint Jean,* M.-F. Berrouard identifies the "animales" as "ceux qui continuent à vivre selon le vieil homme; ils jugent et se comportent comme s'ils n'avaient pas été régénérés par le baptême" (837). There is some evidence that Augustine did not distinguish between the carnal and the animal. Such people are found both in the church and outside the church, though the spirituals are only in the church. On the other hand, the little ones, the *parvuli,* are found only in the church. See Robert J. O'Connell's *St. Augustine's* Confessions: *The*

Odyssey of Soul (Cambridge, Mass.: Belknap Press of Harvard University Press, 1969), 169-72, for an excellent treatment of this puzzling passage.

4. See T. Van Bavel's article on the humanity of Christ as the milk of the little ones, "L'humanité du Christ comme *lac parvulorum* et comme *via* dans la spiritualité de saint Augustin," *Augustiniana* 7 (1957), 245-81.

5. This would be what is generally referred to as an allegorical interpretation. But in *De genesi contra Manichaeos* 2.2.3, Augustine distinguished between historical and prophetic understanding of a text. He says, "According to history facts are narrated; according to prophecy future things are foretold."

6. Cf. *Lib. arb.* 2.12.34. That these forms of knowledge refer to the ideas in the mind of God is acknowledged by Solignac in his note (see above, note 4). "Il n'a pas à juger des 'connaissances spirituelles,' c'est-à-dire, semble-t-il, des 'raisons éternelles' établies dans le firmament ..." (631).

7. Augustine alludes to James 4.11, but the law seems to refer, as we shall see, to the eternal law or to Christ, who is the one legislator and judge.

8. It is interesting that Augustine stresses that it is the abyss of this world or age into which we have fallen and the blindness of the flesh that necessitates the use of such external signs. He still holds the view first present in *De genesi contra Manichaeos* 2.4.5, that before the fall we would not have had need of exterior words and signs, or even of the Book.

9. See O'Connell, *Confessions* p. 171.

10. Augustine does not, of course, explicitly refer to himself as a spiritual, though I think that the implication is clear. The fact that he later still refers to himself as a *parvulus* need not be taken as proof that he did not earlier think of himself as a spiritual. Van Bavel cites *Sermo* 117.5.7 and *Sermo* 53.15.16 and adds, "Mûri par l'experience, Augustin, à soixante ans, n'hésite pas à se compte encore parmi les *parvuli*" (art, cit., 263).

11. "In terms of the classic problematic of church-hierarchical and church-charismatic, the Plotinian flavor of Augustin's anthropology commits him squarely to the latter alternative, to a frankly 'spiritual' Church" (see O'Connell, *Confessions*, p. 172).

12. "Lorsqu'Augustin mentionne les 'spirituels' qui pourront sourire amicalement en apprenant les bizarres erreurs où il est tombé dans sa jeunesse, il songe sûrement à Pauline surtout." (*Recherches sur les Confessions de Saint Augustin*, 2nd ed. [Paris: E. de Boccard, 1968], 31-32). William A. Schumacher, in *Spiritus and Spiritualis: A Study in the Sermons of Saint Augustine* (Mundelein, Illinois: 1957), 283, agrees with Courcelle.

13. There is solid evidence that Augustine believed for a long time that the *Catholica* held an anthropomorphic view of God – not merely that God had human characteristics, but that he was bound by the shape of a human body and had hair and nails (see *Conf.* 3.7.12). Indeed, given the prevalent Stoic materialism of the age, what else could one make of humankind's having been made to God's image and likeness?

14. In *Tractatus in Ioannis Evangelium* 1.1, Augustine describes the little ones, the *parvuli*, as unable as yet to rise to spiritual understanding. Hence, the spirituals, it would seem, are precisely those who can so raise themselves up.

15. In *De Duabus animabus* 9, Augustine uses the phrase, "bonus intellector et, ut divinitus dicitur, homo spiritualis," to refer to one that "necessario faveret veris rationibus, quas de intelligibili sensibilique natura, quantum potui, tractavi atque disserui, immo eas ipse multo melius et ad docendum aptius aperiret, ..." He seems to indicate that the scriptural term for one who understands well is "the spiritual man."

16. See Gerard Verbeke, *L'évolution de la doctrine du pneuma du stoïcisme à s. Augustin* (Paris and Louvain: Editions de l'Institut superieur de philosophie, 1945), and F. Masai, "Les conversions de saint Augustin et les débuts du spiritualism en Occident," *Le Moyen Age* 67 (1961), 1-40.

17. For the existence of the circle of Christian Neoplatonists in Milan, see Courcelle's *Recherches sur les Confessions,* 251-53. Once Augustine discovered such "spirituals" in the Church, he "assumed" that such people had existed in the Church since the apostles, just as some today suppose quite anachronistically that there was right from from the beginning an understanding of the spiritual nature of God and the soul.

18. In 12.27.37, Augustine mentions some interpreters of scripture who, when they read Genesis, think that God, like a man or a power infused in an immense mass, "by some new decision, operating outside himself and as it were, in distant regions, made heaven and earth." They think of words that sound and pass away when they hear, "God said, 'Let there be made,' and the thing was made." They think of these things in accord with ordinary sense operations (*ex familiaritate carnis*). "In such men, still little ones and wholly sense-conscious (*parvulus animalibus*), while their infirmity is carried in this most lowly way of speech as if in their mothers' bosom, faith is strengthened in a healthful manner." But these little ones who think of God as bodily and even as human are the carnals or animals in the church – precisely the opposite of the spirituals.

19. Often when Augustine uses the expression *docti* or *doctissimi* he refers to the Platonists; here the *docti catholicae fidei* would seem to be the Christian Neoplatonists.

20. See Van Bavel, "L'humanité," 266-67, for his concern about the role of the humanity of Christ and of faith for the spirituals who have risen to an understanding of the Word, the solid food of which the spirituals are capable. Only once does Augustine say that the *parvuli* should not be so weaned that they abandon Christ the man and notes that foundation is an *aptior similitudo* than milk since a foundation is not taken away, but built upon. See *Tractatus in Ioannis Evangelium* 98.6.

21. *Con. Acad.* 3.19.42.

22. See my paper, "The *De Libero Arbitrio* Proof for God's Existence," *Proceedings of the Jesuit Philosophical Association* (1987) 15-47, and in a revised form, *Philosophy and Theology,* 2 (1987). 124-42.

23. In *L'intelligence de la foi en la trinité selon saint Augustin. Génèse de sa théologie trinitaire jusqu'en 391* (Paris: Études Augustiniennes, 1966), Olivier Du Roi says, "L'Esprit, ici comme dans le *De moribus* I, rend conforme au Fils (l'homme spirituel 'devient lui-même cette Loi') et unit ainsi à Dieu, c'est-à-dire au Père ('il est avec Dieu').... Dieu, la pure intelligence qu'on en prend dans sa Verité et la totale charité dont on aime ce qu'on comprend,

voilà la Trinité à laquelle se suspend notre esprit lorsqu'il juge les réalités inférieures et se soumet à la Loi qui le domaine (3)."

24. Du Roi (p. 333) says, "Je ne crois pas forcer le texte en y voyant l'Esprit dont l'action est suggérée par ... 'l'homme *spirituel* juge tout' ... et par ... 'quand il aime totalement ce qu'il comprend....'" The phrase "*tota charitate*" surely recalls "*plena et integra charitate*" of *De moribus* 1.13. 22-23, where Augustine would seem to refer to the Holy Spirit.

25. *Con. Acad.* 3.19.42.

AUGUSTINE'S *CONFESSIONS*: ELEMENTS OF FICTION

J.J. O'MEARA

Some readers were somewhat scandalized when Pierre Courcelle wrote that the *tolle lege* episode, the description of Augustine's actual conversion, in the *Confessions* (8.28f.) contains "de fiction littéraire et de symbolism." He indicated the Plotinian allusions; the reminiscence of the famous story of Prodicus, according to which Heracles as a young man, on reaching a crossroads alone, hesitated between the appeal of pleasure and of virtue, each represented by a woman proposing her own way to him; the opposing invitations to Augustine of the vanities on the one hand and continence on the other to follow them, presented in the form of a rhetorical *controversia;* reminiscences of Perseus – and more besides. From which Courcelle concluded that the scene, purporting to describe the hour, so to speak, of his actual conversion, "*fourmille d'intentions littéraires.*" As for the fig tree under which Augustine cast himself in the agony of mind that immediately preceded his sudden yielding to Christ, it could have only a symbolical meaning: it recalled the fig tree under which, according to the Gospel of Saint John (1.48), Nathanael sat, a tree which is constantly interpreted by Augustine as symbolizing the mortal shade of sin that spreads over the human race. Literary forms and symbolism were only half the story: with the exception of the item of the fig tree, the whole scene of the garden in Milan, according to Courcelle, is explained by the influence of the *Life of Anthony* by Athanasius, a life referred to, just before the conversion scene, by Augustine himself.[1]

If one accepts these affirmations of Courcelle on the most critical details recounted in the *Confessions,* one feels invited perhaps to treat more items indicated in the *Confessions* as being possibly fictitious in the same sense. To do this would not necessarily impugn the truthfulness of Augustine, unless one insisted, wrongly, it may be, that "truth" and "fiction" were always mutually exclusive. All description, it might be contended, is to some extent fictitious. All of us, when we set out to describe an event, tell a story – narrate. There is no way we can choose words that correspond exactly to what actually happened; at best they will convey approximately the most objective version to which we can consciously discipline ourselves. This does not make for fluent expression or easy reading. And so we embroider upon our message, we tell a story, we narrate.

The description we give is the description we must choose. Here we are limited, so to speak, by the materials available to us. What we choose at any one time, moreover, will be affected by our present purposes and interests. These purposes and interests will tend to vary as we proceed through life and adjust our picture of it. But for all that, it must be added, there may well be an underlying consistency of purpose and interest reflecting our psychological make-up. What we choose will also depend upon our models – for there is usually some model or some convention. A lawyer will have one way of presenting an account – representing an event; a civil servant, gobbledegooking his way around bills with their sections and sub-sections, another; a guru, a third. We speak within conventions.

Autobiography for example, in the nature of things must compose a story, even more than some other forms of writing. At first blush this seems paradoxical: is it not the autobiographer's sole task to tell the truth, the whole truth, and nothing but the truth about himself? He cannot, of course, tell the whole truth: this would yield *à la rigueur* tedious life-long documentation. This is not acceptable. So choice creeps in. I must choose what I shall recount. Correspondingly I must choose what I shall omit: "I brush them away ... until what I want is unveiled" (*Conf.* 10.12).[2] By the very choice there is already necessarily misrepresentation, that is, insofar as there is non-representation. But there is something more significant – and it is unavoidable – I choose according to some canon, some pattern, some ideal; otherwise, I could not choose at all. Thus, for example, Augustine recounts the story of his stealing pears that he did not need, only because it was symbolical of wilful sin: it was the *symbol* that justified the inclusion of the event, not the event itself, which was trivial. This is tantamount to admitting that in autobiography one is creating oneself anew: one is painting an image of oneself. One chooses, among the events of the past that one can recall, those that seem significant *now,* those that bear some relation, not excluding opposition, to one's present picture of oneself then. This implies that one's earlier view of oneself, then, is identical with one's present view of what one was like then – which is unlikely. One can never recover exactly one's view of oneself at any particular time in the past. We can re-construct it, but we do so only with the help of our more or less faithful memories and our imaginations, which must start from the present. Augustine tells us explicitly that the account he gives of his babyhood and even later childhood in the *Confessions* (1.8) is conjectured.

Telling the truth and nothing but the truth is, at best, an exercise in approximation. Words are never adequate to describe reality. They are a *pis aller!* Fiction is a frequent vehicle for alleged truth.

Bearing such ideas in mind, we may approach the question of the fictional elements in the *Confessions* of Augustine. It is emphasized here that our purpose in this paper is not to attack in any way the general historicity of the *Confessions;* it is rather to draw attention to the considerable element of fiction in the narrative in which this historicity is conveyed.

First, it is important to insist that the *Confessions* does not purport to be, nor does it issue in being, so to speak, a "proper" autobiography. One has only to observe that its last three books are mostly concerned with the interpretation of Genesis to come to the conclusion that they at least have little pretence at constituting any part of a strict autobiography. The intrusion of *so much* confession of faith in, and praise of God, so important for the purposes of the book, tells us something, it is true, but disproportionally little about Augustine's life. The opening of the book dilates upon God and the soul, God's omnipresence, his immensity, and his attributes. It is a slow and indirect beginning.

Georg Misch, the specialist in the genre of autobiography, noted that the project of telling the story of his life yielded in Augustine's *Confessions* to metaphysical and religious preoccupations, to the exercise of his religion, and to the awakening in others of the religious sentiment he himself felt. If the *Confessions* is an autobiography, it is an autobiography of an entirely new form: the story of his past is far from being Augustine's only aim.[3]

But there *is* direct description of events in the *Confessions.* Augustine does give us information on his life, even if he omits many things that he remembers: "I pass over many things because I hasten to those which most urge me to confess to you, and there are many things that I do not remember" (3.21). One must realize that he never set out to give an account of his whole life: he concentrates in fact for the most part on episodes, and even these are diluted with prayers and demonstrations of doctrine (which are reflected in works contemporary with the *Confessions*) on original sin, conversion of the sinner, and the operation of the will. Added too are the heretical opinions of the Manichaeans, and a number of other matters, such as the Neoplatonic theory of the "beautiful," his views on baptism, marriage, love and friendship and a host of other topics. What he set out to write was not so much an autobiography as a *vita,* a "Life," a tale with a moral for others.

The *Confessions* contain not just one *vita,* but many. There are, for example, the "lives" of his mother, of his friend Alypius, of Victorinus, of the public officials of Trier, and of Saint Anthony – all of these lives feature a sudden conversion of some sort, due usually to some intervention of Providence. Monica, while still a young girl, had succumbed to the love of wine. One day a maidservant, quarrelling with her, called her a winebibber: "wounded through and through by this taunt," Augustine tells us solemnly, "she beheld her foul state, and immediately condemned it and cast it off.... But you, O Lord, by means of madness in one soul, ever heal another" (9.18). Alypius was converted from an infatuation with the circus by a sarcastic remark of Augustine's about the circus, which Alypius heard on entering his class: "Upon hearing those words he burst forth from that deep fit in which he had willingly plunged himself. He shook his mind with a vigorous self-control. All the filth of the circus fell off from him, and he never returned there again" (6.12). Augustine remarks that God had worked the transformation through himself, though he did not know it. Victorinus, from being a demon-worshipper, had been convinced of Christianity, but was afraid to become formally a Christian for fear of offending his demon-worshipping friends. The old Neoplatonic-Christian priest, Simplicianus, told him that he would not reckon him among Christians unless he saw him in the church of Christ. This he kept repeating: suddenly and unexpectedly Victorinus said to Simplicianus "Let us go to the church. I wish to become a Christian" (8.4). Augustine attributes this conversion to the grace of Christ. The public officials of Trier chanced to come upon the life of St. Anthony and one of them began to read it: "Suddenly in anguish he said to his companion 'I have determined to serve God, and from this very hour and in this very place I make my start' "(8.15). In his story of the moment of his own conversion Augustine appeals to the experience of Anthony: "For I had heard how Anthony had been admonished by a reading from the gospel at which he chanced to be present, as if the words read were addressed to him: 'Go, sell what you have, and give to the poor ... and come, follow me,' and by such an oracle (*tali oraculo*) he was immediately converted to you" (8.29).

These and other rudimentary lives, such as those of Nebridius (6.17; 9.6) and Verecundus (9.5), also given in the *Confessions,* were much appreciated in the early Christian church, not least of all in North Africa in the time of Augustine. Apart from any inspiration from pre-Christian sources, there were many descriptions in Christian literature of the search for truth, of the confession of sins, conversion by grace (here the story of Saint Paul's sudden and astounding conversion and reversal of roles from enemy to defender of Christianity was dominant), and the recital of visions and revelations experienced, which must have been to some extent models for Augustine. In his case the influence of the *ad Donatum* of Cyprian of Carthage, where Cyprian gives a brief account of his own conversion – of which there are a number of surprising reminiscences in the *Confessions* – and the *Passiones* of such African martyrs as Perpetua, Marian, and Cyprian are of particular interest. The *Confessions,* too, tells us of exhortations, terrors, consolations, directions, dreams, oracles, miracles, and admonitions which issued in the dramatic scene of Augustine's sudden conversion in the garden – itself reminiscent of Christ's agony in the garden and the submission of his will to the Father. Mixed in with all these are the themes of the prodigal son, the wandering of Virgil's Aeneas, and, this reflecting Augustine's philosophic interests and experiences, the Neoplatonic theme of return, *regressus,* to the Father and the homeland.

The overall theme of the *Confessions,* transcending its very many digressions, is not simply Augustine's life, but his life insofar as it illustrates an idea that was uppermost in his mind, as it must be in the mind of anyone who feels that he has been entrusted with a mission, the theme of conversion. It is a salvational theme, one common to Christianity and Neoplatonism and many other religious or philosophical systems of the time. It applied to persons as individuals and to all as a race. It was a near-obsession in Augustine's mind.

Augustine had learned from Plotinus that the most fundamental – in the literal sense of that word – fact and origin of existence lay in conversion – ἐπιστροφῆ. According to Plotinus the first being, Intelligence, came into existence in its turning towards the One to see it: τῆ ἐπιστροφῆ πρὸς αὐτὸ ἑώρα · ἡ δὲ ὅρασις αὕτη νοῦς.[4] That was the philosophical fundament of philosophical, religious, mystical, and all experience. In the very first paragraphs of his first extant work, the *Contra Academicos* (386) Augustine bids his old friend and patron Romanianus to wake up under the providential buffetings of fortune and give himself to philosophy, to which indeed his son, Augustine's student, Licentius, had already been "converted" from the snares and pleasures of youth. The preface to the contemporary *De beata uita* again dilates at length on the function of what appears to be misfortune in bringing us – and Augustine himself – to the beloved homeland. And likewise the notion of conversion is very much present in the other contemporary dialogue – the *De ordine* (1.23; 10.28).

In passing one should observe that the great contrast between the *Confessions* and the *Dialogues* of Cassiciacum arises not only from their different purposes – the one a story of ultimately religious conversion, the others concerned primarily to expound philosophical themes in the forms of Platonic-type dialogues – but also in the more religiously oriented presentation in the one and the more philosophically oriented in the other. The description of his conversion in *Contra Academicos* 2.5 ends by indicating that he discovered that philosophy and religion were at one, but leads to the recommendation of *philosophy* as illuminated by St. Paul: *tunc uero quantulocumque iam lumine asperso tanta se mihi philosophiae facies aperuit.* Similarly in the *De beata uita,* the comparison of the teachings of the Neoplatonists and the divine mysteries is made, but the issue of the event is presented as an escape from the world into the harbour of philosophy: *ergo uides, in qua philosophia quasi in portu nauigem.*[5] There is not only not a conflict between the reports of his conversion as given in the *Dialogues* and the *Confessions* – there is in fact, close correspondence: but whereas in the beginning, while preferring the authority of Christ over all others, he saw no conflict of any substance between the Neoplatonist doctrine that he read and the teachings of Saint Paul and, moreover, expected to understand Christian teaching through Neoplatonist reasoning, by the time of the *Confessions* he had discovered the irreconcilability of both positions on major issues and had elected unambiguously for Christianity, for the incarnation and the crucifixion, which were outlandish doctrines to the Neoplatonists. In other words, the conversion syndrome that always affected him expressed itself in the earlier "professedly" philosophical works as conversion to a religion for the understanding of which he embraced a philosophy. A decade later, in the *Confessions* it expressed itself in terms of embracing a religion in relation to which a certain philosophy could be both a serious help and a serious hindrance. There can be no doubt but that Augustine's initial expectations from Neoplatonism in relation to Christianity were very high. But from an early stage his enthusiasm for the Neoplatonists was diminished, even if never altogether abandoned.

Augustine, then, although presenting the same material without deliberate falsification in the *Dialogues* and the *Confessions,* had not only different purposes – he had different models. The "life," the *vita,* that he gave of himself in the *Confessions* appears, according to the very plausible view of Courcelle,[6] to have been written in response to an interest shown in him by Paulinus of Nola. Augustine's friend Alypius had written to Paulinus in 395 AD to request from him a copy of the *Chronicles* of Eusebius of Caesarea: by way of *douceur* he enclosed five works of Augustine against the Manichees. Paulinus complied with the request but in turn asked Alypius to write for him an account of "the whole story of his holiness's life"[7] and to send it to him. He wanted to know, in the words of Virgil's *Aeneid,* "of what race he was, where was his home," *qui genus, unde sis domo* (8.114), a ritual formula to designate an "autobiography." He was especially interested in Alypius's vocation to the ascetic life, and if he had been converted and ordained to the priesthood by Ambrose, as had been Paulinus himself. Alypius's reply is not extant, but Courcelle supposes that Alypius asked Augustine to fill Paulinus's request. Augustine wrote to Paulinus in the summer of 396 saying that he was completing the requested life of Alypius and that, among other things, he offered himself fully to Paulinus to be known to him – since each so much desired to know the other.[8] The life of Alypius would appear to have been completed – some of it, as we have already indicated, is incorporated in the *Confessions* (6.7-10, 11-16). Courcelle supposes that Paulinus received it and, impressed by it, requested Augustine to do in relation to his own life what he had done for Alypius – where was he born, what was his vocation to the ascetic career, had he been converted and ordained by Ambrose, and so on. Here, it would seem, was given the outline plan of the *Confessions.* In this context one can easily understand why such a large proportion of the book was taken up with Augustine's period in Milan (5.23-9.16), where he was finally converted to the ascetical life and baptized by Ambrose. This Milan period amounts to thirty-eight per cent of the first nine books that constitute the substance of the *Confessions* and corresponds to three years, or nine per cent, of his life to that date. Clearly the conversion episode is the centre of interest of the book and does actually comply with what appears to have been Paulinus's request. Although he omits to speak of his ordination – as Paulinus had requested in the case of Alypius – we know that he had originally planned to describe this.[9]

We should take note, too, of the audience Augustine had in mind for his book: it was not God only or Paulinus – *non enim a te solo illa legerentur:* "for not by you alone will those things be read" (*Ep.* 27.5); it was in general the *spirituales* (5.20; 10.6), those given to the spiritual life within the church who, like Paulinus, would be avid to read of the *vita* and especially the conversion of a prominent convert – the public orator at the Imperial court, one who could well have aspired to the governorship of a province, a former Manichee, one who, presumably, had the intellectual equipment and sophistication to champion the cause of Christianity with and against the Neoplatonists, one baptized by the great Ambrose, and one finally who had had a dramatic conversion. He tells us plainly (11.1.3) why he recounts so many things – not that God should know them, but that he should excite his own love for God and the love of his readers so that they would cry out, "the Lord is great and greatly to be praised." But his critics, indeed his detractors, would read the book, too, and would not derive profit from such a moral tale.

I shall now enter into some detail on what I may call the fictional context or elements of the *Confessions.* The first issue I want to discuss is his use of Scripture, and especially the Psalms, to convey thoughts and information: this is a very indirect, analogical, and to that extent fictional, way of recounting events, and leaves us frequently without any clear idea of the details of what in fact happened.

Take, for instance, the celebrated passage (7.13-15) in which Augustine describes what he read in the Platonist books. He does not say, for example, "I read in some of the *Enneads* of Plotinus, or in the *de regressu animae* (or *Philosophy from Oracles*) of Porphyry, or in these works of both philosophers, translated by Victorinus, of the Father, and Intelligence, and the soul of man and their relations. This enabled me to conceive of a spiritual deity, which released me from a block until then insurmountable to me. It seemed to me as it had seemed to others, that there was a correspondence between these Principles and the Father and the Word of the Christian Trinity." Such a statement would have given us direct information on a crucial episode in Augustine's life where, because of the indirect telling, in spite of the concentrated attention of scholars for a century, obscurity remains. He described the episode indirectly, using the words of the Prologue of Saint John's Gospel to indicate what he had read – and what he had not read – in the books of the Platonists, the *libri Platonicorum.* In the end we are left with little more than questions: did he read something of Plotinus or Porphyry or, as may seem likely, of both? What books or portions of books did he read?

In view of Augustine's general obsession with Porphyry (as seen throughout his works and especially books ten and nineteen of the *City of God*); his omission of mention of the third Neoplatonist hypostasis here in the *Confessions* and his report in the *City of God* (10.23) that Porphyry does not at all or does not clearly speak of this third hypostasis; of his accusation of Porphyry's idolatry, usually with the quotation of Paul's epistle to the Romans (1.21f): "they changed the glory of the immortal God for images resembling mortal man or birds or animals or reptiles" – the text used at this point in the *Confessions* to describe some of what he did read in the Platonist books but did not accept; of his indication that these books did not have – or at any rate that he did not read there – the incarnation and crucifixion; and finally of his report that after reading these books he shared the Porphyrian-Photinian view that Christ was a good man, body and soul, but was not God – it is impossible to exclude Porphyry's *De regressu animae* (or *Philosophy from Oracles*) from the Platonist books read at this juncture. If this were so, then the appositeness of the text of Romans 13.14: "put on the Lord Jesus Christ," which, according to Augustine, wrought his conversion, would become manifest, for it would represent his humble acceptance of the incarnation against Porphyry's prideful contempt of it. But, alas, the process of using Scripture to inform leaves us groping for hypotheses which are only more or less to be approved.

In this passage of the *Confessions* to which I have been referring,

Augustine uses not only the indirectness of Scripture to impart crucial information, he confuses things further by using rhetoric. He sets up a contrast between "what he read" in the Platonist books (*et ibi legi, legebam ibi, inueni haec ibi*), and "what was in them" (*est ibi*), and "what he did not read" (*non ibi legi*), and "what was not in them" (*non est ibi, non habent illi libri*). At first blush the phrases *non ibi legi, non est ibi,* and *non habent illi libri* seem to refer to the *absence* of reference to the incarnation and crucifixion in the Platonist books; but for all that it is impossible altogether to exclude the idea that these books explicitly rejected the doctrines of the incarnation and crucifixion, as did Porphyry: "not *there* did I read," "not *there* is found," "*those* books do not have ..." in the perfectly good sense that these books would be the last place where Augustine, in addition to the teaching on the Principles, would find also the teaching on the incarnation and crucifixion, since they explicitly rejected these doctrines. One should not press this point too far, but it illustrates the obscurity of the indirectness of the use of Scripture to describe something else, especially when reinforced by rhetoric.

There is also the question of the poet that Augustine was. He tells us that he composed poems and entered poetry competitions (3.14; 4.1) in his early manhood. And although we have no extant poem of his, F. Van der Meer has written finely of his poetry – perhaps, indeed, too finely:

> He was an *homme de coeur*.... When one studies Augustine's arguments one is impressed not so much by his powers of reasoning as by the personal passion that lies behind the arguments. One can always sense the man who dared to say to God: It was your *beauty* that drew me to you.... Few saints illustrate so overwhelmingly the thesis that in the existential order of things *prière et poésie* stand next to each other, the one being perhaps simply the continuation of the other. Augustine is the greatest poet of Christian Antiquity, without ever having written any poetry worth mentioning.... He possesses the fifth talent, the most valuable of all, the gift of endless wonderment, remaining in this like the little children to whom the Kingdom of Heaven was promised. [10]

Again, Van der Meer appeals to Pascal that, like Jesus Christ and Saint Paul, Augustine exists in the order of love, not in the intellectual order – for they all aimed to bring fire, not to teach. As we quoted from the *Confessions* already, his aim in writing the *Confessions* was to excite his own affections and those of his readers to God, to declare, "The Lord is great, and exceedingly to be praised" (11.1).

The poetic qualities of the *Confessions* are from time to time distinctly obtrusive. With regard to theme, it is possible to compare, as Augustine does himself, his wanderings in search of God with the wandering of Aeneas in search of Italy and great Rome; Augustine's theme is to that extent compared by him to the Roman epic. The *Confessions* and the *City of God,* both proceeding from considerations of Roman institutions and Greek philosophy to Hebrew revelation, in the one as applied to the individual Augustine, and in the other as applied to the history of humankind, represent each in its own way a view of the mission of Christianity, and each contains distinct reminiscences of the *Aeneid.* The *City of God* right in its first paragraph compares Rome's mission as expressed by Virgil: *Parcere subiectis et debellare superbos* (6.853) to the Hebrew and Christian: *Deus superbis resistit, humilibus autem dat gratiam* (Prov. 3.34; Jas. 4.6; 1 Pet. 5.5) – and there are other significant reminiscences of the *Aeneid.*

The poetry of the diction in the *Confessions,* however, is much more obvious. It is a long time since J. Finaert studied this in his *Evolution littéraire de Saint Augustine,*[11] and I do not propose to repeat his conclusions here. Anyone who has read the *Confessions* in Latin will recall the lyricism caused by the extensive use of the psalms, and how rhetoric is frequently transformed into poetry. That is why, for example, the translation done into French by E. Tréhorel and G. Bouissou often employs the form of free verse. One might reasonably contend, I think, that sometimes the poetry barely escapes, if it does escape, being a rhetorical jingle:

> Veni Carthaginem, et circumstrepebat me undique sartago flagitiosorum amorum. nondum amabam et amare amabam et secretiore indigentia oderam me minus indigentem. quaerebam quid amarem, amans amare, et oderam securitatem et uiam sine muscipulis.... (3.1).

This passage is given a verse translation by Tréhorel and Bouissou, not surprisingly. It borders on an excess of rhetoric: the word *sartago,* although expressive enough, might well not have been chosen if it had not occurred to Augustine as parallelling *Carthago.* The passage is an illustration, although not the only or even the most obvious one, of what I call the incantatory style of the *Confessions.* This passage is not and does not pretend to be a recital of the concrete facts that happened to Augustine on his coming to Carthage: these are *not* detailed, but instead there is conjured up for us an emotional tumult which was of importance in suggesting a state of soul, itself relevant to a moral tale. What is said is, doubtless, true, but it is also an imaginative *reconstruction;* it is partly a fiction.

The influence of the parataxis of the Bible much enhances the lyrical character of the *Confessions: et ibam longius a te ... et sinebas et jactabar et effundebar et diffluebam et ebulliebam ... et tacebas* (2.2). One feels that Augustine's love of such diction arises, not merely from rhetoric and the Bible, but from a strongly artistic temperament, which was preoccupied more with artistic truth than a banal account. Solignac, in the course of discussing the style and poetic elements of the *Confessions,* draws attention also to what he terms the "colour and the ornaments" of its style.[12] The book is full of the poetry of images. Comparisons, metaphors, personifications emerge from Augustine's pen, sometimes as fugitive sparks, sometimes under the guise of small charming *tableaux,* and sometimes as long continuing frescoes. Sometimes there is a strange realism: the soul is described as having a head, eyes, a back, flanks, and a belly. Always there is antithesis, which emphasizes the difficulty of stating truth in words: *in istam dico uitam mortalem an mortem uitalem ... nescio* (1.7).

There is, moreover, an additional consideration which is rather difficult for us to appreciate. Augustine had a profound belief in the workings of Providence. One's actions or words might have the most surprising and even improbable results. We have already seen the instance recounted by Augustine of Alypius – Augustine had seen Alypius enter his classroom, and thereupon illustrated a text on which he was engaged by a biting sarcasm at the expense of the circus, to which his audience (and Alypius) were captive: "You know, O my God, that at that time I had no thought of curing Alypius of his disease. But he applied it to himself, and believed that I had said it only because of him.... I had not rebuked him, but you (God) who make use of all men, both the knowing and the unknowing, in the order that you know ... out of my mouth and tongue made coals of fire by which you cauterized a mind of such high promise and healed it" (6.11, 12). There was the taunt of the maid-servant that converted Monica (9.18), and, the taunt of Simplicianus to Victorinus: "I will not reckon you among Christians, unless I see you in the church of Christ," that was followed by conversion: "Suddenly and unexpectedly he said to Simplicianus: 'Let us go to the church, I wish to become a Christian' " (8.4). Any word might be an oracle: the "Go, sell what you have ... and come follow me" that converted Anthony (*tali oraculo confestim ad te esse conuersum*), and the "take up and read" that brought Augustine himself to the point of conversion (8.29). That latter phrase had seemed to Augustine at the time as likely to be no more than a banal instruction in a children's game. But he took it to be a command of God: *diuinitus mihi iuberi.* As Augustine frequently called the Scriptures "oracles," which he does in the *Confessions* (12.22) and especially in the second half of the *City of God,* to be matched, but in their superiority, with the pagan oracles as appealed to by such as Porphyry, so he reveals himself as a man of his times more profoundly affected than we are likely to be by a sensitivity to possibly oracular expressions. This might extend not only to normal sources for such expressions, but to one's own casual words and writings, too.

Augustine held very open views on the interpretation of Scripture. Various meanings might be found in its words, *all* of which were true: "While every man tries to understand in Holy Scripture what the author understood therein, what wrong is there if anyone understands what you, O light of all truthful minds, reveal to him as true, even if the author he reads did not understand this, since he also understood a truth, though not this truth" (12.27). Once again, in the *Confessions* he asserts that an abundance of meanings can be taken out of the words of Scripture, and that it would be rash to affirm which of them Moses chiefly meant: this would be to offend against charity, for the sake of which Moses spoke what he spoke (12.35). He even considers what he himself would have done if he had been Moses: "I should have wished ... that such power of eloquence be given me, and such ways to fashion words that ... they who can understand, no matter what true interpretation they have arrived at in their thought, would not find it passed over in (my) words: and if some other men by the light of truth had perceived a further meaning, it should not fail to be understood from these same words" (12.36). He is careful to tolerate for readers who are wholly sense-conscious a gross sensible understanding of Scripture: that God, for example, like a man, by some new and sudden decision, operating outside of himself and as it were, in distant regions, made heaven and earth, two great bodies in which all things would be contained. Such readers are like fledglings in a nest who must be content as they are until they can fly: otherwise they may fall from the nest and be trampled on (12.37). As we saw from an earlier remark of his, we must always employ charity – for the sake of which Moses spoke what he spoke.

This reflection on how he would have hoped to write, if he had been

Moses (see also 12.41-43) must suggest that he might have entertained similar purposes in relation to his own actual writing: this, too, could be interpreted in a way that he did not have in mind when he was writing. This is not surprising, for it is at root a commonplace in relation to the interpretation of all authors that are of universal appeal: his own favourite poet Virgil was a case in point. But Augustine speaks with an unusual intensity on this matter, not only in the *Confessions,* from which we have been quoting, but elsewhere. Thus in the *Usefulness of Believing* he asserts that a reader can sometimes usefully understand the contrary of what the writer intended (10f.).

The combination of what we may call this openness to what writing may mean on the one hand, and charity in allowing understandings that elsewhere one might characterize as puerile on the other, cannot but have resulted from time to time for Augustine in what one might call "detachment" from the actual words that he was writing. He allowed Providence, the Spirit, to supplement his words. He had the authority of Paul for this, who wrote that the "Spirit helps our weakness" (Rom. 8.26), this in relation to what words we use in prayer. And so we find an extraordinary number of indefinite phrases in the *Confessions.* We should have a brief look at some of these.

One is a linguistic usage which suggests that Augustine occasionally wished to weaken a reference that one would expect to be particular. He speaks of Aeneas for example, as – *nescio quis* "some Aeneas or other" (1.20) – when it is evident that he knew precisely who Aeneas was. Similarly with regard to Joshua (11.30), and St. Paul (12.20) he uses the term *quidam,* "a certain person," when equally he knew precisely who was involved. Likewise in his description of the fig tree in the conversion scene (8.28) and of the window at which he and his mother stood during the "vision of Ostia" (9.23) he employs the term *quaedam,* "a certain fig tree," "a certain window," when there is no evident need for the indefinite term at all. Attempts have been made to account for such uses of *quidam* by Augustine, but without convincing success.[13] I myself believe that Augustine's use of such terms, intended, as I said earlier in a similar connection,[14] to take the emphasis and concentration off the nouns to which they are attached, in order to heighten the providential in the scene.

And then there is the concentration on indefinite terms in the conversion scene. Here is the passage in Latin:

> *nescio quid* enim, *puto,* dixeram, in quo apparebat sonus uocis meae iam fletu grauidus, et sic surrexeram. mansit ergo ille ubi sedebamus nimie stupens. ego sub *quadam* fici arbore straui me *nescio quomodo* ... et *non quidem his uerbis,* sed in hac sententia multa dixi tibi ... et ecce audio uocem de uicina domo cum cantu dicentis et crebro repetentis *quasi* pueri an puellae, *nescio:* "tolle lege, tolle lege" (8. 28f).

It is obvious that this scene is described in terms conveying great emotion, emotion that affects descriptions of the same event in the dialogues of Cassiciacum, the description of Augustine's first conversion to philosophy by the *Hortensius* of Cicero, and the description in the *Confessions* of the conversion of the public servants at Trier (8.15). It is part of Augustine's psychology not only to have almost an obsession with the same theme of conversion, but equally to employ the same emotional terms in his description of it. The indefinite phrases not only heighten the emotion of the description of the *tolle lege* scene: they are a kind of *incantation.* They deliberately take the emphasis and concentration, nay more, the precision, off the words that are used – for some words must be used – and heighten the supra-rational, the marvellous, the providential in the scene.

This impressionism is marked in Augustine. In spite of the picture of him as the great definer of doctrines in the West, he was also profoundly questioning, profoundly aporetic. He professes this openly and constantly, especially in his mature and non-controversial work (he tended to be dogmatic in controversy) the *De Genesi ad litteram.* Hence it is that texts from him have been confidently used on both sides in the bitter theological conflicts of later ages. Yet even in connection with the question of the origin of the individual soul – how it is found in the body and whether or not it comes through Adam – he had to write at the end of his life: "I did not know this then, and I still do not know it now."[15] Similarly in relation to the beatific vision, when he was discussing it at the very end of the *City of God,* he countenanced two possibilities, one more Platonic and one more scriptural, which latter, he said, was easier to hold. But he declares that, to tell the truth, he must confess his ignorance on the topic.[16]

The charity, moreover for which he appealed in dealing with those less able to reason and understand, increased, as did his approbation of miracles, as life went on. Thus, in a letter of the year 408, the belief (based on a fundamentalist reading of Scripture), that in the beatific vision we would see God with corporeal eyes, which he appears to favour in the *City of God*, is simply put aside.[17] But by the year 413, although he still maintained this position, he allowed for the anthropomorphic views on the matter held by a fellow bishop.[18] And in book twenty-two of the *City of God* (written in the mid- to late 420s) he appears to favour those views.

Some of his tolerance for the less intelligent he could relate to his understanding of the esoteric and exotic doctrines practised by the philosophers. He had a real *penchant* for attributing to those whose opinions he controverted their actual lack of belief in the doctrines they espoused. There are many instances of this, which I have detailed elsewhere;[19] in, for example the first half of the *City of God:* Posidonius in 5.2 is represented as not likely to have been sincere in a certain astrological explanation. Varro in 6.4 and 9 is said not to have spoken his mind plainly on the matter of religion in Rome; Apuleius is also said in 9.8 to have concealed his full opinion – and so on. It is ironic that Joannes Scottus Eriugena, when he encounters in Augustine a doctrinal opinion which does not accord with one accepted by himself from a Greek father, attributes to Augustine the process of concealing his true opinion: "And so," he says, "it is more credible that (Augustine) wrote according to the capacity of this audience than to have disagreed with Ambrose...."[20]

The most significant case of this presumption by Augustine that authors might not believe what they explicitly teach is found in his very first extant work, the *Contra Academicos:* there (3.43) he supposed that the professedly sceptical New Academy was not only not sceptical at all but preserved within itself the true doctrine of Plato. He immediately adds a phrase that may tell us a great deal about him: *hoc mihi de Academicis interim probabiliter, ut potui, persuasi. Quod si falsum est, nihil ad me* – "this opinion about the Academics I have meanwhile adopted, as far as I could, as probable. If it is false, it does not affect me." It is difficult not to judge his attitude as more than a little debonair.

Augustine, then, indulged from time to time in a measure of make-believe, accommodation, detachment – whatever one cares to call it. It arose to some extent from a profound belief in Providence which he felt had been significantly at work in his own life – "You (God) worked within me so that I might be persuaded to go to Rome ... the most hidden depths of your providence must be proclaimed" (5.14). When in turn he left Rome for Milan and all that was to follow, neither his Manichaean friends in Rome nor he himself knew the significance of what was happening (5.23). Likewise God had ordained in his secret ways that he and Monica should commune together at Ostia on a day before she died: "a day that you (God) knew, although it was unknown to us" (9.23). There are innumerable instances in the *Confessions* of Augustine's professions of one's unawareness of the secret workings of Providence. One did not know what apparently chance word would work some unexpected and significant result. Hence it was perhaps unnecessary to insist overmuch on precise formulation of what one might say in any conjuncture: "the Spirit helps our weakness" (Rom. 8.26). Is there some explanation here of Augustine's bias against nature in favour of grace?

The *Confessions* has also its share of credit in dreams, visions, and miracles. He urged his mother to discover in a vision his future marriage: "both at my pleading and by her own desire, each day with a mighty cry from her heart she besought you (God) to give her in a vision some sign as to my coming marriage" (6.23). But the vision never came, although she did have some revelations on that occasion which she discerned as not coming from God. The extent of Augustine's belief in Monica's visions cannot be determined,[21] but he evidently had some belief in them (3.19). Likewise he had reason to report that she could dream what was to be. Augustine's belief in miracles at this time is also clearly demonstrated.[22]

In short, the necessary indirectness of poetry and particularly of the use of the Psalms, and Scriptures generally, to describe things, added to cultivated detachment from particulars, leaves one frequently uninformed where one might very much wish to be informed. What was the name of Augustine's mistress? What was the name of the friend of his early youth who died and left him disconsolate? What Platonist books or excerpts did he read? Did he get to know Ambrose at all well? The method of the *Confessions* is not that of even direct narrative.

The accumulation of the considerations that I have advanced, to show how qualified must be our expectation of strict historicity in the *Confessions*, does not mean that Augustine tells untruths. Much of what he wants to say has reference to states of soul rather than to any particular facts; and these states of soul involve imaginative reconstruction and for him imaginative, indeed emotional, and poetical expression. Much of the description is borrowed from the Psalms, and so is indirect and unclear as to its precise intent. In view of the scope of the work, relatively few precise facts are conveyed. The aim of the work is not to inform, but to arouse the minds and hearts of his readers. Some of the states of soul described are perceived by him, as he would say, in his inner ear.[23] Is the scene of his conversion in the garden simply deeply affected by fiction in *its expression,* as Courcelle would have it? Or is it wholly fictional, both as to expression and fact? Has it been sufficiently noted that, when he writes of his sorrow immediately on his mother's death (9.29) he again speaks of a youthful voice, his heart's own voice: "something childish in me was by a youthful voice, my heart's own voice, checked"? This voice was clearly internal to him. What he heard in his inner or interior ear had to be bodied forth in some way – did he invent this? Or did it "occur" to him much as he described it?

There are innumerable records of alleged experiences similar to that of Augustine's hearing the *tolle lege* in the garden in Milan. Many are recounted with explicit guarantee of their total truth – that is, of the total authenticity of the agent's perception. Take this one for example, told by a recent English Poet Laureate, C. Day Lewis. He had been speaking with unusual fervour and eloquence at a meeting in London. Half-way through his speech, he tells us: "I seemed to detach myself from the man who was so eloquently holding forth, to hover above my own shoulder, and with x-ray eyes to look penetratingly down. I heard myself speaking with sincerity and fervour ... to my detached self up there it was as though reality had evaporated out of the performance. When I sat down, all in one piece again, I distinctly heard above the applause a small voice saying three or four times within my head, 'It won't do, it just won't do.'"[24] Day Lewis is clear that the small voice spoke its short and repeated instruction *within his head.* If one followed Courcelle in preferring in the conversion scene in the *Confessions* the reading *de diuina domo,* "from the divine house," from Heaven, that is from the invisible God, in his inner ear, one would have an interestingly close correspondence in the case of Augustine – but it raises a difficult question.

If experiences of this kind, proceeding from highly emotional states, are to be described, they can be described only in terms of a subjective internal perception. Augustine, interestingly enough, reports that he sought at the time of the experience to relate it to an external objective circumstance: was *tolle lege* used in some children's game? He could not verify that it was. It seems unlikely that Augustine "invented" the scene. Conversions of the kind described involve a long gestation, but a moment does come when, to use Augustine's own constantly repeated word, suddenly all is changed, and utterly. But as the experience is a mental one, so its process has no external dimension. Yet the converted can have a perception which he, and only he, can describe. The truth is a subjective truth and the reader cannot control it.

It has not been the purpose of this paper either to attack or defend the historicity of the *Confessions.* What I have tried to do is to draw attention to the extraordinary amount of "fiction" or fictional elements that are used as a vehicle in the narrative. There still remains the question of assessing the historicity of each episode in the light of outside evidence, Augustine's other works, his techniques, and purposes.

NOTES

1. *Recherches sur les Confessions de Saint Augustin* (Paris: E. de Boccard, 1950), 188-202.
2. I make general use of John K. Ryan's translation of the *Confessions,* (New York: Image Books, 1960).
3. *Geschichte der Autobiographie,* I, 1, 482 ff.
4. See Paul Aubin, *Le Problème de la conversion* (Paris: Beauchesne, 1962).
5. *En.* 5. I, 7, ff. See Augustine, *Gen.Litt.* 4.50.
6. Op. cit., 29 ff.
7. *Ep. ad Alypium* 3, 4.
8. *Ep.* 27. 5.
9. Courcelle, 32, n.l.
10. *Augustine the Bishop* (London: Shead and Ward, 1961), 567.
11. (Paris: Société d'édition Paris 'les Belles Lettres', 1939), 54 ff. See also A. Solignac in *Les Confessions, BA,* vol. 13 (Paris: Etudes Augustiniennes, 1962), 207-33.
12. Ibid., 226-28.
13. See A. Solignac, *ibid.,* 667.
14. *The Young Augustine* (London: Longmans, Green and Company, 1954), 10 f.
15. *Ret.* 1.1.3.
16. *Civ. Dei.* 22. 29.
17. *Ep.* 92, 2 f.
18. 47. 15.37.
19. "Augustine the Artist and the *Aeneid,*" *Mélanges Christine Mohrmann* (Utrecht-Anvers: Spectrum, 1963), 253 ff.
20. *Periphyseon, PL* 122, 992A; see also 968 D.
21. See also *Conf.* 5.17 and 6.1.
22. See, e.g. ibid., 13.26, 29 and 42.
23. See ibid., 12. 11, 12, 18; 13.44.
24. S. Day Lewis, *Cecil Day Lewis* (London: Weidenfeld and Nicholson, 1980), 110.

BEYOND AUGUSTINE'S CONVERSION SCENE

LEO FERRARI

Sixteen hundred years ago, almost to the very month, on the 24th of April, Aurelius Augustinus was baptized and so entered the Church which he was to transform profoundly forever afterwards. Of the deepest sincerity of the conversion which preceded that epochal baptism, there can be no reasonable doubt. Saint Augustine's conversion back to the Catholicism of his childhood has been described in an unforgettable manner in the eighth book of his *Confessions.* [1] Indeed, so vivid is that description, that, as the eminent Irish scholar, J.J. O'Meara, has well observed, the scene remains with the reader long after all other details in the book have been forgotten. [2] Yet, as I aim to show here, there are substantial reasons for at least questioning the concrete realism of that well-known conversion scene. This will involve summarizing and extending work which I have already published or which is in the process of being published. In following this aim, I shall attempt to go beyond the given, as is implied in the title of this paper.

Prior to the appearance in 1950 of Courcelle's *Recherches sur les Confessions de saint Augustin* [3] the factuality of the conversion scene was challenged mainly by the more quixotic scholars. [4] However, Courcelle's immense erudition and his careful analysis of the conversion scene in the light of the literary tradition were both achievements which could not be lightly dismissed. Consequently, his espousal of the fictional interpretation of the famous conversion scene meant that the so-called "fictionalists" had at least acquired an impressive figurehead. Later, in 1968, Buchheit produced a fine study which further substantiated Courcelle's conclusion about the fictional nature of the conversion scene, and again by scholarly recourse to the literary tradition. [5]

In the more recent past, I had an idea for a completely different approach to the question about the factuality (or fictionality) of the conversion scene. This new approach, which I call "reference analysis," involved the construction of a data bank of all of Augustine's scriptural allusions and citations[6] from the first writings of 386 up to, and including, the writings of the year 401, when he completed the *Confessions.* This new idea concerned the significance of the now well-known text of Rom. 13.13-14, which, when read, effected Augustine's conversion. If this episode had in fact really occurred, then the passage must have been greatly cherished by Augustine. The basic problem was how to prove, or disprove, this consequent.

Now Augustine's conversion occurred in the year 386, while the *Confessions* was written some ten to fifteen years later, in the period of 397 to 401. In the total period, from the conversion of 386, up to and including 401, Augustine produced many works in which he often quoted from the same Epistle to the Romans. Indeed, I have counted up to some eight hundred and fifty verses cited or alluded to from this epistle in that same timespan. Yet, with one notable exception, the verses Rom. 13.13-14 are conspicuously absent from all these citations. It would therefore seem to follow that these verses were not of any special significance to Augustine prior to writing the *Confessions,* and so were not an integral part of the real, original event which the conversion scene claims to portray. Such, in brief, is the conclusion of a study which I published in 1980.[7]

Against this conclusion it can be argued that it is based on an argument *ex silentio* and therefore proves nothing. In reply, first of all, it should be objected that silences can be most significant, as a little reflection will verify.[8] Secondly, the same argument would seem to be fallacious in that it is implying that since silence is nothing, it can produce nothing and so prove nothing, which is false.

Again, it can be argued that in the time period of 386 to 401, the occasion simply had not arisen for Augustine to quote from Rom. 13.13-14.[9] This is contradicted by Augustine's eagerness for citing Scripture and especially Paul. Again, there are many occasions in the same time period when Augustine repeatedly quotes Pauline passages which are similar in tone to part, or all, of Rom. 13.13-14. The more popular of these texts, as well as their chronological distributions, are worthy of consideration for suspected emanation from any supposed conversional readings of Rom. 13.13-14 in 386.

For present purposes of brevity, the period 386-395 will be termed "the earlier period" and 396-401 "the Confessions period," with this latter allowing a year of forethought prior to writing the *Confessions*. The former is ten years, while the latter is only six; a fact to be borne in mind in the figures which follow. It is noteworthy that a few works pose problems in that the dates of their compositions are uncertain. To begin, and for the purposes of comparison, the text of Rom. 13.13-14 is as follows: "[Let us conduct ourselves becomingly as in the day] not in revelling and drunkenness, not in debauchery and licentiousness, not in quarrelling and jealousy, but put on the Lord Jesus Christ, and make no provision for the flesh to satisfy its desires."[10] Among the Pauline citations of similar tone, the most popular is 1 Cor. 15.53-54 with its injunction for the perishable nature to put on the imperishable and the mortal to put on immortality. These verses are found forty-four times, of which twenty-two belong to the Confessions period. Fifteen are earlier than 396, two occur some time after 392, while five are of uncertain dates. Therefore, their distribution favours the Confessions period, rather than the earlier period. Again, the text of Eph. 5. 8 is as follows: "Once you were darkness, but now you are light in the Lord; walk as children of light." Of the eighteen occurrences of this text, fourteen are found in the Confessions period, one in the earlier period, and three are of uncertain dates. In Col. 3. 10 Paul charges the Colossians to put off the old nature with its practices and put on the new nature. This text is cited fifteen times by Augustine. Nine cases occur in the Confessions period, and four in the earlier period, while two citations are of uncertain dates. Finally, Eph. 2. 2 concerns the sins in which the Ephesians once walked, following the course of this world and the prince of the power of the air. This passage is cited ten times, with six cases occurring in the Confessions period, two in the earlier period, and two of uncertain dates. Therefore, the majority of the above texts occur in the Confessions period, so discounting any emanation from the supposed reading of Rom. 13.13-14 in 386.

The above texts are but the more numerously quoted ones of similar tone to Rom. 13. 13-14 from the conversion scene. Their very occurrences in such numbers contradict the claim that the occasion had not arisen for Augustine to quote Rom. 13. 13-14. Further, and most significantly, it can well be asked why Rom. 13. 13-14 not only does not find a prominent place among such citations, but is entirely absent. These facts are all the more amazing in view of the text's climactic role in the conversion scene.

By way of rejoinder to this question, it could be submitted that because of the experience in the garden scene, Rom. 13. 13-14 had touched Augustine too intimately to be touted in public. If this were indeed so, then verses of similar tone would have been suitably substituted and so explain the popularity of the above-mentioned verses. But the most frequently cited of such verses, as selected above, display a most inconvenient distribution for supporting such a claim.

In view of the soul-searing drama of the conversion scene, the verses should be most frequently cited in the earliest years of the earlier period, when the effects of the conversion scene would have been most recent, and therefore most intense. But, as has been seen, they tend rather to be more frequently cited in the very period when Augustine was writing the *Confessions,* which supports a fictional, rather than a realistic, interpretation of the conversion scene. So much, then, for the objections to a fictional explanation of the reading from Rom. 13. 13-14 at the climax of the conversion scene. As has been seen, they fail to account for the incredible absence of Rom. 13. 13-14 in the earlier period; an absence which becomes all the more remarkable in view of the popularity of the above verses of similar tone in that same period.

Again, while working on that study, I was struck by many points of similarity between Augustine's conversion and that of his beloved apostle, Paul. As a result, in 1982 I published a study entitled "Saint Augustine on the Road to Damascus"[11] which, by the same technique of reference analysis, showed that Paul's conversion was not of detectable interest to Augustine until the very same years that he was working on the *Confessions,* when an impressive cluster of some seventeen references to Paul's conversion is to be found in Augustine's other writings. Thereafter, the episode is mentioned only rarely in firmly dated works.

If Augustine's conversion scene had been a faithful recount of a personal experience that he had undergone in the year 386, then the very similar, earlier conversion of Paul must have been constantly before the mind of Augustine. In view of his spontaneous tendency to cite the Scriptures, and especially Paul, then the biblical citations of the earlier period would have been rich in allusions to the conversion of Paul. The absence of such allusions makes it virtually certain that Augustine was not preoccupied with that other conversion and therefore had not himself undergone a remarkably similar experience in the year 386.

Complementing this argument *ex silentio* is an argument of a more positive nature concerning the cluster of seventeen allusions to the conversion of Paul during the very same years that Augustine was working on his *Confessions.* This is positive evidence that Paul's conversion had suddenly acquired significance for Augustine during the period of 397-401, and I claim that it had acquired such significance precisely because he was using it as a paradigm for the story of his own conversion in the eighth book of the *Confessions.*

In this regard, it is most relevant that Sermon 89, firmly dated as deriving from the Confessions period, contains a unique combination of two important elements from Augustine's own conversion scene. Courcelle saw Augustine's depiction of himself beneath the fig tree in the conversion scene as a symbolic identification with Nathanael in the same condition, and all that that implied.[12] Sermon 89 not only treats of this latter episode, but, most significantly, joins it with another episode – that of the voice calling Paul – "Saule, Saule, quid me persequeris?" Realization of this rare combination makes one feel very close to the actual origins of the episode of Augustine under the fig tree with the mysterious voice calling him: "*tolle lege, tolle lege.*"

Regarding possible objections to the significance imputed to that unique cluster of references to Paul's conversion in Augustine's works precisely at the time that he was writing the *Confessions,* it is significant that a similar cluster applies to another important ingredient of that same work. In 1977 I published a study devoted to the leitmotif of the prodigal son in Augustine's *Confessions.*[13] Not only does Augustine there state that the story used to bring tears to his eyes, but the work contains seven references to that parable.[14] Added to these is the sudden appearance of seven references to that parable in other works of the Confessions period.[15] In addition, there are three references to the parable in the *Enarrationes* dating from some time after 392.[16] There is only one very brief allusion dating from somewhere in Augustine's earlier period.[17] Therefore, the importance of the parable of the prodigal son to Augustine's *Confessions* and also the allusions to that parable which occur virtually for the first time during the same period that Augustine was working on the *Confessions* are both facts yielding yet further confirmation of the validity of the technique of reference analysis.

I trust that I have shown that this technique, when used with discretion, can offer valuable insights into Augustine's peripheral preoccupations while authoring texts. Indeed, his paratextual world, filled with thousands of biblical allusions and citations, has been explored somewhat in the past, but not with the speed and thoroughness made possible by the new age of computers and the construction of data banks. In my opinion, the verdict of reference analysis upon the justly famous conversion scene of Augustine's *Confessions* is in accord with the viewpoint championed by the eminent Courcelle and further substantiated by Buchheit. For yet a third time and by a completely different approach, it must be concluded that the well-known conversion scene in the eighth book of the *Confessions* is essentially fictional in nature.

That Augustine was profoundly and permanently converted is a basic fact beyond all reasonable doubt. But so too is the scrupulous honesty that he displays in all his writings. These facts raise the question of how this latter quality of honesty can be reconciled with the conclusion that his account of his conversion is essentially fictional. According to that conclusion, he is presenting as fact that which is not fact. His inconsistency is all the greater in that it concerns the climax of his brilliant autobiography.

It seems that the solution to this problem must begin with an appreciation of the cultural chasm which separates our age from that of Augustine. As I have pointed out elsewhere,[18] the *Confessions* was written long before *The Guttenberg Galaxy* appeared on the horizon of history. Consequently, both books and readers were extremely rare and the coming together of the two made of reading a highly social occasion.

We must therefore begin by realizing that the *Confessions* was written to be read aloud before an assembled audience, as Augustine himself repeatedly says of it.[19] This means that the text is really a script for a dramatic performance, which throws an entirely different light on the whole question about the factuality or fictionality of the conversion scene.

Writing factual autobiography destined for the silent reading so common today, a person of Augustine's scrupulous honesty would aim at what Courcelle describes as *l'exactitude sténographique.* But as script for a dramatic performance, the presentation, to be dramatically effective, must subordinate factuality to the canons of dramatic presentation – a craft incidentally in which it should be recalled that Augustine had been well schooled – and so a certain romanticizing of reality becomes inevitable, whence the Courcellean *mode de présentation romanesque.*

On this point of the dramatic character of the *Confessions,* the rhetorical structure of the eighth book has been carefully analyzed by Schmidt-

Dengler.[20] As the narrative approaches the climax of the *tolle lege* episode, Schmidt-Dengler sees the abandonment of rhetorical artifice and the simplicity of language as preparing for the sudden intrusion of the present tense in the famous words of *ecce audio vocem de vicina domo*. This tense change Schmidt-Dengler sees as part of the evidence for the factuality of the voice episode. On the other hand, once it is realized that the text is a script for a dramatic performance, the intrusion of the present tense would seem to have no other significance than sharpening the attention of the audience and underscoring the climactic nature of the voice episode.

One objection to the notion of the *Confessions* as a script for a dramatic performance could be derived from the text itself when Augustine roundly condemns the drama of the theatre in the third book (3. 2. 2-4). This objection is easily answered by pointing out that the theatre is there condemned for its portrayal of lust. Again, it is also significant that Augustine there condemns theatre for promoting grief, not over real people's misfortunes, but over mere fictions. However, the matter is quite otherwise in the case of the *Confessions* where the audience is invited to grieve, not over some fiction, but over the undeniable truth of Augustine's past sinfulness and his flight from God.

It follows, then, that the *Confessions,* while being a dramatic text, is also basically about undeniable truths in Augustine's own life. Noteworthy is the fact that the question of truth in the work arises in the tenth book (10. 3. 3-4. 6) in regard to how Augustine's audience will know that he is telling the truth. He points out there that his confession is not addressed to those who are merely curious about other people's lives, while inert about improving their own; but rather to those whose ears are opened to him by charity. This point is significant.

In the treatise *On Lying,* written in 395, or just two years before he began working on the *Confessions,* Augustine states the need for sinners, not only to repent, but also to speak the truth in confessing their past sinfulness (para. 35). Further, the truth is spoken not merely with the tongue, but in the heart (para. 31). Those whose ears are opened by charity will hear and understand. This has also been said by Augustine of his *Confessions,* as noted above.

Moreover, it is also important to notice that in the treatise *On Lying,* Augustine readily admits the legitimacy of allegory and figurative speech as expressions of the truth, particularly in regard to spiritual matters, as in the case of the Bible (paras. 7-9, 26 and 42). I believe that if there were any further need to justify the dramatic liberties of the conversion scene, it would be found under this category and by a special justification, as will be seen. Meanwhile, the demonstrable similarities of Augustine's conversion to that of Paul would not only increase the impact upon his audience, but such similarities would leave no doubt about the origins of his own conversion and the spiritual tradition to which it belongs. In this regard, it is most relevant that Augustine's audience belonged to a culture which, unlike the present age, looked to the past, rather than to the future. Therefore, where the modern mind suspects plagiarism, Augustine's audience would have savoured authenticity. On this matter of authenticity, there is yet another, and probably the most powerful reason, for the masterful portrayal of the conversion scene, as has just been hinted. That reason must wait till the conclusion of this paper.

If it be conceded then, that the conversion scene is basically fictional in character, the question arises as to what, if anything, can be known about the real conversion so long eclipsed by that justly famous description of the conversion in the garden of Milan in the eighth book of the *Confessions.* Looking beyond this latter conversion scene, there does indeed seem to have been an important episode in the real life of Augustine upon which that scene was based. The *Confessions* contains another and earlier seizing upon the writings of the apostle Paul. This other episode is found towards the end of the seventh book, when Augustine describes how he seized "most eagerly" upon the writings of the Holy Spirit, but especially upon those of Paul.[21]

There can be no doubting the factuality of this action, since, like the Hortensius episode, it is described in several other places in Augustine's works.[22] However, unlike the reading of Paul in the conversion scene, this other seizing upon Paul's writings follows, not from the instructions of some mysterious voice, but from the reading of certain plenteous books of the "Platonists," as the context makes quite clear. For this, and other reasons, it would be doing violence to the text of the *Confessions* to attempt to identify this episode with the later description of seizing upon the volume of Paul in the conversion scene.[23] Rather, the episode in the seventh book seems to be the personal source for Augustine of the better known seizing upon the book of Paul in the famous conversion scene, so that this latter scene does indeed have a foundation in fact.

As to the real conversion which resulted from that first seizing upon the works of Paul, some interesting details can still be gleaned from

Augustine's writings. Thus, it would appear that he was not enthusiastically received back into the Church of his childhood. Ambrose's silent rebuffs of *Conf.* 6.3.3 would seem to justify such a conclusion. Reasons for these rebuffs are not hard to find. Besides being a Manichee (even if secretly disillusioned), Augustine, by his own admissions, had habitually vanquished Christians in debates.[24] Consequently, like his beloved Paul before him, he was probably a notorious character in the eyes of the Christian community. For this reason, it seems, having been rebuffed by Ambrose, Augustine sought entry into the Church through the intervention of Simplician.[25]

On this matter of authenticity there is yet another, and probably the most powerful, reason for the masterly portrayal of the conversion scene, as has just been hinted. The converted Augustine of the early dialogues was a fervent Neoplatonist and vastly different from the author of the writings subsequent to the *Confessions.* With more justification than he probably realized, Anton Pegis remarks upon the two different Augustines in an article entitled "The Second Conversion of St. Augustine."[26] As I have explained elsewhere,[27] in my opinion, the change was more than quantitative. It was qualitative in that Augustine's faith had acquired new foundations. The tremendous transformation had been brought about not merely by spiritual growth, but, as Augustine himself says, by a direct revelation from God.[28] This momentous revelation concerned what became Augustine's famous doctrine of divine predestination, and meant that everything, from the very first stirrings of grace onwards, came entirely from God and from God alone. The rest, as they say, is history.

Augustine's divine revelation came as he was struggling to answer some exegetical problems concerning Rom. 9. 10-29; problems directed to his attention by Simplician. Consequently, as Brown has well observed,[29] the reply to Simplician became a charter for the *Confessions,* and, I might add that in its turn the *Confessions* became the charter for Augustine's doctrine of divine predestination. This, then, is the powerful reason, previously hinted at, for the drama of the conversion scene. But this dramatic text has long eclipsed the divine revelation which inspired and justified it. That revelation, I have described elsewhere as Augustine's final conversion.[30] It occurred in the year 396. In closing therefore, I would respectfully suggest the fittingness of a sedecentennial celebration in 1996 to mark the final conversion of Augustine, a conversion in which he earnestly believed that he had received a privileged revelation of a universal divine predestination – a belief which was increasingly to influence all his subsequent writings.

NOTES

1. For the place of this particular conversion in the other conversions of Augustine, see my *The Conversions of Saint Augustine* (the Saint Augustine lecture, 1982), (Villanova: Villanova University Press, 1984). This work is hereinafter referred to as "The Conversions."

2. *Augustinus Magister* I (Paris: Etudes Augustiniennes, 1954), 59.

3. A second edition appeared in 1968. Subsequent references to *Recherches* are to this edition.

4. For an overview of the famous debate about the historicity of the conversion scene, see my "Saint Augustine's Conversion Scene: The End of the Modern Debate," *Studia Patristica* (Leuven, 1989), 235-50.

5. "Augustinus unter dem Feigenbaum," *Vigiliae Christianae* 22 (1968), 257-271.

6. The references were gathered from the appropriate works in the Benedictine Maurist edition of the *Opera Omnia* (Paris: J.P. Migne, 1841-1849).

7. "Paul at the Conversion of Augustine (*Conf.* 8.12.29-30)," *Augustinian Studies* 11 (1980), 6-20.

8. Consider, for instance, the important role of silence in the famous vision of Ostia (*Conf.* 9.10.25), or, on a more mundane level, the trepidation of a mother whose young child does not answer her call.

9. See A. Solignac, *Les Confessions*, Notes complementaires, *BA* vol. 13 (Paris: Etudes Augustiniennes, 1962), 549.

10. This, and all biblical quotes are taken from the Revised Standard Version, ecumenical edition (New York, Glasgow and Toronto: Collins, 1973).

11. *Augustinian Studies* 13 (1982), 151-79.

12. *Recherches*, 193.

13. "The Prodigal Son in St Augustine's *Confessions*," *Recherches Augustiniennes* 12 (1977), 105-18. As I showed in this study, there were virtually no references prior to the *Confessions*, but some fourteen references during the same years that this work was being written.

14. *Conf.* 1. 18. 28; 3. 4. 7; 3. 6. 11; 4. 16. 30; 8. 3. 6 (which contains a reference to the tears); 8. 3. 8 and 10. 31. 45.

15. *Qu. Ev.* 2, 45 and 51; *Ann. Job* 9; *Doct.* 3.7.11; *Con. ep. Parm.* 2; *Serm.* 330. 3; *Con. Faust.* 15.6.

16. *Enn.* 18. 2. 3, 6 and 15; 32. 2. 28.

17. *En.* 24. 5.

18. "Ecce audio vocem de vicina domo (*Conf.* 8.12.29)," *Augustiniana* 33 (1983), 232-45, especially 235f.

19. *Conf.* 10.3.3 and 4; 10.4. 6.

20. "Der rhetorische Aufbau des achten Buches der Konfessionen des heiligen Augustinus," *Revue des Etudes Augustiniennes* 15 (1969), 195-208.

21. See my "Truth and Augustine's Conversion Scene," *Collectanea Augustiniana* (in press).

22. *Beat. vita* 4; *Con. Acad.* 2.2.5.

23. This was done by O'Meara in his "Arripui, aperui et legi," *Augustinus Magister* I (Paris: Etudes Augustiniennes, 1954), 59-65. See, however, my "Paul at the Conversion of Augustine," *Augustinian Studies* 11 (1980), 5-20 and also my *The Conversions*, 59-63.

24. See my *Conversions*, 70ff.

25. See *Ad Simp.* 1.2.

26. *Gesellschaft, Kultur, Literatur; Rezeption und Originalität im Wachsen einer europäischen Literatur und Geistkeit.* (Stuttgart, 1975), 79-93

27. See *Conversions*, 70ff.

28. *Praed.* 4, 8. See also *Conversions*, 77ff.

29. Peter Brown, *Augustine of Hippo; a Biography* (Berkeley and Los Angeles, 1969), 78.

30. *Conversions*, 70.

AUGUSTINIAN PLATONISM IN EARLY MEDIEVAL THEOLOGY

R.D. CROUSE

Let me begin by admitting quite frankly that the title I have proposed for this paper is both pretentious and question-begging. Early medieval theology is, after all, a vast and still inadequately charted territory, richly productive of theological literature of many different kinds, and replete with controversies of enduring interest and importance. To speak of Augustine's influence there is either to utter platitudes, or to embark upon a long and difficult enterprise; for, throughout those early medieval centuries, the voice of Augustine was echoed everywhere. "Clarissimus idemque suavissimus auctor Augustinus," said Servatus Lupus: "Vir ille divini ingenii," "whom you do not know whether to admire more for his discoveries, or for his felicity in expressing them." [1]

Augustine's voice was not, of course, the only one. There were the other Latin Fathers, and a few of the Greeks as well, and some survivors from pagan Greek and Latin literature, useful as sources of philosophic doctrine, and as providing grammatical and dialectical instruments of exegesis. But it was Augustine's voice that dominated, whether in biblical interpretation or in doctrinal definition. At least from the time of the Synod of Orange, in 529, both sides in any controversy felt constrained to claim Augustine as their patron, as, for instance, in the eucharistic and predestination controversies of the ninth century. As Notker Balbulus expressed it, "Si Augustinus adest, sufficit ipse tibi." [2]

Obviously, even the most anaemic sketch of the influence of Augustine's thought through six centuries of the early middle ages is beyond our present scope, and I think you must forgive me if I reduce my topic rather drastically, to speak only of the influence of Augustine in the two most important speculative theologians of the period, namely, Boethius and Eriugena. I hope to find there something of the history of a consistent development of Augustinian Platonism, which seems to me important not only for our understanding of early medieval theology, but also of the theologies of "the renaissance of the twelfth century," and the Christian Platonism of the high and later middle ages.[3]

"Augustinian Platonism" is undoubtedly a question-begging term. After a century or so of modern controversy about Augustine's Platonism, there is still no clear agreement as to what, precisely, such a term might mean. Was Augustine, perhaps, a Christian theologian, who found in the language and conceptual forms of Platonism a convenient and essentially indifferent lexicon for the exposition of Christian doctrine? Or was he, perhaps, intellectually a Platonist, who found in Christianity the missing element of moral inspiration? Or ought we, perhaps, to divide between philosophy and theology, and call him a Platonist philosophically, and a Christian theologically?

None of those familiar and still current hypotheses seems really satisfactory as an account of Augustine's Platonism.[4] Augustine is not a Christian who simply borrows elements from Platonism, as though from some external source, to expound his Christian doctrine. The doctrine he expounds, as he finds it in the Scriptures and in his Christian predecessors, is for him unrecognizable and unthinkable in abstract separation from those modes of Platonic speculation which, long before his time, belonged already to the Christian *intellectus.* Nor is it possible, in Augustine, to distinguish between a Platonic intellectuality and a Christian moral inspiration; for him, as indeed for pagan Platonists, and for Christian Platonists before him, the intellectual and the moral are inextricably related, and his problems with pagan Platonism are surely as much intellectual as moral. Nor is there, for Augustine, any proto-scholastic division of philosophy from theology: Christian *sapientia* is one, and is at once both Christian and Platonic. Intellectually and morally, philosophically and theologically, Augustine is both Platonist and Christian.

As Professor O'Meara has remarked, "there is no simple statement to describe Augustine's use of the Neoplatonists."[5] At least from the time of his reading of Cicero's *Hortensius* – that lost Platonic-Aristotelian exhortation to the philosophic life, which, he tells us, changed his prayers and called him to return to God[6] – Augustine's thought never ceased to be nourished by the theology of Platonism, which he found in many sources: not only in the notorious *libri platonicorum* of book seven of the

Confessions, but from a multitude of sources, some of which we know, because he mentions them (especially in *De civitate Dei*), and others, perhaps, about which we can only guess. It is difficult to measure the influence of specific forms of Platonism – for instance, Plotinian and Porphyrian[7] – but it is clear that Platonism, in one form and another, belongs to Augustine's whole formation, not only at one moment, but throughout his life, not just as an alternative to Christianity, but as a form of Christian understanding. In his conversion, Platonism is not abandoned, but is continually converted with him, in the continual conversion of his intellect and will. Augustine thinks of Christianity Platonically, and Platonism in the light of the word of revelation; and it is to that conversion of Platonic thought that we refer when we speak of "Augustinian Platonism."

The story of Augustine's conversion of Platonic doctrine is, of course, in the first place, the story of his own conversion, as he tells it in the *Confessions,* where the word of God, spoken outwardly in the Scriptures and the preaching of the church, and inwardly received with the humility of faith, provides the key to resolution of the most profound dilemmas of Platonic thought, in regard to the nature of the divine principle, the meaning of creation, and the *via* and the goal of human aspiration. All that becomes explicit in the last three books of the *Confessions,* where the phenomena and the psychological theory of conversion, expounded earlier, are given their full theological dimension in the doctrine of the *conversio* of all creation.[8]

That doctrine of *conversio* is, of course, Platonic; familiar especially from the fifth of the *Enneads* of Plotinus.[9] The similarity is obvious; but the difference is altogether crucial. For Augustine, *conversio* means conversion by and to the Holy Trinity of Father, Word, and Spirit – a doctrine expounded fully in *De Trinitate,* but also present, at least in embryo, as the fundamental pattern of his thought in the *Confessions,* and clearly enunciated in book thirteen of that work.[10]

There are, indeed, in pagan Platonism, as Augustine sees it, adumbrations, vague intimations, of that doctrine: "quasi per quaedam tenuis imaginationis umbracula," he says, in *De civitate Dei,* with reference to Porphyry's doctrine of hypostases;[11] and Porphyry's doctrine of hypostases does, indeed, move in the *direction* of a trinitarian formulation. According to the perspective of Augustine, the doctrine of the Trinity is implied – indeed, demanded – by Platonic speculation, as its own clarification and completion; and yet, as he insists, at the beginning of *De Trinitate,*[12] it is not attainable apart from the revealed Word, grasped first by faith, and only later demonstrated.

The *intellectus fidei,* then, will not be simply an alternative to Platonism, but rather a divinely given fulfillment of the aims and tendencies of that theology. In fact, it involves a revision, or conversion, of Platonic thought, at its most central point – a conversion *in principio.* And that trinitarian conversion is of incalculable importance, both for Augustine, and for all the later history of philosophy.[13]

One of the many major implications of that doctrine, and one to which we must now turn our attention especially, as we look towards the influence of Augustinian Platonism in early medieval theology, is in regard to the theory of creation. In the light of the conversion of Neoplatonic hypostatic doctrine to an understanding of the divine principle as Trinity in unity, as "inseparabilis distinctio," as "simplicitas" which is also "multiplicitas,"[14] Augustine elaborates, progressively, in the last three books of the *Confessions,* in *De genesi ad litteram,* and in books eleven and twelve of *De civitate Dei,* a metaphysic of the cosmos[15] in which Platonic emanation theory receives a profound reorientation, and a resolution of the dilemmas typically inherent in the Platonic opposition of unity and multiplicity.

Certainly, for pagan Platonism, as Augustine clearly recognises, creation is creation in the Word. But while for them the Word (or "Nous") must be somehow a subordinate, derivative principle of distinction, outside the absolute unity of the purely actual, transcendent One (in a manner analogous to that of some forms of Arian Christology), for Augustine the Word is absolutely God. That is to say, the Word, as the principle of the intelligible distinction in which all things are created, and the Spirit, as governing their distribution or relatedness, are hypostases belonging equally and eternally to the essential unity of the divine Trinity. There is, quite literally, and in the most radical sense, nothing outside the unity of the triune activity: no irrational element, no "errant cause," no quasi-independent matter; and, therefore, creation can in no way be seen in terms of successive diminutions of divinity, but only in terms of the efficient causality of the divine will. As Augustine puts it, with sublime simplicity, the only reason of creation is that a good God makes good things.[16]

This trinitarian metaphysic of Genesis, this Christian Platonic reconception of the nature of the cosmos, worked out in the trinitarian exegesis of the first few verses of the biblical creation narrative, in the *Confessions,* and more fully in *De genesi ad litteram,* finds its most mature statement in *De civitate Dei;* and there its implications are eloquently illustrated: for instance, in the marvellous passages in book eleven, where Augustine celebrates the unmitigated goodness, harmony, and beauty of the *universitas rerum,* the *res publica* of God.[17] The cosmos becomes, on every level, the translucent mirror of divine goodness; it becomes, indeed, if one may be forgiven a somewhat anachronistic term, "theophanic" – the revelatory sphere of the triune unity in distinction. And this involves, of course, a positive re-assessment of the value of the external and sensible, and (as one sees especially in book thirteen of *De Trinitate*) a Christian re-possession of *scientia,* as not in opposition to, but embraced within *sapientia: ratio* with *intelligentia,* creation within the unity of triune divine activity.

All this is not simply Platonic; but neither is it simply un-Platonic. There is an ambiguity there, suggested, for instance, in the fact that in Augustine's debate with Manichaeism on these matters, in *De civitate Dei,* Plato's *Timaeus* is really on both sides of the argument. I think that indicates Augustine's assessment not only of the deficiencies of pagan Platonism, but also of what he discerned to be the intention, the essential tendency, the internal logic of its own development. That he was right in that assessment of its tendency is surely to some extent borne out in the developments of post-Plotinian Neoplatonism which in some ways parallel quite strikingly the thought of Augustine: for instance, in the development (which he may have known) of the doctrine of God as Being and cause of being, especially in the anonymous commentary on the *Parmenides,* which Hadot ascribes to Porphyry;[18] and in the treatment of the problem of evil, and the re-evaluation of matter as divinely created, in Proclus's commentaries on the *Parmenides* and the *Timaeus,* in the *Elements of Theology,* and especially in the *De malorum subsistentia.*[19]

Certainly, the tendency is not complete without the Christian reconception of the divine principle as Trinity; in fact, the problems of a mediation hierarchy which cannot really mediate remain. But the tendency is there, expressed in a more positive assessment of the sensible, and the value of *scientia.* We have no evidence that these developments of pagan

Platonism have anything particular to do with Christian influences; nor, if Augustine is right about the internal logic of Platonism, have we really any reason to suspect it. But the fact of a considerable measure of *rapprochement,* on certain points, between the theses of Augustinian Platonism and those of Proclan Platonism, must inevitably complicate the task of evaluating the relative weights of those influences upon the Christian theologians of the early middle ages.

Thus, in Boethius, in the *Consolation of Philosophy,* we encounter what Hilary Armstrong has well described as a "concordist Platonism":[20] concordist, indeed, to such a degree that the old debate continues as to whether the author of that work must be seen as a pagan or a Christian.[21] Certainly, the predominant tendency of recent studies has been to focus upon what Boethius appears to owe to such pagan Neoplatonists as Ammonius and Proclus, especially in the interpretation of Aristotelian logic, which was, of course, a matter of special interest in those late Platonic schools.[22]

Yet, at the same time, I think it remains true to say, with E.K. Rand, that in the *Consolation,* "there is nothing ... for which a good case might not have been made by any contemporary Christian theologian, who knew his Augustine."[23] And might one not see some significance in the fact that in the whole of the *Consolation* and the *Tractates,* Boethius never makes mention of an author more recent than Cicero, with the sole exception of Augustine? I refer, of course, to that passage in the prologue of Boethius's *De Trinitate,* in which he asks Symmachus to judge "whether the seeds of reasons (*semina rationum*) coming from the writings of St. Augustine have borne fruit."[24]

Obviously, the doctrine of Boethius in the *Tractates* is explicitly Christian and Augustinian;[25] but I think that also in the *Consolation,* in the cosmic metaphysic which governs the argument of that work, one must see the germination of the "seeds of reasons" from Augustine. I think especially of Boethius's easy dismissal of any concern about intermediaries between the goodness of the divine creative principle and the goodness of created things, and the reduction of all such to the simplicity of providence;[26] and also of how, in the resolution of the argument of the *Consolation,* the order of *ratio* is immediately contained within the simplicity of divine *intelligentia, uno ictu.*[27]

In such matters, Boethius is surely very far from both the spirit and the letter of Proclan Neoplatonism; and if we may regard the *Tractates* as adding theological precision to what Professor Starnes well describes as the "theology of Christian humanism"[28] of the *Consolation,* I think we may see in the tractate, *De hebdomadibus,* the fundamental reason of the difference. That tractate is principally concerned with the presentation of the dilemmas of Platonic participation theory; and the resolution of the question – whatever it may own, as Hadot suggests, to a Porphyrian conception of essence and existence[29] – is finally worked out in terms of the Augustinian conclusion, that the only reason of creation is that a good God, by his efficient will, makes good things from nothing.[30]

When we turn to Eriugena, who is in some degree a disciple of "magnificus Boetius,"[31] within this context of the development of Christian Platonism, our problems are somewhat different than with Boethius. Here there is no scarcity of sources, but rather, generous quotations from a host of authors, Greek and Latin; predominantly from Augustine, and from Pseudo-Dionysius and other Greek fathers. The tendency of scholarship has been to emphasize the differences between the Proclan Neoplatonism of Pseudo-Dionysius, and the older (supposedly Plotinian) Neoplatonism of Augustine, and to ask which side Eriugena distorts in favour of the other. But no decision on that point is easily forthcoming. Sheldon-Williams, in his editing of the *Periphyseon,* came to the conclusion that Augustine is everywhere misrepresented in that work;[32] but that is a judgement which must depend, of course, upon a certain view of what constitutes the true, historical Augustine. A number of other recent studies have suggested, rather, fundamental and extensive influence of Augustine in the formulation of Eriugena's position in scriptural exegesis and theology.[33]

Certainly, Eriugena goes beyond Augustine in some ways: for instance, in the systematic thoroughness with which, in the commentary on Genesis in the *Periphyseon,* the doctrine of creation is worked out within the context of the doctrine of the Trinity. That is, indeed, the whole burden of the second book. "Simul enim Pater et sapientiam suam genuit, et in ipsa omnia fecit". At once – *simul* – says Eriugena, the Father both begot his wisdom, and in that wisdom made all things; for God's understanding of all things *is* their essence; for God knowing and making are the same thing.[34] All creation, in all its levels of *esse, sensus, ratio* and *intellectus,*[35] in its descent and its return, is essentially and eternally contained within the unity of the divine thinking and willing of it. The whole of the *Periphyseon* has the point of showing how the unity and the divisions of created and uncreated "nature" can be coherently understood according to a trinitarian logic of unity in multiplicity; and the texts of Genesis are thoroughly and systematically interpreted in that light. Thus, for instance, the six days of creation must be understood as atemporal, intelligible days,[36] as moments of logical distinction in what is created *simul et semel,*[37] *in momento oculi.*[38]

On these, and indeed on all essential points of doctrine, Eriugena makes continual appeal to the texts of Augustine, especially *De genesi ad litteram* and *De civitate Dei,* and it is difficult to see that he wanders very far from what any discerning Christian Platonist must find in those texts. The form of expression bears Eriugena's characteristic signature, and the argument becomes more fully systematic, but the import is fundamentally Augustinian.

And if, turning to the Greeks, one finds Eriugena interpreting the thought of Pseudo-Dionysius in the direction of an essentially Augustinian formulation of trinitarian doctrine, is that really untrue to the sense and implications of Pseudo-Dionysius's Christian conversion of Proclan metaphysics?[39] Eriugena is certainly aware of differences in this matter, but they are differences of words, he claims, and not of fundamental meanings.[40] And if Eriugena's constant labours towards consensus suggest a Pseudo-Dionysius and an Augustine who have rather more in common than a narrower philological criticism might easily allow, may that not be because Eriugena penetrates, in fact, more deeply the theological sense of these several strains of Christian Platonism?

If one is looking for what is sometimes called the "historical" Augustine, obviously one does not look to Boethius or Eriugena. What one finds in these early medieval authors is an interpretation, which is also a development of Augustinian Platonism. I think it is a development consistent with the direction of Augustine's own development of Christian Platonism, particularly in *De genesi ad litteram* and *De civitate Dei;* but, whatever one might make of its fidelity to Augustine, it is a development of vast importance for the history of Augustinianism, by virtue of the constant influence of Boethius in the work of later medieval students of Augustine, and also by virtue of the more occasional, but nonetheless powerful, impact of Eriugenian interpretation of Augustine, as, for instance, in the theology of creation in the twelfth-century schools, or in the ready alliance between Augustinian and Proclan interests evident in various forms of Platonism in the thirteenth century, and throughout the later middle ages, in some of which, at least, the mediation of Eriugena is evident and well established.[41]

The interpretation of Augustinian Platonism in the speculative theology of the early middle ages is, thus, a necessary chapter in the history of the development and influence of Christian Platonism, and in the general history of Christian thought.

NOTES

1. Servatus Lupus, *Epist. 4; Epist. 5; Liber de tribus quaestionibus* (PL, 119, 444; 446; 634); see M. Grabmann, *Die Geschichte der scholastischen Methode* 1 (Freiburg im Br.: Herder, 1909), 183.

2. Notker Balbulus, *De interpretibus divinarum scriptuarum,* 5 (PL, 131, 998); see Grabmann, op. cit., 183.

3. See my article, "Anselm of Canterbury and Medieval Augustinianisms," *Toronto Journal of Theology,* 3/1 (1987) 60-68; and "A Twelfth Century Augustinian: Honorius Augustodunensis," *Studia ephemeridis "Augustinianum"* 26 (1987), 167-177.

4. I have discussed these problems more fully in "St. Augustine's *De Trinitate:* Philosophical Method," in E.A. Livingstone, ed., *Studia Patristica,* 16 (Berlin, 1985), 501-510; and "The Conversion of Philosophy in St. Augustine's *Confessions,*" *Dionysius* 11 (1987), 53-62; see also, A.H. Armstrong, *St. Augustine and Christian Platonism* (Villanova, Pa.: Villanova University Press, 1967); J.A. Doull, "Augustinian Trinitarianism and Existential Theology," *Dionysius* 3 (1979), 111-59; H. Dörrie, "Die andere Theologie," *Theologie und Philosophie* 56 (1981), 1-46; D.K. House, "St. Augustine's Account of the Relation of Platonism to Christianity in *De civitate Dei,*" *Dionysius* 7 (1983), 43-48; R. Russell, "The Role of Neoplatonism in St. Augustine's *De civitate Dei,*" in H.J. Blumenthal and R.A. Markus, eds., *Neoplatonism and Early Christian Thought, Essays in honour of A.H. Armstrong* (London: Variorum Press, 1981), 160-70; C. de Vogel, "Platonism and Christianity: A Mere Antagonism or a Profound Common Ground," *Vigiliae Christianae* 39 (1985), 1-62; M.T. Clark, *Augustine of Hippo. Selected Writings* (New York and Toronto: Paulist Press, 1984), "Introduction."

5. J.J. O'Meara, "The Neoplatonism of Saint Augustine," in D.J. O'Meara, ed., *Neoplatonism and Christian Thought* (Norfolk, Virginia and Albany, N.Y.: State University of New York Press, 1982), 34-44.

6. *Conf.* 3.4.7. See M. Testard, *St. Augustin et Cicéron,* vol. 1: *Cicéron dans la formation et dans l'oeuvre de saint Augustin* (Paris: Etudes Augustiniennes, 1958), 19-39.

7. On the Porphyrian character of the *libri platonicorum,* the recent comment of A.H. Armstrong: "I am inclined to wonder whether both Platonism and the understanding of what Platonism is in the West, from Augustine to our own times, have had a stronger and more distinctive Porphyrian colour than we have realized." A.H. Armstrong, *Expectations of Immortality in Late Antiquity.* The Aquinas Lecture, 1987 (Milwaukee: Marquette University Press, 1987), 35.

8. See R.D. Crouse, "Recurrents in te unum: *The Pattern of St. Augustine's Confessions,*" in E.A. Livingstone, ed., *Studia Patristica* (Berlin: Akademie-Verlag, 1976), 389-92.

9. Plotinus, *Enneads,* 5.3.49. See Armstrong, *St. Augustine and Christian Platonism,* 39, n. 7.

10. See C.J. Starnes, "The Place and Purpose of the Tenth Book of the *Confessions,*" *Studia ephemeridis "Augustinianum"* 25 (1987), 95-103; R.D. Crouse, "The Conversion of Philosophy in St. Augustine's *Confessions*" (n. 4, above).

11. *Civ. Dei* 10.29.

12. *Trin.* 1.2.4.

13. See P. Hadot, "L'image de la Trinité dans l'âme chez Victorinus et chez saint Augustin," in *Studia Patristica* 6 (Berlin, 1962), 409-42; R.D. Crouse, "In multa defluximus: *Confessions* 10, 29-43, and St. Augustine's Theory of Personality," in Blumenthal and Markus, op. cit., 180-85.

14. *Conf.* 13.11.12.

15. See A. Solignac, "Exégèse et Metaphysique. Genèse, 1, 1-3 chez saint Augustin," in *In Principio. Interprétations des premiers verses de la Genèse* (Paris: Etudes Augustiniennes, 1973), 153-75; E. Zum Brunn, "L'exégèse augustinienne de 'Ego sum qui sum' et la 'métaphysique de l'Exode,'" in *Dieu et L'Être. Exégèse d'Exode 3, 14 et de Coran 20, 11-24* (Paris: Etudes Augustiniennes, 1978), 141-64: "... des derniers livres des *Confessions* et *De genesi ad litteram,* où il élabore une théogonie chrétienne en utilisant la métaphysique de l'*epistrophe*" (155).

16. See *Civ. Dei* 10.21. St. Augustine wonders how Plato (*Timaeus,* 28) arrived at a similar statement: whether it came to him directly or indirectly from the Scriptures, or from his own or someone else's penetrating understanding of created things (ibid., 94-96).

17. See especially *Civ. Dei* 11.22. These terms, which may be traced through Eriugena, became watchwords of the Christian Platonic conception of nature characteristic of twelfth-century Christian humanism, which M.-D. Chenu describes as "a religious discovery of the universe." *La théologie au douzième siècle* (Paris: J. Vrin, 1957), 51.

18. See P. Hadot, "Fragments d'un commentaire de Porphyre sur le Parménide," *Revue des Études Grecques* 74 (1961), 410-38.

19. On these points, with the appropriate Proclan references, see R. Padellaro de Angelis, *L'influenza del pensiero neoplatonica sulla metafisica di S. Tommaso d'Aquino* (Rome: Abete, 1981), 139-45.

20. A.H. Armstrong, *St. Augustine and Christian Platonism,* 32-34, n. 2.

21. See R.D. Crouse, "*Semina Rationum:* St Augustine and Boethius," *Dionysius* 4 (1980), 75-86.

22. For a thorough and critical account of the recent literature, see L. Obertello, "Boezio e il neoplatonismo Cristiano, gli orientmenti attuali della critica," *Cultura e scuola* 87 (1983), 95-103.

23. E.K. Rand, *Founders of the Middle Ages* (Cambridge, Mass.: Harvard University Press, 1928), 178; see L. Obertello, *Severino Boezio,* 2 vols. (Genoa, 1974), Vol. 1, Ch. 8, "Boezio pensatore cristiano" (746-81).

24. Boethius, *De Trinitate, Tractates, De consolatione philosophiae,* H.F. Stewart, E.K. Rand, S.J. Tester, eds. (Cambridge, Mass. and London: Harvard University Press, 1978), 4.

25. Cf. A. Trapé, "Boezio teologo e S. Agostino," in L. Obertello, ed., *Atti. Congresso Internazionale di Studi Boeziani* (Rome: Accademia Ligure di Scienze e Lettere, 1981), 15-26 (concerned only with the tractates on the Trinity and Christology).

26. Boethius, *De consol. phil.,* 4, pr. 6 (356-62).

27. Boethius, *De consol. phil.,* 6, pr. 6 (422-34).

28. C.J. Starnes, "Boethius and the Development of Christian Humanism: The Theology of the *Consolatio,*" in L. Obertello, ed., *Atti*, 27-38.

29. P. Hadot, "Dieu comme acte d'être dans le néoplatonisme. A propos des théories d'É. Gilson sur la métaphysique de l'Exode," in *Dieu et l'Être,* 57-63.

30. See R.D. Crouse, "The Doctrine of Creation in Boethius. The *De hebdomadibus* and the *Consolatio,*" in E.A. Livingstone, ed., *Studia Patristica,* 18 (Oxford and New York: Pergamon Press, 1982), 417-21.

31. John Scottus Eriugena, *De divisione naturae,* 1.55; 1.61 (PL, 122, 498B, 503B).

32. I.P. Sheldon-Williams, "Eriugena's Greek Sources," in J.J. O'Meara and L. Bieler, eds., *The Mind of Eriugena* (Dublin: Irish University Press for the Royal Irish Academy, 1973), 1-15, especially 5; and note the reservations expressed by E. Jeauneau, 15.

33. See the remarks of E. Jeauneau, in the introductions to his editions of Eriugena's Johannine commentaries, *Jean Scot, Homélie sur le Prologue de Jean,* Sources Chrétiennes, vol. 151 (Paris: Editions du Cerf, 1969), 65; *Jean Scot, Commentaire sur l'évangile de Jean,* Sources Chrétiennes, vol. 180 (Paris: Editions du Cerf, 1972), 27, 38, 52-53; on Eriugena's following of Augustine in Genesis interpretation, see especially J.J. O'Meara, " 'Magnorum Virorum Quendam Consensum Velimus Machinari' (804B): Eriugena's Use of Augustine's De Genesi ad litteram in the Periphyseon," in W. Beierwaltes, ed., *Eriugena. Studien zu seinen Quellen* (Heidelberg: C. Winter, 1980), 105-16. G. Madec has recently provided a very useful instrument for the comparative study of Augustine and Eriugena: "Le dossier augustinien du Periphyseon de Jean Scot," *Recherches Augustiniennes* 15 (1980), for Books 1 and 2; 18 (1983), for Books 3 and 4.

34. Eriugena, *De divisione naturae,* 2, 20 (PL, 122, 557A, 559AB).

35. Ibid., 2, 22 (PL, 122, 565D).

36. Ibid., 2, 20 (PL. 122, 556A).

37. Ibid., 3, 24 (PL, 122, 690C); III, 27 (PL, 122, 699AB).

38. Ibid., 3, 24 (PL, 122, 699C).

39. On Pseudo-Dionysius's conversion of Proclan metaphysics, cf. M. Ninci, *L'universo e il non-essere, I. Transcendenza di Dio e molteplicità del reale nel monismo dionysiano* (Rome: Edizioni di storia e letteratura, 1980), especially 143-225; S.E. Gersh, *From Iamblichus to Eriugena* (Leiden: E.J. Brill, 1978).

40. Eriugena, *De divisione naturae,* 5, 31 (PL, 122, 942A).

41. See P. Lucentini, *Platonismo medievale. Contributi per la storia dell'Eriugenismo,* 2 ed., (Florence: La Nuova Italia, 1980); R.D. Crouse, "*Intentio Moysi:* Bede, Augustine,

Eriugena and Plato in the *Hexaemeron* of Honorius Augustodunensis," *Dionysius* 2 (1978), 135-37; M.-O. Garrigues, "Honorius Augustodunensis, *De anima et de Deo,*" *Recherches Augustiniennes* 12 (1977), 212-79; W.J. Hankey, "The *De Trinitate* of Boethius and the Structure of the *Summa theologiae* of St. Thomas Aquinas," in L. Obertello, ed., *Atti* (Congresso Internazionale di Studi Boeziani), 367-75. A remarkable fourteenth-century conflation of Augustinian and Proclan interests (Eriugena present by way of Honorius Augustodunensis, *Clavis physicae*) is to be seen in Berthold of Moosburg, *Expositio super elementationem theologicam Procli* (ed. L. Sturlese; "presentazione" by E. Massa, Temi e Testi, 18, Rome: Edizioni di storia e letteratura, 1974).

PELAGIUS ANTICIPATED: GRACE AND ELECTION IN AUGUSTINE'S *AD SIMPLICIANUM*

JAMES WETZEL

Augustine accorded the second part of his first book of responses to Simplician a magisterial place in the evolution of his own theology of grace. In *De praedestinatione sanctorum* (4.8), a late work in what is known as his anti-Pelagian writings, he directs brethren who are confused about the workings of grace to *Ad Simplicianum,* where they can discover for themselves the resolution to his own former and similar confusions. In *De dono perseverantiae* (20.52), Augustine further commends his earlier work of 396, citing *Ad Simplicianum* as essentially his first anti-Pelagian work – a striking commendation, certainly, considering that the Pelagian heresy did not exist in 396. These retrospective judgements are remarkably high praise for what amounts to a few pages of commentary on the ninth chapter of Romans, where Paul discusses the election of Jacob over Esau. I have no wish to impugn the honour of *Ad Simplicianum,* but I do think that we might be puzzled by the work's supposed prescience, even when this prescience has been acknowledged by as considerable a critic as Augustine himself. Surely the voluminous tide of Augustine's writings directed deliberately against Pelagians come to more than an elaborate footnote to the views on grace and election espoused in *Ad Simplicianum.*

A number of prominent scholars have in fact noticed some incongruities between *Ad Simplicianum* and at least some of the anti-Pelagian writings. In their contributions to *Augustinus Magister,* Jean Lebourlier and Guy De Broglie both claimed that Augustine changes his views about the workings of grace as he settles himself into the long struggle against the seductions of Pelagian soteriology. At some point during the controversy – Lebourlier offers the year 418 – Augustine begins to cast regeneration by grace as a transformation of the human will from within, whereas in

Ad Simplicianum he had apparently depicted only an external operation of grace, one which shaped and influenced the will without disrupting its essential character.[1] More recently, J. Patout Burns has charted with great sophistication and care several twists and turns in the evolution of Augustine's doctrine of operative grace.[2] His study casts the most doubt on whether Augustine's position in 396 contained the resources, however unrefined, to forge any essential link to the theology of grace developed during the Pelagian controversy. Indeed Burns goes as far as to suggest that *Ad Simplicianum* could have given encouragement to the discerning Pelagian reader.[3]

In light of this scholarship, our suspicion that Augustine indulged in some creative reinterpretation of *Ad Simplicianum* deepens. I want to test that suspicion, but not with the object of either flatly rejecting or accepting Augustine's retrospective judgements. A more edifying course would be to consider in what sense there could be a kinship between *Ad Simplicianum* and the anti-Pelagian writings. It might turn out to be only a relationship between distant cousins, but whatever the outcome, we would likely gain some further insight into the deeper motivations behind his thinking on grace and election. In turning our attention back to *Ad Simplicianum,* a work written well before the emergence of the Pelagian heresy, Augustine invites us to consider his theology of grace as something more than the artifact of a protracted and sometimes rancorous debate. It is an invitation worth accepting.

I will therefore proceed by first trying to see what Augustine saw in *Ad Simplicianum.* I will not be searching for everything of interest that he had to say against the Pelagians, but I will be looking for a key turn of mind which would have established and fixed a clear direction for Augustine's future ruminations on the work of grace. If and when a candidate for this role emerges, I will briefly consider for purposes of contrast how Augustine's understanding of grace deepens after *Ad Simplicianum.* Lebourlier, De Broglie, and Burns were quite right, I think, to note that Augustine does not dwell on the deeply transformative effects of grace until late in the Pelagian controversy, 418. The anti-Pelagian emphasis on inwardly working grace is conspicuously absent from *Ad Simplicianum.* Nevertheless, I suspect that when Augustine moves the locus of grace's operation to deeper recesses within the human personality, he does so in a way that maintains an essential continuity with the framework of *Ad Simplicianum.* I will offer the basis for that suspicion in a comparison of *Ad*

Simplicianum with *De spiritu et littera,* another of Augustine's forays into Romans, though this one was conducted with Pelagius in mind.[4]

In his *Retractationes* (2.1) Augustine refers to his efforts in the second part of *Ad Simplicianum* as a labour on behalf of the free choice of the human will, the upshot of which was the victory of grace. Though it is difficult to say exactly what should be included under the victory, there is one notable understanding of free choice that clearly ends up on the losing side. In earlier reflections on Paul's Epistle to the Romans, which Augustine gathered into an *Expositio* not long before *Ad Simplicianum,* he had already given some consideration to the election of Jacob over Esau. Following Paul, he had concluded that God's election could not have been based on God's foreknowledge of Jacob's good works. Those good works were themselves the consequence rather than the cause of election. Augustine's alternative was to view the election as turning on God's foreknowledge of Jacob's freely willed acceptance and Esau's freely willed rejection of redemptive assistance. *Ad Simplicianum* roundly rejects this view of the *Expositio* as depending on an overweening distinction between a good work and the acceptance of faith.[5] Augustine rereads Paul as suggesting a more radical view, one which could not be accepted by human pride without having a certain sobering effect. Election is not to be based on any distinction between persons. It is wholly gratuitous.

The gratuity of election is the victory of grace in *Ad Simplicianum.* For a turn of Augustine's mind on a crucial theological issue, it would be hard to find a more conspicuous example than that of his revised interpretation of Romans 9. The significance of the change, however, remains elusive if we take election's gratuity in too narrow a sense. Minimally Augustine means us to understand that human beings do not in any way merit redemption. God is free to dispense mercy apart from what might be termed juridical constraints. In other words, the interests of justice do not oblige God to favour one person over another or, indeed, to favour anyone at all. Aside from juridical constraints, it is also possible to imagine limitations on election that would have more to do with the pathology of a human will than with its degree of moral worth. If a person were so deeply mired in depravity as to be in effect beyond hope of redemption, then he or she, owing to a pathology of the will, could not be considered even a candidate for election. God's election would thereby be limited by what might be called volitional constraints.

In *Ad Simplicianum* Augustine is concerned to disencumber God's sovereignty over the work of redemption from constraints of any stripe. Juridical constraints are eliminated over the course of his somewhat notorious argument that after the original fall from grace, human beings no longer exercise a claim on God's justice. Volitional constraints are also disposed of in *Ad Simplicianum,* handily enough by appeal to divine omnipotence, but not without first running through an illuminating array of the human will's pathological conditions. Three basic kinds of pathology are considered by Augustine, which for purposes of reference I will call the conflicted will, the perverse will, and the obdurate will.

I want to pause to consider Augustine's descriptions of those conditions, for it is in the triumph of God's mercy over the abundant iniquities of the human will that the idea of election's gratuity finds its connection to substantive claims about the work of grace. That the overcoming of volitional constraints should be relevant in this regard is a consequence of how volitional constraints are thought to pose a possible limitation on election. Augustine could have claimed that severe pathologies of the will are merely indicative of ultimate reprobation. But he does not want to make that claim, at least not for all cases of pathology, because he would be imposing a constraint on how the work of redemption could proceed once election had been decided. Specifically, he would be suggesting that God could not allow the disease of sin to become too severe in one of the elect without also risking that election would be frustrated by a terminal volitional pathology.

Two cases of severe pathology which are not considered by Augustine to pose a threat to the efficacy of grace are those of the conflicted will and the perverse will. A conflicted will designates a person who experiences an inability to act upon his or her own recognition and desire for the life of *beatitudo,* or blessedness. The conflict has its source in what Augustine understands as the Pauline struggle between the spirit and the flesh, a condition he discusses at some length in the first part of *Ad Simplicianum* under the rubric of the person *sub lege.* Grace resolves the conflict by weakening the hold of problematic desires upon the human will, so that fledgling desires for the genuinely good life have at least the opportunity of coming to maturity. Augustine's own conversion in the garden scene of the *Confessions* is the *locus classicus* for resolutions of this sort. A perverse will designates a person whose desires lead him or her farther away from the possibility of *beatitudo,* though without any accompanying inner turmoil. The exemplar of perversity in *Ad Simplicianum* is Saul of Tarsus, whom Augustine describes as having a "blind, mad, and savage will."[6] When God deems to reorient this sort of will, the results tend to be dramatic, as was certainly the case on the road to Damascus.

We are not to suppose that Augustine hopes to explain how God manages to effect a conversion from these pathological conditions. His aims are considerably more modest. When he presents the will paralyzed by internal conflict or corrupted by perversity as a suitable object for conversion and regeneration, he reminds us that what appears as an insurmountable obstacle to *beatitudo* from the human point of view need not be thought so from God's point of view. Thus reminded, we can gratefully acknowledge the miracle of human redemption and God's power over the iniquity of the human will.

Unfortunately the reminder is not enough in the last and most difficult case of pathology – that of the obdurate will. The person afflicted with obduracy rejects God's influence and becomes one of the many who are called but not chosen. Esau serves as Augustine's paradigm case here, since Augustine assumes that Esau's rejection of God was final and irrevocable. The theological difficulty presented by Esau's situation, aside from the thorny issue of God's justice, is that Esau's rejection of his calling seems to constitute a breach of divine sovereignty. How else could a mere mortal frustrate God's redemptive purposes, unless God did not in fact exercise full control over the human will? Augustine answers this question by suggesting a way in which Esau's rejection of God could be construed as God's rejection of Esau.

The reversal depends upon a distinction in how calls are delivered. When the person called happens also to be one of the elect, God structures the calling in such a way as to ensure the person's acceptance. In that case, a calling may be said to be suitable (a *congrua vocatio*).[7] When Esau is called, however, his calling fails to suit him and he does not follow.[8] From Esau's rejection of God, we can conclude only that a divine judgement is taking its toll. What Augustine expressly forbids us to conclude is that Esau's obduracy circumvents his election and regeneration. Esau could have been called suitably, but in fact he wasn't. The case of the obdurate will is the one pathology which Augustine will accept as a sign of ultimate reprobation.[9]

Through his efforts to shore up divine sovereignty over the human will, Augustine finds himself committed to a very strong conclusion about the work of redemption. Namely, grace must be irresistible.[10] If grace were not irresistible, human beings would sometimes be in a position to refuse God's influence regardless of how that influence was presented. Esau's reprobation would then be as much a rebuke to God as a warning to prideful humanity. It is important, however, that Augustine's commitment to the irresistibility of grace not be confused with a theory of conversion. Although Augustine supplied us with at least a rudimentary psychology of consent (1.2.10 and 1.2.21), and discusses the nature of a calling (especially in 1.2.13), there is no theory of conversion in *Ad Simplicianum.* What little Augustine has to say about the effect of grace on the will is reserved for those who would confuse irresistibility with force and turn conversion into a mockery of human freedom.

Augustine rejects the confusion by pointing out that if the will itself is the subject of transformation in conversion, then the language of force is misplaced. Force implies that the natural or customary determinations of a will are frustrated by external opposition. Conversion, on the other hand, implies that the customary determinations are changed in response to a new object of attraction. It makes no sense, then, to say that a conversion could take place by force.[11]

Augustine's recognition that the will is the arena of redemptive transformation is crucial for his future reflections on what that transformation amounts to. Thanks to his change of mind on Romans 9 in *Ad Simplicianum,* he will develop those reflections along a route quite free of hazardous Pelagian detours. I have already elaborated upon the line of thought that yields this result. All that remains is to display the connections. The rejection of God's foreknowledge of faith as a basis for election leaves Augustine with a doctrine of the gratuity of election. When the gratuity of election is tested against juridical and especially volitional constraints, he is left with a doctrine of grace's irresistibility. The irresistibility of grace, properly understood, is equivalent to the doctrine of the sufficiency of grace – the idea that God's redemptive work can succeed on any human will, whatever the severity of its pathology. Human beings do not have to begin to cure themselves in order for God to get involved.

As of the second part of book one of *Ad Simplicianum,* the gratuity of election and the sufficiency of grace are enshrined as axioms within Augustine's theology of grace. It would be difficult to imagine foundations more anti-Pelagian in their implications.

The next time that Augustine turns to sustained exegesis of Romans, he is ready to draw some of those implications. *De spiritu et littera,* written in 412, shows subtle yet significant divergences from *Ad Simplicianum.* In his earlier exegesis, Augustine had associated the killing power of the law with the just punishment owed to sinful and disobedient humanity. According to Augustine, naked human ability invariably withers before the demands of the law and falls prey to fear and carnal servitude. God gives his Spirit in order that persons may come to love the law and fulfill its demands. Charity in *Ad Simplicianum* remains ancillary to the law, insofar as the primary end of charity is the restoration of sinners to obedience. Fear, by contrast, finds expression in disobedience, rebellion from God, and guilt.[12] In *De spiritu et littera* Augustine modifies these views when he suggests that obedience is sometimes carried out in a spirit of servitude – without love and hence without value.[13] Once Augustine has come to see that sinful dispositions do not always express themselves in acts of outright disobedience, obedience loses its status as a guarantee of charity's presence and at best serves as a fallible sign of God's work of redemption. He subsequently shifts his main attention to charity itself and its transformation of sinful sensibilities into sensibilities desirous of pleasing God. Charity does not thereby gain in importance over the law; it becomes the law rightly understood.

In a way that simply was not evident in *Ad Simplicianum,* Augustine in *De spiritu et littera* takes aim against all externalist views of grace, views which presume to understand the work of regeneration as a mop-up operation against bad habits. Pelagian theology is externalist because it tends to identify the gift of grace with a person's providential placement within an environment conducive to virtue.[14] Presumably that environment would be the church. Once inside the church, an individual would be responsible for taking full advantage of the salutary instruction, example, and encouragement offered. Pelagius is never mentioned by name in *De spiritu et littera,* but he looms in the background.

Augustine's alternative to an externalist view of grace emerges in tandem with his critique of Pelagian-style theology. Two lines of attack can be discerned. First there is Augustine's criticism of any attempt to situate human efforts directed toward *beatitudo* outside the scope of divine initiative. Attempts of this sort always betrayed an all-too-human desire to draw a limit to divine sovereignty in order to make room for human pride. He had already made this case in *Ad Simplicianum,* and although *De spiritu et littera* continues the theme, its primary emphasis resides elsewhere. The critical preoccupation of *De spiritu et littera* is with Augustine's criticism of theologies which misidentify the locus of human redemptive transformation. Pelagians are guilty of this when they restrict the operation of grace to the surface of the will, where the play of free choice and habit produce an observable panoply of actions. The life of faith is thereby fit a little too snugly into a life of works, the will loses its depth, and the Pelagians are seduced by a Christian positivism. They miss the deeper penetration of grace, whose expression resists too facile a reduction to practical consequences. To a certain extent, Augustine is guilty of the same sin in *Ad Simplicianum,* when he ties the gift of charity too strongly to the palpable consequences of human obedience. *De spiritu et littera* loosens this tie and uses the slack to follow the penetration of grace down to where the will is not so much rehabilitated as recreated from within.

It is difficult, I think, to attach the proper significance to the inward turn of anti-Pelagian works such as *De spiritu et littera* without also noticing why *Ad Simplicianum* cannot ultimately be tarred with an anti-Pelagian brush. There is a world of difference between Pelagius's mistake, which is a ground-level mistake about the nature of grace, and the occasional short-sightedness of Augustine in *Ad Simplicianum,* which is an excusable manifestation of the untidiness surrounding any new and great discovery whose implications are initially only dimly perceived. Our failure to take sufficient note of the difference stems from the temptation to read too much novelty into the anti-Pelagian writings. If we notice there only Augustine's new interest in the direct and immediate influence of grace upon the will, we will tend to lose the intricacies of the work of redemption to a preemptive emphasis on divine power. An inwardly working grace, seen only *sub specie dei,* diverts our attention away from the involvement of the human will in its own regeneration. The work of redemption consequently emerges as a gratuitous infusion of new desires and dispositions, which are implanted in the human will through the work of the Spirit. Those desires and dispositions become the raw material for the will's reconstruction. Such an understanding of regeneration sacrifices any continuity between the old depraved self and the new redeemed self (opening Augustine to Julian's charge of Manichaean sympathies) and encourages a strict separation between inward and external operations of grace. Regeneration in *Ad Simplicianum,* which centres on the response to a calling, comes off by comparison as externalist and Pelagian.

But Augustine was too good a psychologist to be seduced by conversions which took the humanity out of the conversion and too good a theologian to rest very comfortably with appeals to divine omnipotence. In *De natura et gratia,* a work written only a few years after *De spiritu et littera,* he raises a profoundly relevant question for our comprehension of the work of grace. If pride is at the root of all sinfulness, then why doesn't God merely wrench pride completely out of the soul in an instant? That would certainly be the most obvious and magnificent display of an inwardly working grace. Augustine merely hints at an answer. He observes that pride will always reassert itself on the very occasions that we would take to celebrate its banishment from our hearts. Pride will raise its head from the midst of our celebrations in order to mock our hollow triumph.[15] In even the most radical self-overcomings, there is, according to Augustine, a trace of the old self remaining. That trace will continue to cast its shadow upon the soul until the final noontide of judgement spoken of in the Psalms.[16]

Augustine's observation does not conjure up a limitation on God's redemptive power, nor does it suggest that God is simply too mean spirited to give sinful souls a quick cure. Instead Augustine is referring us, I think, to an inescapable feature of the human side of the redemptive process. No matter how radically our wills may be reoriented, we still remain creatures who exist *in time.* No new will, regardless of its source or manner of arrival, could ever constitute a new self without first becoming part of the story of a single, temporally extended person. The past, in one way or another, will find its entry into the converted will. It is best to meet it honestly.

The *Confessions* is perhaps the greatest literary account of a self attempting to understand its past from the perspective of its conversion. What is not always noticed is that this process of retrospective reinterpretation is actually constitutive of Augustine's conversion.[17] Without some success at reinterpretation, his self-understanding would have disintegrated into a series of discrete and unrelated events. There would have been no inward transformation, no change of heart, no conversion, no self.

The point I am suggesting is that Augustine's emphasis on inward transformation in his anti-Pelagian theology of grace has less to do with how God dispenses grace than with how human beings are understood to receive it. Furthermore, this emphasis is at bottom a deepening of a psychological insight at the heart of both *Ad Simplicianum* and *De spiritu et littera.* In each of those works Augustine insists that the one inalienable contribution that human beings make to their own redemption is the consent that they give to the divine influence at work within them.[18] After *Ad Simplicianum* this consent is never understood by Augustine to be a veto power exercised from outside the redemptive process. In his mature theology of grace, consent emerges as the delicate task of self-integration faced by all those who discover themselves changed by the grace of God. God can guarantee this consent, but he cannot do it for us.

Pelagius's ground-level mistake about the nature of grace was to exempt the human contribution to redemption from divine control. That starting point narrowed his attention to *liberum arbitrium* – the nub of human autonomy – and his theology resolved itself into a lonely and heroic moral asceticism. Augustine had opted for an entirely different starting point. After *Ad Simplicianum* he ceased to search for the place of human entry into grace. The gratuity of election and the sufficiency of grace freed his attention to probe the depths of the will's transformation, the ground below the expression of free choice. It took him a career to realize fully that his own theological starting point ruled out the presumption of admitting God into the drama of redemption only at its climax and not also during its setting and dénouement. For its part, *Ad Simplicianum* was only a promise of Augustine's final insight. But we can trust the hindsight of a genius to show us where his foresight had begun.

NOTES

1. Jean Lebourlier, "Essai sur la responsabilité du pécheur dans la réflexion de saint Augustin," *Augustinus Magister* 3 (Paris: Etudes Augustiniennes, 1954), 287-307, especially 299, and Guy De Broglie, "Pour une meilleure intelligence du De correptione et gratia," *Augustinus Magister* 3 (Paris: Etudes Augustiniennes, 1954), 317-37, especially 332, n. 1.

2. J. Patout Burns, *The Development of Augustine's Doctrine of Operative Grace* (Paris: Etudes Augustiniennes, 1980).

3. Burns, *Operative Grace,* 8, 112.

4. What each of Lebourlier, De Broglie, and Burns would identify as the source of the rift – an inwardly working grace – is already quite evident in *De spiritu et littera.* Consider, for example, 3.5 (*CSEL* 60, 157, 10-19):

Nos autem dicimus humanam voluntatem sic divinitus adiuuari ad faciendam iustitiam, ut praeter quod creatus est homo cum libero arbitrio praeterque doctrinam qua ei praecipitur quemadmodum vivere debeat accipiat spiritum sanctum, quo fiat in animo eius delectatio dilectioque summi illius atque incommutabilis boni, quod deus est, etiam nunc cum per fidem ambulatur, nondum per speciem, ut hac sibi velut arra data gratuiti muneris inardescat inhaerere creatori atque inflammetur accedere ad participationem illius veri luminis, ut ex illo ei bene sit, a quo habet ut sit.

5. See, as well, Paula Fredriksen Landes, "Introduction" to *Augustine on Romans* (Chico: Scholars Press, 1982); and William S. Babcock, "Augustine's Interpretation of Romans, A.D. 394-396," *Augustinian Studies* 10 (1979), 55-74.

6. *Ad Simp.* 1.2.22 (*CCSL* 44, 55, 798-99).

7. See, e.g., *Ad Simp.* 1.2.13 (*CCSL* 44, 38, 377-78): Cuius autem miseretur, sic eum vocat, quomodo scit ei congruere, ut vocantem non respuat.

8. *Ad Simp.* 1.2.13 (*CCSL* 44, 38, 369-71): Illi enim electi qui congruenter vocati, illi autem qui non congruebant neque contemperabantur vocationi non electi, quia non secuti quamvis vocati.

9. Commentary on the problematic status of divine justice in *Ad Simplicianum* can be found in Jean Lebourlier, "Essai sur la responsabilité du pécheur," 293-96, and "Misère morale originelle et responsabilité du pécheur," *Augustinus Magister* 3, 301-307. Also note Babcock, "Augustine's Interpretations of Romans," 66-67.

10. See Etienne Gilson, *The Christian Philosophy of Saint Augustine,* trans. L.E.M. Lynch (New York: Random House, 1960), 155-56; and John M. Rist, "Augustine on Free Will and Predestination," *Journal of Theological Studies* N.S. 20 (1969), 429; and my "The Recovery of Free Agency in the Theology of Saint Augustine," *Harvard Theological Review* 80 (1987). 1-27.

11. For further reflections on the distinction between force and irresistibility, see Athanase Sage, "Praeparatur voluntas a Domino," *Revue des études augustiniennes* 10 (1964), 15; and Xavier Léon-Dufour, "Grâce et libre arbitre chez saint Augustin," *Recherches de science religieuse* 33 (1946), 157-58.

12. Consider *Ad Simp.* I,i,17 (*CCSL* 44, 22-23, 354-64):

Cur liberati sumus a lege, mortui in qua detinebamur, ita ut seruiamus in nouitate spiritus et non in vetustate litterae, si lex bona est? Quoniam lex littera est eis qui non eam implent per spiritum caritatis, quo pertinet testamentum nouum. Itaque mortui peccato liberantur a littera, qua detinentur rei qui non implent quod scriptum est. Lex enim quid aliud quam sola littera est eis qui eam legere nouerunt et implere non possunt? Non enim ignoratur ab eis quibus conscripta est; sed quoniam in tantum nota est, in quantum scripta legitur, non in quantum dilecta perficitur, nihil est aliud talibus nisi littera.

This passage is representative of the position Augustine holds on the relationship between the spirit and the letter in book one, part one, of *Ad Simplicianum.* Although the

Latin is not entirely unambiguous, it seems fairly clear that charity is presented as a means or precondition for obedience rather than as the ground or source of what makes obedience valuable. Servitude under the letter of the law is consequently wed to disobedience. Augustine is less moralistic in *De spiritu et littera.*

13. *Spir. litt.* 14.26 (*CSEL* 60, 180, 22-25): "Quod mandatum si fit timore poenae, non amore iustitiae, serviliter fit, non liberaliter et ideo nec fit. Non enim fructus est bonus, qui de caritatis radice non surgit."

14. For a detailed and highly illuminating picture of Pelagian soteriology, see Peter Brown, "Pelagius and his Supporters: Aims and Environment," *Journal of Theological Studies* N.S. 19 (1968), 93-114.

15. *Nat. grat.* 31.35 (*CSEL* 60, 258, 16-19): "Ubi enim laetatus homo fuerit in aliquo bono opere se etiam superasse superbiam, ex ipsa laetitia caput erigit et dicit: 'ecce ego vivo, quid triumphas? et ideo vivo, quia triumphas.' "

16. Ps 37.6 (Vulg. 36.6). Augustine cites this verse in *Nat. grat.* 31.35.

17. But see "Paul and Augustine: Conversion Narratives, Orthodox Traditions, and the Retrospective Self," *Journal of Theological Studies* N.S. 37 (1986), 3-34.

18. See *Ad Simp.* 1.2.10 (*CCSL* 44.3. 297-299): "Aliter enim deus praestat ut velimus, aliter praestat quod voluerimus. Ut velimus enim et suum esse voluit et nostrum, suum vocando nostrum sequendo."

And *Spir. litt.* 34.60 (*CSEL* 60.220.17-20): "Profecto et ipsum velle credere deus operatur in homine et in omnibus misericordia eius praevenit nos, consentire autem vocationi dei vel ab ea dissentire, sicut dixi, propriae voluntatis est."

In his celebrated article (cited in n. 11), Léon-Dufour argues that Augustine's assignment of consent to the will in *De spiritu et littera* can be taken as normative for his considered view of the human contribution to redemption. I believe that this reading is quite defensible provided that descriptions of the work of grace are kept distinct from worries about putative preconditions for the reception of grace. When descriptions are confused with preconditions, Augustine's claim about the ownership of consent begins to look like a claim about the resistibility of grace. It would be extremely implausible, however, to read Augustine as arguing for the resistibility of grace in *De spiritu et littera* (thus making an anti-Pelagian work a throwback to his position in *Expositio quarundam propositionum ex Epistola ad Romanos*).

THE HUMAN AND THE ANGELIC FALL: WILL AND MORAL AGENCY IN AUGUSTINE'S *CITY OF GOD*

WILLIAM S. BABCOCK

I.

In Book fourteen of the *City of God,* Augustine's account of the fall of the first human pair proceeds in two stages.[1] He first discusses the evil deed in which Eve and then Adam ate of the fruit of the forbidden tree.[2] Their action took place in and through a complex set of circumstances involving the interaction of a variegated cast of characters. There is, first of all, the devil, engorged with pride and activated by a deep and rancorous envy of the unfallen human couple. Through the serpent the devil approaches the woman and, playing upon her gullibility, convinces her to eat of the fruit. Eve then approaches Adam and leads him to eat in his turn. In Adam's case, however, this is not a question of gullibility or of error about the moral import of what he is doing.[3] He joins the woman in sin in full knowledge that he is, in fact, committing sin, disobeying the command of God. But the woman is his partner, provided for him by God; and he has no wish to be left alone. His love for and loyalty to her outweigh his knowledge that the deed is evil, that he ought not to do what he does. And in one respect, at least, Adam too is in error. He mistakenly believes that the deed, even though he knows it to be wrong, is not of any great significance. He does not realize that the outcome, the penalty imposed by God, will be so harsh as to alter the whole condition of human existence, plunging human beings into captivity to sin and subjecting them to the bitterness of death.

This rendering of the first humans' evil deed, their transgression in eating the forbidden fruit, has, it seems to me, an appealing plausibility. It offers a reckoning of character and circumstance that permits us to understand how and why these agents, set in this situation, come to act as they do. We can recognize the interaction of demonic deceit (providing an opening to evil in an environment otherwise wholly good) and human gullibility (providing a vulnerability to evil in a person wholly innocent) that brought Eve to take the fruit and eat. We can resonate to Adam's plight: caught in a conflict of loves and loyalties, he "refused to be separated from his only companion, even if it involved sharing her sin."[4] In addition, even if Adam was not deceived in the same sense in which Eve was, he was as yet inexperienced (*inexpertus*) in the severity of God and was thus capable of error about the harshness with which God would judge his action.[5] Of course none of this – neither deception nor conflicting loves nor ignorance of consequences – excuses either Eve or Adam or relieves them of moral culpability. The deed was theirs and so was the moral responsibility for it.[6] But Augustine has painted the characters of the actors and the circumstances of their action in such a way that what they did makes sense. It is a plausible outcome, an outcome that fits together with their dispositions and motivations and that coheres with the setting in which they acted.

II.

In the beginning, however, was not the deed. In the beginning, Augustine insists, was the will.[7] Neither Adam nor Eve would have committed the deed if they had not already been evil in will.[8] It is important to note that Augustine does *not* mean that, because Eve believed the serpent's blandishments, her will turned to the evil and so she committed the deed or that, because Adam put loyalty to his partner above loyalty to God, his will turned to the evil and so he committed the deed. Rather he means that, unless Eve's will had already been evil, she would not have accepted the serpent's words as true and correspondingly that, unless Adam's will had already been evil, he would not have preferred his partner's will to his creator's.[9] The start of human evil, in Augustine's view, does not lie in the open and public forum of the deed; it lies rather in the hidden and secret chamber of the will.[10] And so there must be a second stage in his account of the human fall. The interplay of characters and tensions and circumstances that gives the first stage its appealing plausibility, it turns out, does not actually illuminate or explain the becoming-evil of human beings. It shows us only how, already evil, they enacted their first misdeed. The evil tree brings forth the evil fruit; the evil fruit does not make the tree evil.[11] If we are to understand the start of human evil, we must look behind the deed to the will, already evil before any act or action had occurred.

When Augustine turns to the becoming-evil of the will, however, there also takes place a sharp change in the cast of characters and the setting of the scene in his discussion. For one thing, the devil no longer has a role to play. However the opening toward the evil, realized in the hidden places of the will, is to be explained, it is not by appeal to an intervention from outside. The turn of the will from the good to the evil is not to be reckoned in relation to external agents or deceptions worked from without. For another thing, the differences between Eve and Adam also disappear. She is no longer the one who is gullible and therefore vulnerable to deception and self-deception; he is no longer the one who is resistant to deceit and mistake about what is right and what is wrong, but vulnerable in his love for his partner and in his wish not to be separated from her. What Augustine has to say about the becoming-evil of the will neither requires nor permits any differentiation between the woman and the man; and so he no longer speaks of them separately. The distinction between the two is relevant only to the deed, not to the will. In fact, to note a third and final point, there is no social interaction at all, whether between devil and human beings or among human beings alone, in Augustine's account of the will's turning from the good to the evil. This turning is a hidden, a secret happening. It transpires between the human will and God (although even God's role is limited: God simply is the supreme good from which the human will turns away); but it has no other social dimension or social context. The turning of the will from good to evil is not a public, and therefore it is not a social, event.

How then are we to construe the will's fall? The will's turn from the good to the evil is to be understood, first of all, as a fault, a defect, or a flaw in a nature that was originally good and that, in other respects, remains good even after its fall.[12] The defect is not inherent to the nature, as if the nature were defective from the start or were directed toward the evil from its very origin. This point is critically important for Augustine's view. In speaking of the will as the evil tree that bore evil fruit in its public deeds, he had come dangerously close to the Manichaeanism he had rejected some thirty years before. According to the Manichees, evil, both in the cosmos at large and in the willing and acting of human beings, arose from an evil principle independent of and opposed to God.

Such a view, Augustine maintained, undercut the divine power and control (by admitting an agency in the universe that was not subject to God), impugned the goodness of the created order (by ascribing especially its material elements to the evil principle) and denied the moral responsibility of created agents for their actions (by assigning those actions to an evil will belonging not to the agents themselves but to the evil principle active within them). The dyke that prevented Augustine's thought from flowing into this Manichaean mould was his insistence that evil has no independent reality, no separate ontic standing from which it might issue forth to do battle with the good. "Evil" is simply a word for the failure of a created good to realize or to enact its goodness.[13] The evil of the human will, therefore, is simply its turn from the good. The elaborate Manichaean ontology and cosmology of evil do not come into play. There is only the will's own turn from the highest good to a lesser good; and for that turn the will itself is alone – and fully – responsible.

Augustine characterizes this turn, on the one hand, as an act of self-deprivation. It deprives the will of the divine light in which it could see and understand; and it deprives the will of the fire of the divine love with which it could love its supreme good, the true source and goal of its fulfillment. Thus the turn leaves the will darkened and chilled, darkened in understanding and chilled in affection, so that Eve could take the serpent's words as true and Adam could place loyalty to his partner above loyalty to God.[14] On the other hand, Augustine represents the turn as an act of self-assertion. The lesser good to which the will turns is, in fact, itself. Instead of taking pleasure in God, the will takes pleasure in itself. Instead of directing its love to God, it directs its love to itself. Instead of keeping God as the principle of its existence, it makes itself the principle of its existence. Instead of living according to God's will, it follows its own will. And in pleasing itself, loving itself, making itself the principle of its own existence, and following its own will, it makes itself the evil tree that bears evil fruit in its deeds. The double act of self-deprivation and self-assertion is the "original evil," the evil that "came first, in secret" and whose result was "the other evil, which was committed in the open."[15]

This second stage of Augustine's account of the human fall, however, presents a problem that the first does not. Instead of providing a coherent linkage between actor, circumstance, and action, it seems rather to stress the sheer discontinuity between actor and circumstance, on the one hand, and action, on the other. Consider the following points. (1) The first human beings, before their fall, inhabited a paradise that was at once material and spiritual. It provided, in full supply, not only the goods of the body but also the goods of the spirit; it was a place to be enjoyed not only through the external, corporeal senses but also through the internal senses of the mind.[16] In this paradise, there was no threat of death or fear of harm to distress the first human pair; nor was there anything lacking that the good will might desire.[17] Consequently the dialectic of fear and desire that operates universally in fallen humanity, interrupting and distorting its affective and moral life, was not yet at work before the fall. (2) Furthermore, Augustine maintained that the first humans, as created by God, did in fact have a good will: "God made man upright" [Eccles. 7:29], and therefore possessed of a good will – for he would not have been upright, had he not possessed a good will. Good will then is the work of God, since man was created with it by God."[18] Thus it is not that the first humans longed to do what had been forbidden to them and abstained only because they feared the punishment that would follow. It was love of righteousness (*amor iustitiae*), not fear of pain, that ordered their affections and governed their behavior.[19] They lived in unshadowed love for God and for each other; and since the object of their love was always present to enjoy, they had great gladness.[20]

(3) The absence of fear and desire and the presence of the object of love are not incidental or unimportant features of Augustine's portrait of unfallen humanity. They represent a manipulation of the classical theory of the four passions – joy and grief, desire and fear – designed to support the picture of a humanity originally ordered wholly to God and to the good. According to the classical theory, joy is the affection that accompanies possession (or actual occurrence) of something that we take to be good, and grief comes with the possession (or actual occurrence) of something that we take to be evil. Correspondingly desire is the longing for something that we take to be good but do not yet have (or which has not yet come about); and fear is the distress that we feel at the prospect of something that we take to be evil. Augustine departs from the classical theory, however, in treating the passions not as irruptions into the mind from the body or from the lower, irrational part of the soul, but precisely as forms of will. Desire and joy are the affective shapes of the will when it is in accord with what it anticipates or what it actually has on hand; fear and grief are the affective shapes of the will when it is not in accord with what it anticipates or what it actually has on hand.[21]

The passions, then, are not disrupting incursions from below – prompted by external stimuli – into the otherwise rightly functioning life of the higher soul by which human beings ought properly to direct and order their lives. They are rather functions of the will, giving affective expression to the soul's own orientation, in its willing, to what it takes to be good and evil. In this light, the basic question about the passions is no longer whether and how a person exercises control over their disrupting and essentially external influence, but whether the will itself is rightly directed. If the will is rightly directed, its desire will be for and its joy will be in what is truly good, while its fear will be fear of and its grief over what is genuinely to be considered evil. Otherwise, a person's affective life will take its shape and play out its dynamic in relation to a false scale of goods and evils. The key to the matter, then, is not the elimination of the passions or of their influence, but rather the right ordering of the passions as the affective expressions of a will rightly directed – i.e., a will whose love carries it toward the truly good, for the direction of the will is its love.[22]

In the light of this more general discussion of the passions, it seems clear enough that Augustine's description of the affective state of the first humans is meant to do more than simply to display the paradisaical character of their initial environment. It also – and more importantly – serves the purpose of emphasizing that Adam's and Eve's wills were rightly ordered and their loves rightly directed before the fall. If the pair were without desire, that means not only that their paradisaical setting provided for all their wants, but also that they wanted nothing other than the one true and supreme Good present to them in paradise. If they were without fear, that means that there was no sense in which their wills were out of accord with an environment wholly ordered by and to the supreme Good. If their affective state was one of great gladness, that means not only that they enjoyed the immediate and unfailing presence of the object of their love, but also that their love was directed to its true and proper object, the very God who had created them. And since the passions are, in Augustine's view, to be construed as forms of will, the entire description underlines the uprightness of the human will as created and prior to the fall.

It is, however, precisely this emphasis on the right-ordering of the affective and volitional life of the human pair in paradise that creates the difficulty in Augustine's rendering of the fall of the human will. In effect, he has made the first humans' withdrawal from God and turn to themselves utterly inexplicable, an action so thoroughly discontinuous with the actors' prior dispositions, motivations, and circumstances that we cannot link it to the actors at all. How are we to understand such a turn on the part of an upright will whose affections are entirely a function of its rightly ordered love? There is, in Augustine's discussion of the will's fall, no demonic intervention to provide an opening to evil. There is no interplay of social tensions to define a conflict of loves and loyalties forcing choices that may go wrong. There is not even any distortion or disturbance of the internal life of the self from which a turn to the evil, a preference of self to God, might emerge. There is only the upright will, activated by love of righteousness, inexplicably making itself rather than God the principle of its existence. What Augustine fails to provide, in this second stage of his account of the human fall, is the linkage that connects agent and act, the upright will and the defection from the supreme Good; and, lacking such connection, it is difficult to see how the agent can be considered morally responsible for an act that seems far more to have happened to him than to have been produced by him.

III.

Augustine himself can hardly be said to have been unaware of the problem. He explicitly addresses the question of the origin of the evil will, however, not at the level of the human but at the level of the angelic fall. The evil angels, of course, were no more created evil than were the first human pair; their evil, too, is a function and a result of a movement of the will, not of an evil origin. They were the first, even before the human fall, to turn away from the supreme Good and toward a lesser good, away from God and toward themselves, in an act of pride. In this connection Augustine declares that, if we look for the efficient cause (*causa efficiens*) of the evil will, we will discover that there is nothing to be found. The evil will is the cause of the evil act; but of the evil will itself there is no (efficient) cause at all.[23] His argument runs as follows.[24] Anything one might suppose to be the cause of an evil will will either itself have a will or it will not. If it does, its will will be either good or evil. If it is good, however, one is driven to the foolish and absurd conclusion that a good will is the cause of an evil will, that a good will is the cause of sin. If its will is evil, on the other hand, one is faced with the same question all over again: how did this will become evil? What caused it to be evil? *Ex hypothesi,* however, we are dealing, in the case of the evil angels, with the first evil will; and it would not be the first if it had a cause in some prior evil will.

The fact that the evil will has no (efficient) cause does not mean that it has no origin, that it existed forever. The evil, in Augustine's view, does not and cannot exist independently; it can only exist in a nature which was antecedently good and to which it does harm by depriving it of some of its initial good. And since there can be no evil without an antecedent good for it to harm, we cannot claim that the evil has no origin, no beginning. Consequently we cannot avoid the problem of the origin of the evil will by claiming that, in fact, the evil existed from all eternity and therefore had no beginning.

There remains, then, only the possibility that the cause of the evil will was something that itself had no will. But this option, too, turns out to be unsatisfactory. If, on the scale of being and value, this something is superior or equal to the angelic nature, then it too must have a will and that will must be good. A nature without will or a nature whose will is evil cannot be reckoned better or even equal to a nature that does have will and whose will is good. If something without will is the cause of the evil will, then, it could only be something inferior to the angels. But even things inferior, since they have being in their own modes and degrees and since they are natures created by God, are good; and the good cannot be the cause of evil. When the will turns from a higher to a lower good, it is not the lower good that is evil or that causes the evil. The evil is rather the will's own turn, its perverse and inordinate desire for the inferior good; and we cannot say that the inferior thing causes that inordinate desire. With all the possibilities exhausted, we can only say that there is no efficient cause of the evil will.

To reinforce his point, Augustine proposes that we consider the case of two persons, identical in cast of mind and in bodily disposition (*aequaliter affecti animo et corpore*), who sees the beauty of one and the same body. The sight stirs one of the two toward illicit enjoyment, while the other remains firm in chastity of will. How then are we to explain the difference between the two? What caused the evil will in the one and not in the other? The answer cannot be the body's beauty itself; each had the same view of it, and yet they responded differently to it. Nor can the answer lie in either the flesh or the mind of the viewer, since there is no difference between the two in either of these regards. Perhaps the one, but not the other, was tempted by the secret prompting of a malign spirit? But this suggestion has the double disadvantage of intimating that the one tempted was not acting of his own will (*propria voluntate*) and of deflecting our attention from the main question which is not where the temptation came from but why the viewer consented to it. Consequently Augustine eliminates the notion that there was some externally derived point of differentiation between the two viewers by proposing that both were equally subject to temptation. In effect, he removes every variable from his imaginary case except the individual wills of the two viewers themselves; every other factor in the situation is treated as a constant, equally at work in and on both viewers and therefore not the determinant of the evil will of the one who chose to defect from chastity. Why does the one will, acting in its own right, consent to the evil and the other not? No matter how closely we examine the matter, no answer comes to mind.[25]

We are left, then, with a perfect parable of the problem of the angelic fall: how is it that, of a group of apparently identical agents, sharing the same condition and showing the same initial disposition to the good, some acted in one way and some in another? Augustine obviously wants to eliminate every variable except the will itself, every appeal except the appeal to the will's own willing. In doing so, however, he simply makes the problem all the more acute. We can understand how it is that some good angels remain in goodness; in this case, the action stands in continuity with the actor. But can we understand how it is that some good angels turn to the evil? In this case, since all the angels were presumably equally good to start with and since there was no prior moral differentiation between them, we cannot discern the continuity between action and actor; and it begins to look as though we are dealing with a random distribution of outcomes rather than the moral action of moral agents. Some good wills just happen to turn evil; others just happen to remain good.

IV.

In the eleventh book of *De Genesi ad litteram,* written shortly before he began *The City of God,* Augustine had proposed an interpretation of the devil's fall that did not bring this problem in its wake. Prompted by Jn. 8.44 – the devil "was a murderer from the beginning and did not stand fast in the truth" – he insisted that the devil had sinned from and at the very moment of his creation without ever having participated in the truth or having enjoyed the bliss of the holy angels.[26] Any claim that the devil had enjoyed the angelic bliss would have created major difficulties. The angels' bliss includes the certain knowledge that their beatitude is secure and will endure eternally (for uncertainty on this point would introduce an element of apprehension that would cast a dark shadow over their enjoyment of God and keep their felicity from being full and complete). Now if the devil had no foreknowledge of his sin and of his punishment, then he must have been in a state of uncertainty about whether or not his bliss would endure (since he could not have known that it would endure when, in fact, it would not). And if the devil, before his fall, was not equally and fully blessed with the other angels, there immediately arise questions about the divine justice:

> what demerit did [the devil] have to be thus distinguished from the others so that God would not reveal the future to him, even the future that pertained to him? Surely God did not punish him before he sinned, for God does not condemn the innocent.[27]

The crux of the matter lay here: Augustine could neither find a way to make the devil a full participant in the angelic bliss (and thus to put him on the same moral footing as the good angels) nor stipulate a just principle of distinction on the basis of which to set the devil apart from the good angels prior to his fall (thus avoiding intimations of injustice on God's part or hints that the devil had somehow sinned even before he had sinned).

Faced with this dilemma, Augustine hesitantly adopted the solution suggested in the wording of Jn. 8.44. The devil fell from the beginning, from the very moment of his creation. Consequently he never tasted "the sweetness of the blessed life of the angels" at all. "He did not receive it and then scorn it; rather, being unwilling to receive it, he forsook it and lost it."[28] The devil fell not from the beatitude he possessed, then, but from the beatitude he would have possessed if he had willed to receive it instead of turning from it. In taking this view, Augustine achieved a double end. By locating the devil's fall at the very moment of his creation, prior to any participation in the angelic bliss, he avoided the dilemma of having to show either how the devil could have shared the felicity of the good angels or that the devil was justly set apart from the good angels even before his fall; and, at the same time, he blocked the question about how the good could give rise to the evil, how an agent characterized by an upright will could engender an evil will. In the version of the *De Genesi ad litteram,* the devil, although created good in nature, was never good in any recognizably moral sense. Created in what might be called a morally neutral position – i.e., neither morally good nor morally evil but capable of becoming either – he perverted his good nature with an evil will from the outset. In this case, then, there is no turn of a good will from the good to the evil. Instead there is only the realization of an evil rather than a good will by an agent whose moral character is indeterminate prior to that realization.[29]

V.

By the time Augustine came to write *The City of God,* however, he had given up the interpretation he had tentatively adopted in the earlier commentary. Characteristically he argued directly against himself. "Now perhaps someone will quote" Jn. 8.44, he writes, and "will suggest ... that even from the beginning of his own creation the Devil did not stand fast in the truth, and for that reason he never enjoyed felicity with the holy angels, because he refused to be subject to his creator, and in his arrogance supposed that he wielded power as his own private possession and rejoiced in that power."[30] The "someone," of course, is Augustine's own former self. In the interval between the two writings, however, he had become convinced that the most natural interpretation of "he did not stand fast in the truth" (Jn. 8.44) is precisely that the devil "*was* in the truth, but did not continue in it." Consequently "the devil sinned from the beginning" (1 Jn. 3.8) will mean "not that we are to think that he sinned from the first moment of his creation, but from the first beginning of sin, because sin first came into existence as a result of the Devil's pride."[31]

In altering his interpretation of the devil's fall, however, Augustine was also saddling himself with the two problems that he had managed to avoid in his earlier commentary on Genesis. He would now have to provide some explanation as to how a will that once was in the truth could turn from the truth, how a good will could make the evil turn from the supreme Good to a lesser good. In addition, he would now have either to sort out the question of the devil and participation in the angelic felicity or to supply a reason for marking the devil off from the other angels prior to his fall, yet without violating the justice of God or introducing sin prior to sin. It is this complex problematic that governs Augustine's discussion of the fall of the evil angels in the twelfth book of *The City of God.*

Augustine's response to the first of the two problems that he had imposed upon himself is a *tour de force,* a brilliant display of verbal pyrotechnics the actual import of which remains unclear. As we have seen, he argues that there is no efficient cause of the evil will. The cause is not something that makes the evil will, but rather, he proposed, a defection on the part of the will itself. The cause *non enim est efficiens sed deficiens quia nec illa* [the evil will] *effectio sed defectio.* [32] It is difficult to reproduce in English the full nominal and adjectival play on words *efficiens* and *deficiens* that Augustine packs into this brief sentence. The sense, however, seems to run something like this: the cause is not an efficient but a deficient cause because the evil will itself is not something effective, but something defective, a defect.

Yet the meaning of *deficiens* and *defectio,* which I have so far rendered with the English cognates "defective" and "defect," is qualified and altered in the very next sentence: *Deficere namque ab eo quod summe est ad id quod minus est, hoc est incipere habere voluntatem malam.* [33] Now we are to think not so much of a deficiency or defect as of a defection, a withdrawal on the part of the will from one thing and toward another. But can these two senses – "defect" and "defection" – really be held together simply on the ground that a single Latin word can express either the one or the other? And, in any case, how are we to know what a "deficient cause" is? To want to discover deficient causes, Augustine claims, is like wanting to see darkness or to hear silence. We can only perceive darkness by not seeing and can only perceive silence by not hearing. Similarly we can only recognize deficient causes by not knowing the causes that bring things about. As silence is known by not hearing, so deficient causes are known by not knowing. In each case, we catch a glimpse of the thing we want to know (silence, deficient cause) only by recognizing the field that is left unoccupied when something else (sound, efficient cause) is absent. [34] If there is any cause of the evil will, then, it is only the cause of which we catch a dim glimpse when we acknowledge that there is no efficient cause. But do we catch a glimpse of anything at all?

The evil of mutable spirits, Augustine claims, begins with the will itself, by which the good of nature is diminished and perverted; and nothing causes such a will except the defection by which it abandons God, a defection itself without cause (*cuius defectionis etiam causa utique deficit*). [35] To say that the will's defection from God is without cause, however, amounts to saying that it is simply inexplicable. It amounts to saying that "it just happened that" the will turned from God. But if the will's turn "just happened," we are left without the crucial link between the agent and the act. We do not see how such an agent, good in nature and good in orientation of will, could actually have begun to will a lesser good in place of a higher, or rather the highest, good. The same implausibility that besets Augustine's account of the fall of the human will seems also to plague his account of the fall of the evil angels. The will's defection from God seems rather to have happened to it than to have arisen from it. And we do not hold agents morally responsible for things that happen to them.

As it turns out, however, it is not quite correct to say that the will's defection from the supreme Good simply happened to it. Augustine has still to address the second of the two problems that he brought upon himself by altering his interpretation of the moment of the devil's fall. He must either provide an account of the creation of the angels in which the good angels do not receive full bliss until after the fall of the evil angels (so as to keep the evil and the good angels on the same moral footing before the formers' fall) or find some way of marking the evil angels off from the good even prior to their fall (so as to justify a precedent difference in moral footing) yet without violating the divine justice or intimating sin before there is sin.

The point of departure for Augustine's argument – and it seems virtually to determine the outcome – is his insistence that there is a kind of asymmetry between the origin of the evil and the origin of the good will. From the fact that the one lacks any efficient cause we are not to conclude that the same is true of the other. The good will is not uncaused; it is caused by God. Since the angels were created, Augustine claims, "it follows that their will must also be created."[36] Given this starting point, there are two possibilities: either their will was created with them, i.e., at the very moment of their creation, or they first existed, for some brief interval, without it. In the first case, since their will was created by the good creator, it was obviously created good; "and as soon as they were created they adhered to their creator with that love with which they were created."[37] In this instance, the evil angels too were created with a good will; they too adhered to their creator with love. Their fall, then, was a fall "from fellowship with the good" in which their will became evil in virtue of "the very fact that they fell away from that good will."[38] But how could they have fallen from a good will created by God and ordered to God in love? What in them yielded that possibility and so distinguished them from the others who remained constant in the good?

When we turn to the second case, we discover that it is further divided into two alternatives. If the good angels were at first without a good will and subsequently gained a good will on their own, apart from divine aid, then it could be said that they improved on God's creation through their own independent action. But this possibility, for Augustine, is "unthinkable." The goodness of creation stems entirely from God and not in any sense from improvements independently supplied by other beings. Consequently, since the good angels could not, on their own, "have improved upon the work of the best possible Creator," they "could only have gained possession of a good will, by which they would be improved, by the assistance of the Creator's activity."[39] In addition to the possibility that the good angels were created with a good will, then, there remains only the possibility that they subsequently obtained a good will through divine assistance. But what accounts for the failure of the evil angels to receive the same divine aid? If they had no will prior to God's intervention, how could their will have become evil by turning from the good?

How, then, are we to regard the fall of the evil angels in the light of these two possibilities? Augustine continues to maintain that it came about "through a voluntary falling away from the good."[40] But his discussion of the case of the good angels has now made it impossible for Augustine to avoid all reference to any further, external factor over and above the sheer defection of will on the part of the evil angels. Either the evil angels

> received less grace of the divine love than did the others, who continued in that grace; or, if both were created equally good, the one sort fell through their evil will, while the others had greater help to enable them to attain to the fullness of bliss with the complete assurance that they will never fall away.[41]

In either case, then, whether or not both classes of angels were created equally good, the critical point of distinction between the two rests in something that God has given to the one and not to the other. Augustine has made the good will of the good angels so much a function of the divine activity in giving and shaping their will that he has made it impossible to construe the evil will of the evil angels as anything other than a result of the absence of the divine activity (or the full degree of the divine activity) in their case. Speaking paradoxically, we might say that the vacuum left by the *causa deficiens* of the first evil will has now been filled by an absence of another sort, the absence of the full measure of the grace of the divine love. In the end, Augustine took the option of marking the evil angels off from the good – not, however, by intimating that they might somehow have sinned before they had sinned, but rather by locating the point of distinction in God, in the unexplained and inexplicable presence or absence of divine aid.

To the inexplicable conundrum of the good will's turn from the supreme Good, then, Augustine has added the inexplicable mystery of a God who gives and withholds aid without apparent regard for considerations of justice. In doing so, he has doubly cast into doubt the notion that the becoming-evil of the will is an action of the willing agent for which the agent can rightly be held morally responsible. We cannot understand how a good will, rightly directed to the supreme Good and rightly ordered in its love for God, should "just happen" to turn from the greatest to a lesser good. Nor does Augustine's reference to the divine aid help in this respect. It serves only to suggest that what accounts for the evil angels' fall is something that lies entirely outside their own control: the presence or absence of that assistance by which God causes the will of the good angels to be or to become good. Where the link between agent and action can neither be discerned nor specified, it seems, the principle that determines the goodness or badness of the will turns out to be extrinsic to the agents themselves, lying either in the *causa efficiens* of divine aid or in the *causa deficiens* of pure happenstance. For all the profundity of Augustine's treatment of the human and the angelic fall in other respects, it is not clear that he has actually helped us to understand either the operation of the will or the moral responsibility of the agent in the primal sin of the evil angels and of the first human beings.

NOTES

1. My aim in this study is simply to expose and to explore what I take to be a problem in the view of the fall, both human and angelic, that Augustine sets out in the relevant sections of *De civitate Dei* (*Civ. Dei*). Consequently I make relatively few references to Augustine's other works. In an essay entitled "Augustine on Sin and Moral Agency," *Journal of Religious Ethics* 16 (1988) I offer a more extensive analysis of the developments that led to the difficulty in Augustine's mature position and a more fully developed assessment of the difficulty itself.

2. *Civ. Dei* 14.11.

3. We are not to suppose that Adam believed Eve to be speaking the truth; he was rather led to transgress God's law by *sociali necessitudine,* by the link of intimacy between one human being and another, *uni unum, hominem homini, coniugem coniugi* (*Civ. Dei* 14.11).

4. *Civ. Dei* 14.12; tr. Henry Bettenson, *Augustine: The City of God* (Harmondsworth, England: Penguin, 1972).

5. *Civ. Dei* 14.11.

6. *Civ. Dei* 14.14: *Neque enim hoc propterea non fecerunt, quia id mulier serpente suadente, vir muliere impertiente commisit....*

7. See *Civ. Dei* 14.11: *Mala vero voluntas prima, quoniam omnia opera mala praecessit in homine ...*; note also 14.13: *Non enim ad malum opus perveniretur nisi praecessit voluntas mala.*

8. *Civ. Dei* 14.13: *Non ergo malum opus factum est ... nisi ab eis qui iam mali erant.*

9. *Civ. Dei* 14.13.

10. *Civ. Dei* 14.13: *In occulto autem mali esse coeperunt ut in apertam inoboedentiam laberentur.*

11. *Civ. Dei* 14.13: *Neque enim fieret ille fructus malus nisi ab arbore mala;* see also 14.11.

12. It is a *vitium* which is not *secundum naturam sed contra naturam* (*Civ. Dei* 14.11). Such fault or defect is possible only in a nature created *ex nihilo* and therefore subject to change. In this sense the will's failure to be what it is (*ut ... ab eo quod est deficiat*) is due to the fact that it was made from nothing (*Civ. Dei* 14.13). But creation from nothing does not make the nature itself evil; and, while it accounts for the possibility of flaw, it is not itself a flaw.

13. See, for example, *Civ. Dei* 11.9, 22.

14. *Civ. Dei* 14.13.

15. *Civ. Dei* 14.13, tr. Bettenson.

16. *Civ. Dei* 14.11.

17. *Civ. Dei* 14.10. Augustine here emphasizes paradise as a place of happiness, *locus beatitudinis,* untouched by any external threat or internal distress that might have muted human felicity or scarred human motivation.

18. *Civ. Dei* 14.11.

19. *Civ. Dei* 14.10. We are not for a moment to suppose that there was any sin where there was no sin – *Absit ut hoc existimemus fuisse ubi nullum erat omnino peccatum* – as if the fall cast a backwards shadow over pre-fallen human existence in the form of an unfulfilled lust for the forbidden tree. There was no sin before there was sin.

20. *Civ. Dei* 14.10.

21. *Civ. Dei* 14.6.

22. See the discussions in *Civ. Dei* 14.7 and 14.9.

23. *Civ. Dei* 12.6: *Huius porro malae voluntatis causa efficiens si quaeretur, nihil invenitur ... mala voluntas efficiens est operis mali, malae autem voluntatis efficiens nihil est.*

24. Augustine develops the argument at length in *Civ. Dei* 12.6.

25. *Civ. Dei* 12.6: *propriam igitur in uno eorum voluntatem malam res quae fecerit scire volentibus, si bene intueantur, nihil occurrit.*

26. *Gen. litt.* 11.16-17, 23.

27. *Gen. litt.* 11.17, tr. John Hammond Taylor, *St. Augustine: The Literal Meaning of Genesis*, 2 vols. (New York: Newman Press, 1982).

28. *Gen. litt.* 11.23, tr. Taylor.

29. Augustine was, in this respect, adapting to the angelic case an interpretation with which he had already toyed in the human case, imagining human beings created neither wise nor foolish but in an intermediate position from which they might become either the one or the other (*Lib. arb.* 3.24.71-73). In neither case, however, did he ultimately adopt this "moral neutrality" view.

30. *Civ. Dei* 11.13, tr. Bettenson.

31. *Civ. Dei* 11.16, tr. Bettenson.

32. *Civ. Dei* 12.7.

33. *Civ. Dei* 12.7.

34. *Civ. Dei* 12.7: *Causas porro defectionum istarum, cum efficientes non sint, ut dixi, sed deficientes, velle invenire tale est ac si quisquam velit videre tenebras vel audire silentium, quod tamen utrumque nobis notum est, neque illud nisi per oculos neque hoc nisi per aures, non sane in specie, sed in speciei privatione. Nemo ergo ex me scire quaerat quod me nescire scio, nisi forte ut nescire discat quod sciri non posse sciendum est. Ea quippe quae non in specie, sed in eius privatione sciuntur, si dici aut intellegi potest, quodam modo nesciendo sciuntur ut sciendo nesciantur.... Ita etiam non ad aliquem alium sensum, sed ad solas aures pertinet sentire silentium, quod tamen nullo modo nisi non audiendo sentitur. Sic species intellegibiles mens quidem nostra intellegendo conspicit; sed ubi deficiunt, nesciendo condiscit.*

35. *Civ. Dei* 12.9.

36. *Civ. Dei* 12.9: *Cum ergo malae voluntatis efficiens naturalis vel, si dici potest, essentialis mulla sit causa ... si dixerimus mullam esse efficientem causam etiam voluntatis bonae, cavendum est ne voluntas bona bonorum angelorum non facta, sed Deo coaeterna esse credatur. Cum ergo ipsi facti sunt, quo modo illa non esse facta dicetur?*

37. *Civ. Dei* 12.9, tr. Bettenson.

38. *Civ. Dei* 12.9, tr Bettenson.

39. *Civ. Dei* 12.9, tr. Bettenson. It is here that Augustine most decisively rejects the "moral neutrality" view. What, he asks, could the good angels have been *sine bona voluntate nisi mali?* The idea of an intermediate position, neither good nor evil, no longer comes into his reckoning at all.

40. *Civ. Dei* 12.9, tr. Bettenson.

41. *Civ. Dei* 12.9, tr. Bettenson.

GOODNESS AS ORDER AND HARMONY IN AUGUSTINE

PETER SLATER

As is well known, in the Platonic and Neoplatonic philosophical traditions which influenced many of the early Fathers of the Church, a key image for absolute goodness was the sun. Seemingly unchanging, the sun gives off light and energy all about it, and so stirs into life what otherwise remains dormant in its universe. The closer to the sun, the more light and life there seems to be. Besides the notion of the unchanging source, consequently, there developed also the assumption of a chain of being, stretching from what is ethereal to what is dense, and held together by the integrating power of the source.[1] The assumption is of a metaphysical dualism between spirit and matter which shaped religious consciousness for centuries. But the conception allows for many gradations of composite beings, so that reality as we perceive it consists of a great variety of species, yet bonded together by varying degrees of dependency. As he wrestled with the problem of evil, as posed by the Manichees, it was this set of images and ideas which Augustine embraced and used to discredit their version of religious dualism.

Augustine added two important conclusions to the traditional conception, which are essential to his solution of the problem of evil. The first is that the spiritual source is itself simple, not composite.[2] This means, among other things, that the attributes of the absolute are coincident and, so to speak, coterminous.[3] If we know God to be good from one set of experiences, therefore, we may infer that God is always good. As simple, the divine being is timeless and must be always and everywhere the same. Identifying the God whom he learned to worship at his mother's knee with this spiritual source, Augustine was thus able to argue that what God ordains is good, even when we cannot see that this must be so. No one doubted that God is good, since by definition God is the one who saves. The problem concerned the scope of this goodness and the nature of the opposition to it evident in our world. Can goodness be entrapped and compromised, at least for a time, as Mani assumed? Platonism enabled Augustine to argue that God in essence cannot be compromised.[4] Yet, like the light of the sun, God's goodness may be *reflected* in material things. That *derived* goodness is attributed to beings which are changeable and which, therefore, may change for the worse. The *possibility* of evil rests metaphysically on this concept of the privation of goodness, which some critics take to be Augustine's sole basis for an answer to the question of evil.

The second conclusion from the traditional conception of divinity is religiously the more important and what identifies Augustinianism in theology, that is, the conception of spirit in terms of will.[5] As his speculations on the doctrine of the Trinity show, Augustine broke with any notion of the emanation of being *within* the godhead. For him originating, redeeming, and harmonizing goodness are in essence identical expressions of divine will. The hallmark of willpower is love, contained in the concept of *bonum* on the divine side and *amor* on the human.[6] Again as is well known, Augustine did not consistently work through what this aspect of his thinking implies for our conception of goodness. His ideas were developed in the course of arguments on different fronts. The formal definition of goodness belongs to this early debate with the Manichees of North Africa. The explication of willpower undergoes revision in the course of his anti-Pelagian writings. Between earlier and later writings, Augustine's attention shifted from the individual odyssey of the soul portrayed in the *Confessions* to the communal record sketched in the *City of God.* In the famous book nineteen of this latter work, Augustine shared a vision of being in an ideal harmony of wills. In this paper, I want to argue that, implicit in this later vision is a theologically more acceptable conception of goodness than that with which Augustine earlier demolished the Manichaean position on good and evil. The conception of goodness as harmony flows out of the earlier conception, as the key idea of willpower is developed. But it was never systematically articulated and examined by Augustine.

In an early work, *De libero arbitrio* I and II, Augustine set out to argue that there is one greatest good – *summum bonum* – by reference to which all other goods are judged (2.9.27). In keeping with his age, he assumed that the key to this must be some conception of human happiness, not as psychologically determined, but as theologically defined. In most instances, there is a difference between what we think to be true happiness and what is actually so. Furthermore, what I call happiness you may not. At times, Augustine simply asserts that the only conception worth considering is the kind of blessedness discerned by the wise (*Civ. Dei* 5.9, 10.1). They have learned which satisfactions can be lasting, according to a hierarchically ordered series of objects of desire. Only right desire, objectively considered, can lead to true happiness. Since for human beings, such desire depends upon an act of will, hinging on what and how we love, loving justly is the key to happiness. But, according to Augustine, after the Fall, as we shall note shortly, we no longer have the power to love the good except through divine grace. For blessedness, as for life itself, we are utterly dependent on God, the source of all.[7]

When arguing with other Christians, however heterodox, who accept the authority of Scripture, Augustine could simply establish that God is the source of all blessedness by appealing to mutually acknowledged biblical texts (*Mor. ecc.* 8.13). But in the work on free choice he developed a metaphysical argument which he never repudiated. It trades on the contention that reason is superior to lack of reason. It is therefore plausible to assert that human being is superior to that of animal being. Moreover, reason may reflect on ideas without reference to physical objects. It is, in this respect, self-sufficient. Yet our own reasoning is fallible. We have within ourselves a sense of what is unchangeably and unchangingly good, i.e., what is inviolably so. This must be superior in being to ourselves. In fact, we are only true and good insofar as we participate in this greater good (II.3-12). True happiness consists in enjoying this eternal good eternally. As eternal, it is unchangeable, indivisible, one. There *is* one highest being, through participation in which we find true blessedness.

For Augustine the Neoplatonist, judging truly means grasping mentally the unchanging form which exists independently of the mind and which is the norm for our accurate perception of it. The Good is not just the Form of Good, in Plato's sense, but God's contemplation of the Form in himself and his conception of how whatever is good is informed by this pattern (*Lib. arb.* II, 15.39). The rule for the use of "good" is thus not some pattern to which we refer in isolation but the essence of what God determines to be the good of each created nature. For humanity, the conclusion is that, "as the soul is the life of the body, so God is the happy life of the soul." (*Lib. arb.* II.1 p. 161. Compare Plotinus, *Enn.* I.iv).

Both God and the soul are understood to be spiritual substances, that is, intelligible entities not extended in space. The soul is like God in being relatively indivisible. There is as much life or soul in my little finger as there is in my heart or head (cf. *Conf.* VII, 9, 142f., *Fund. Epist.* 16:20). Notice, in passing, that the line between Creator and human creature is *within* the class of spiritual substances, not between spirit and matter (cf. *Civ. Dei* 8.6). Metaphysically speaking, the relevant line is between what is sensed and what is grasped by the mind's eye. Augustine simply assumed, incidentally, that because our mental pictures of things cannot have the same extension in space as the things pictured, then they must have no extension in space at all (*Conf.* 7.1, *Civ. Dei* 8.5 and 7, and *passim*).

So far what we have is a strictly metaphysical conception of goodness, based on the assumptions that what judges is superior to what is judged and that self-sufficiency is good. God is the ultimate or highest good because God is unchangeably and self-sufficiently so. It is God's indivisibility which rules out the Manichaean idea that divinity can be separated off from itself and trapped in matter (*Fund. Epist.* 19.21, and *passim*). Augustine was aware that Scripture occasionally portrays God as changing his mind and as ruler of a divided house. But from Ambrose he learned to allegorize such portrayals in ways that made their meaning consistent with his foundational conception that being as such is good (*Conf.* 13.29, *Util. Cred.* 18.36):

> The chief good is that which is properly described as having supreme and original existence *(summum bonum esse quod summae ac primitus esse rectissime dicitur)*. For that exists in the highest sense of the word which is throughout like itself, which cannot in any part be corrupted or changed, which is not subject to time, which admits of no variation in its present as compared with its former condition. This is existence in its true sense *(Id enim est quod est verissime dicitur)*. For in this signification of the word existence there is implied a nature which is self-contained and which continues immutable *(Subest enim huic verbo manentis in se atque incommutabiliter sese habentis naturae significatio)*. Such things can be said only of God, to whom there is nothing contrary in the strict sense of the word (*Mor. Man.* 1.69).

Notice here that while it follows that evil as such does not "exist," neither do we. Only God is being in and of himself.

For Augustine there appeared to be an asymmetry between evil and good due to the fact that there can be good without evil, but not evil without good. This is "fact" if one gives Augustine his definition of evil as corruption. For every process of corruption presupposes a prior uncorrupt state, at least according to his argument against the Manichaeans. Here he traded on an ambiguity. It is true, for instance, that a rotten apple was previously whole and tasty. But it is only as food that we would consider a rotten apple to be bad. As seed ready for planting, it may be good. Yet Augustine rejected the assumption that human preference is what identifies anything as good or bad (*Civ. Dei* 11.16). In fact, he operated with two conceptions of goodness apart from that of personal preference. One is the metaphysical and the other is the moral. The distinction is necessary because, according to him, a fallen angel may be metaphysically superior in being to a human. Yet a good human being is morally better than a fallen angel. Indeed, against the Platonists, Augustine would argue that it is the highest created spirit, not matter as such, which is the source of corruption in creation. The devil, after all, is pure spirit. The divisibility of matter makes corruption possible. But the *origin* of evil lies in perversion of the will, not the privation of goodness in any passive sense (ref. *Nat. bon.* 5).[8] In God, of course, the metaphysical and moral good coincide, but not in creation.

Whatever the root of evil may be, for Augustine it cannot be another substance standing over against God, as the Manichaeans supposed (*Fortunatum* II.21). Every substance is either God or some being dependent on God and good by participation, presumably, in the goodness of God.[9] When any substance other than God loses its goodness, it at the same time loses existence and "falls" towards absolute nothingness *(omnino nihil)*. Among goods, Augustine lists

> life potency, health, memory, virtue, intelligence, tranquillity, plenty, sense, light, sweetness, measure, beauty, peace ... (in sum) especially those things which are found universally in spiritual or corporeal existence, (namely) measure, form and order.... (*Nat. bon.* 13.329; cf. Plotinus, *Enn.* I.7.2)

Metaphysically, the criterion of goodness is the presence of measure, form, and order. It is the supposed order in the kingdom of darkness which leads Augustine to insist that it cannot be considered wholly evil. Nothing exists without some form and order which, as such, is good. Nothing is evil *by nature,* Augustine concluded, since to have a nature or be substantial is to have some measure, form, and order. Moreover, something which in itself has very little good may be part of a larger whole, which is on a larger scale of organization and, as such, good. Hence the shadowy side of our existence fits into a final harmony which is good according to Augustine, even if it does not seem so to us.

To us it seems far from evident that an ignorant man, for instance, was previously knowledgeable. But Augustine shared his generation's assumption that the dawn of history was a golden age. In particular, Adam prior to the Fall was as omniscient as a human can be. Adam is both archetype and individual. Since we were "in" Adam when he fell from grace, we share in his disordered existence. What to us seems evil, as often as not, is in reality the punishment meted out to humanity which should, had Adam willed perfectly, be now in paradise, having eaten from the tree of immortality. Instead, we have to return to this predetermined state by means of another "tree," the Cross of Christ. Christ in the flesh reverses the trend set by the devil in the spirit. The whole saga of salvation is one of diversion, conversion, reversion, for those who receive grace. For those who do not, good is still upheld, in that those in sin do not go unpunished. Augustine even suggested at one point that the number of redeemed will simply match the number of fallen angels, so that heaven may have its full complement. Goodness as order is triumphant to the end, even if such goodness means that most of us are predestined for hell. In this idea we have the germ of the doctrine of double predestination, which Calvin adopted and Barth so roundly criticised (in his *Church Dogmatics* II.2).

Although Augustine's conception of that nature which is essentially good is based on his high estimation of measure, form, and order, with reference to human nature he had to wrestle with the phenomenon of free choice. The Manichaean conception was of two wills, two substantive forces, warring in us. Augustine would allow only one substantive being, which must take responsibility for its waywardness. He attempted to explain this, as we all know, by distinguishing between the faculty of choosing and the power to act on our choice. Since it takes no willpower to go on sinning, he could again posit an asymmetry between our choices of good and evil. To act on a good choice, once we are falling, requires another power than our own to reverse our fall. After Adam, this is possible only by grace. (In Hindu terms, Augustine here opted for the cat, where Pelagius and Aquinas later followed the monkey – the image is of mother cat carrying the kitten to safety by picking it up in her mouth, as contrasted with the baby monkey, which must jump on the mother's back, by its own effort, in order to be carried to safety.) By humbling himself and assuming our flesh, Christ reverses the devil's proud spiritual act of self-assertion and so turns us around to love once more in the right order, that is, God, then self.[10]

Augustine gave us two glimpses of what it would be like to will rightly in an unfallen or fully redeemed world. One is the sex act of the male. At present, according to Augustine, this exemplifies our fallen state, in that the body is not fully obedient to the soul. In a perfect state, evidently, the reason, will, and physical act of the individual would be fully harmonious. Body would obey spirit. The other vision embraces the whole person and the whole social order, when we are neither at war within ourselves nor at odds with our neighbours, but at peace.[11] Such peace is the end for which we all strive. In book nineteen of *The City of God*, Augustine described it this way:

> The peace of the body ... consists in the duly proportioned arrangement of its parts. The peace of the irrational soul is the harmonious repose of the appetites, and that of the rational soul the harmony of knowledge and action. The peace of the body and the soul is the well-ordered and harmonious life and health of the living creature. Peace between man and God is the well-ordered concord. Domestic peace is the well-ordered concord between those of the family who rule and those who obey. Civil peace is a similar concord among citizens. The peace of the celestial city is the perfectly ordered and harmonious enjoyment of God, and of one another in God. The peace of all things is the tranquillity of order. Order is the distribution which allots equal and unequal to its own place ... (*Civ. Dei* 19.13.409)

Emerging through this account of ultimate peace is a second criterion of goodness particularly relevant to willful beings. It is harmony. For Augustine, harmony was still a subset of order. But I submit that, if he had followed through consistently on his conception of spiritual being, he would have had to allow for a more dynamic conception of harmony, appropriate to his vision of heaven as the City of God. His conception was still dominated by the idea of knowing and keeping one's place in a fallen world. Disorder was still thought of as being when the appetites drive the body beyond its appropriate limits and the will becomes enslaved by desire. The focus in the discussion of the power to be free was on the consequences of disobedience. The reverse move does not really allow for any significant exercise of the will to do more than obediently assent to the divine plan for all concerned. Under the heavenly king, the godly prince is the one who seeks to discern God's will in each instance and carry it out. The thought that part of our existing in God's image might involve our own freedom to plan, experiment, and become partners in the work of creation is not there. Despite the fact that the fall originates in a spiritual being who has no bodily appetites, on the level of spiritual pride, Augustine's vision of the final harmony remained true to an age in which the ultimate goal is otherworldly. Given the world in which he lived, this is not surprising. The seeds of the Augustinian concept of personality would have to await its philosophical maturation centuries later, in the romantic movement following the age of enlightenment. But in the idea of peace in the city we can detect its presence.

In support of my interpretation, let me conclude by recalling that in his classic analysis of Christ and culture, H. Richard Niebuhr claimed Augustine as his theological authority for his fifth type, Christ the transformer of culture.[12] The suggestion for this type is not that error is always avoided, but that through evil good may come. However, in Augustine himself the aesthetic ideal of harmony prevailed over the moral one. The Augustinian tradition, especially in Calvin, is never as comfortable with the idea of creaturely freedom as it is with creaturely finitude. When the former is finally given its due in philosophical theology, the conception of God's goodness is much more pregnant with creative possibilities than that which leads to the doctrine of double predestination. I submit that, as Niebuhr contends, the seeds for this richer harvest of thought are to be found in Augustine, even if he himself did not fully grasp the implications of his conceptions of goodness as harmony of wills and spiritual being as fully incarnate. Augustine's own cultural milieu and polemical situation prevented him from exploring what we might fairly take to be his own best insights.[13]

NOTES

1. On this topic see A.O. Lovejoy, *The Great Chain of Being* (Cambridge, Massachusetts: Harvard University Press, 1936).

2. On the indivisibility of spiritual substance see *Lib. arb.* II.8.22; *Mor. Man.* 11.20.

3. On this topic in connection with Augustine's doctrine of creation see the essay by William A. Christian in Roy W. Battenhouse, ed., *A Companion to the Study of St. Augustine* (New York: Oxford University Press, 1955), xii.

4. On Augustine's use of Platonist authors I follow Robert J. O'Connell.

5. On the importance of this conception see C.N. Cochrane, *Christianity and Classical Culture* (New York: Oxford University Press [Galaxy pb], 1957), p. 446-53.

6. On this topic I follow John Burnaby, *Amor Dei* (London: Hodder and Stoughton, 1947).

7. For a recent discussion of Augustine's significance for western thought on this point see Alasdair MacIntyre, *Whose Justice, Which Reason?* (Notre Dame, Indiana: University of Notre Dame Press, 1988). In general, see Ragnar Holte, *Béatitude et Sagesse: Saint Augustin et le problème de la fin de l'homme dans la philosophie ancienne* (Paris: Etudes Augustiniennes, 1962).

8. For comparison of Augustine and Tillich on this topic see my article, "Tillich on the Fall and the Temptation of Goodness," *Journal of Religion,* 65.2 (April 1985), 196-207.

9. For fuller discussion see Burnaby, op. cit., p. 40-41.

10. See Oliver O'Donovan, *The Problem of Self-Love in St. Augustine* (New Haven and London: Yale University Press, 1980), ch. 2.

11. On this topic see most recently Peter Brown, *The Body and Society* (New York: Columbia University Press, 1988), ch.19 on "Sexuality and Society."

12. H. Richard Niebuhr, *Christ and Culture* (New York: Harper & Row, 1956), ch. 6.

13. See in this connection my article contrasting Augustine and Tillich on the origin of evil: "Tillich on the Fall and the Temptation of Goodness," *Journal of Religion* (April 1985), 196-207.

CHRIST AND THE HOLY SPIRIT IN AUGUSTINE'S THEOLOGY OF BAPTISM

J. PATOUT BURNS

Augustine's early writings do not provide a developed theology of baptism or of the other sacraments and rituals of the church. Even in the *Confessions,* the convert submits to the teaching authority and the rituals of the church as an act of humility, in reverence for the incarnation of the divine Word. Through this discipline, the Christian hopes to purify mind and heart and so become capable of the sustained contemplation of Truth. Augustine explained no further effect of the sacrament. [1]

Once Augustine had returned to his native Numidia and become the leading Catholic spokesman in the controversy with the Donatists, he had to give greater attention to the sacraments and their role in the economy of salvation. Even in these controversial writings, however, one searches in vain for the exposition of baptism and the eucharist which are to be found, for example, in Tertullian's *On Baptism,* Gregory of Nyssa's *Catechetical Address* or Ambrose's *On the Mysteries.* Augustine was respectful of the requirement of baptism based upon the gospel of John and the tradition of the church. [2] His explanations, however, are limited to the sinfulness of a rejection or refusal of baptism by one, such as Cornelius, who had already received grace. [3] They do not move beyond the perspective of the *Confessions* to explain the consecration effected in the sacrament which then serves as a basis for a relationship to Christ and access to his kingdom. Nor was the forgiveness of sins a necessary or exclusive effect of baptism in his theory, as we shall see in greater detail.

To one aspect of baptism, however, Augustine devoted significant attention: the role of Christ and of the Holy Spirit in conferring the sacrament and producing its salvific effects. By a genetic study, I hope to clarify the development of the inter-related aspects of the theory.

The works of the Donatist controversy – letters, controversial writings, reports of the conference at Carthage and of other conversations with Donatist leaders – might seem poor objects for a developmental study. Augustine seems to have considered himself duty-bound to reply, individually, in detail, and even in kind, to every pamphlet placed in circulation by a Donatist author. As a consequence, his writings are exceedingly repetitious: the same arguments are presented in successive treatises and even within the books of individual treatises. Over and over again, he rehearsed historical questions such as the innocence of Caecilian and the guilt of his accusers, the successive appeals for imperial intervention, and the Donatist dealings with their own schismatics. The primary theological arguments – the fulfilment of the promise to Abraham that all nations would be blessed in Christ and the imperfect purity of the church before the return of the judging Christ – evince little change during the two decades of his involvement in the controversy. The efficacy of the sacraments, the subject of our investigation, was considered episodically. Sustained analyses are to be found only in *On Baptism,* the treatise in which he commented on the writings of Cyprian rather than answering a Donatist author.

The basic lines of Augustine's theory are, of course, well known. Christ himself confers the consecration of baptism through the minister who performs the visible sacrament. Through the charity which establishes the unity of the church, the Holy Spirit confers the forgiveness of sins. In this essay, I would like to offer a proposal: that this latter part of the theory, the role of the Spirit in the church, developed out of the former, the agency of Christ in the ministry. The essay will focus on the successive treatments in *On Baptism.*

The Donatists had followed the theology of Cyprian which highlighted the role of the Holy Spirit in the baptismal forgiveness of sins. Cyprian seems to have thought that only baptism guaranteed the gift of the Spirit and the forgiveness of sins. A person who had sinned significantly, particularly by denying the faith, thereby lost the presence of the Spirit. That individual might undertake penance and might even be readmitted to the communion of the church. Since no bishop could be certain of the sincerity and adequacy of the repentance, he could not be sure that the imposition of hands through which the person was readmitted to communion restored the presence of the Holy Spirit.[4] Hence the repentant sinner could not be entrusted with the exercise of sacramental ministry through which the Holy Spirit was transmitted.[5] Cyprian also restricted the sanctifying presence of the Holy Spirit to the unity of the church. Because heretics and schismatics could not confer the Spirit, those they attempted to baptize received no salvific effect and thus had to be given true baptism when they converted to the one, holy church.[6]

Against the Donatists, and indeed against Cyprian himself, Augustine insisted that Christ, not the bishop, is the sanctifying agent in baptism. Christ alone confers its consecration and holiness, no matter who invokes the divine name, receives the profession of trinitarian faith, and performs the ritual washing. The scriptural text regularly used to underline this point is the testimony of John the Baptist in John 1.33, "this is he who baptizes with the Holy Spirit." Augustine sometimes quoted only the first part, omitting the reference to the Holy Spirit, to assert that Christ baptizes when his disciples act. In these instances, the activity of Christ through the minister was elaborated in three different ways. Unlike the disciples of John the Baptist, the disciples of Christ are not given a baptism of their own: they confer only the one baptism which bears the name and power of Christ.[7] Moreover, among the pagans the efficacy of a religious ritual is expected from the god rather than from the priest. Thus the African version of Sirach 34.25, "If one is baptized by the dead, his washing does not help" properly applies to rituals attributed to gods who are actually dead humans rather than to Christian baptism which is performed by the risen Christ.[8] Finally, baptism can be compared to the name of Christ or the gospel itself: power for casting out demons, working miracles, and even engendering faith come from Christ, not from the unbeliever invoking the name or the false apostle preaching the word for personal gain.[9] In one way or another, Augustine argued throughout the controversy that Christ is the true and only agent of baptism, no matter whose ministry he uses in the ritual.

A second use of this Johannine text argues that Christ alone baptizes with the Holy Spirit and thereby guarantees the sanctifying power of the sacrament. This argument, however, did not remain stable throughout the controversy. Augustine gradually loosened the link between the sanctifying work of the Holy Spirit and the baptismal consecration effected by Christ. Though he never asserted the independence of forgiveness from baptism, he explained that Christ baptizes true and feigning converts alike through good and evil ministers, while the Holy Spirit cleanses and sanctifies the good convert through saints and spiritual persons. Let us follow the changes in this argument.

In *Against the Letter of Parminian,* the text, "He is the one who baptizes with the Holy Spirit," was introduced to establish that the baptismal forgiveness of sins within the Catholic communion does not depend upon the sanctity of the minister. It comes directly from the Holy Spirit, with whom Christ himself baptizes even through the ministry of evil bishops.[10] Please note that in this instance Augustine made no reference to charity or to the unity of the church.

In the first book of *On Baptism,* the same argument is extended to baptism administered in separation from the Catholic church. The Donatists used Cyprian to assert that baptism cannot be separated from the forgiveness of sins, the operation of the Spirit, and the communion of the Church.[11] Augustine responded by linking the forgiveness of sins to the acceptance of charity. He proposed two ways of explaining the effect of baptism received outside the unity of the church. The schismatic, an enemy of the peace and love of Christ, refuses the Spirit's gift of charity. Baptism in schism, therefore, might not forgive sins unless or until the person is reconciled to the unity of the church. Alternately, baptism might forgive sins even outside the unity of the church because the baptizing Christ acts with the Holy Spirit. These sins, however, would immediately return because of the baptized person's continuing ill will, evident in the sin of schism. An elaboration on the parable of the two debtor servants supported the assertion that forgiven sins would return when pardon is sought by a person who does not practise Christian love.[12]

In this analysis, Augustine began to amplify the assertion that Christ baptizes with the Holy Spirit. By using the Spirit's gift of charity as a sort of middle term, his explanation would link the forgiveness of sins to the unity of the church. A schismatic's hatred of fellow Christians constitutes a rejection of charity, which would in turn either prevent the forgiveness of sins or make them return immediately. If the baptized person subsequently removes this obstacle by true conversion to unity, the sacrament then works a lasting forgiveness. Through its relationship to charity, unity was made a condition for the forgiveness of sins but not for baptism. As is evident, Augustine's focus was still very much on the work of Christ in the sacrament.

In the next four books of *On Baptism,* Augustine turned to the letters of Cyprian which the Donatists used to support their position. In this attack on his theory of church and baptism, Augustine repeatedly called attention to Cyprian's practice. He had refused to break off communion with those of his episcopal colleagues who continued to admit to the communion of the church converts who had been baptized only in heresy and schism, without giving them what he, Cyprian, considered the only true and effective baptism, that conferred by a bishop sharing the Spirit in the unity of the church.[13] In the second book of *On Baptism,* Augustine observed that through those colleagues Cyprian would have been in communion with persons whom he, and the Donatists who followed his theory, considered both unbaptized and guilty of schism.[14] Yet Cyprian judged that such persons, whom he regarded as unbaptized, could win God's pardon and eternal life through the bond of unity in the church. The Donatists themselves had followed this practice, Augustine argued, in readmitting to their communion the bishops who followed Maximian into schism and those they had baptized in that separation from the Donatist communion.[15] He urged them to go the further step and return to the unity of the church. They should trust that unity would win forgiveness for both those who had rebaptized and those who had been rebaptized.[16]

In this argument, Augustine advanced his analysis on two points. He had earlier made the acceptance of charity in the unity of the church a condition either for receiving or for retaining the forgiveness of sins. Here, in elaborating Cyprian's opinion of the efficacy of unity, he cited the assertion of 1 Peter 4.8 that charity covers a multitude of sins. The Donatists, he explained, could gain forgiveness for the sin of schism and the sacrilege of rebaptism through the charity they would share in union with the Catholics. Thus he argued that the power of charity was the basis for Cyprian's belief that unity would win pardon even without baptism.[17] In this argument, charity moved toward becoming the active principle through which remission is effected rather than a condition for its reception or continuation.

Augustine also noted a second effect of charity. As the foundation of concord, it makes prayer effective, according to Matthew 18.19. The prayer offered by disciples gathered in the unity of Christ will placate God and gain forgiveness for the schismatics.[18] This observation could serve as the foundation for his subsequent proposal that the prayers of the society of saints are the medium of forgiveness of sins.

In the third book of *On Baptism,* Augustine began an extended commentary on Cyprian's letter to Jubian on the rebaptism of heretics.[19] In the course of that exposition, he returned to the question of the forgiveness of sins when baptism is conferred outside the communion of the church. Again he argued that in separation from the church, discord and dissension either prevent forgiveness or make sins return immediately. When corrected schismatics come to the unity of the church, he explained, they become worthy of that cleansing from sin which charity accomplished in the bond of unity.[20]

In comparing this discussion of the efficacy of baptism in schism to that found in book one of the treatise, one discerns the continuing shift toward the efficacy of charity. Here, however, charity is named as the cause of forgiveness rather than as the condition for gaining or keeping it. Because the Johannine text affirmed that Christ baptizes with the Holy Spirit, Augustine still hesitated to deny outright the forgiveness of sins through baptism conferred in schism. Increasingly, however, he identified the sanctifying power of the Spirit with the gift of charity, which is operative in the unity of the church.

In the continuing exposition of Cyprian's letter to Jubian, we note a further development of the connection between the Holy Spirit, charity, and the unity of the church. Augustine used Romans 5.5 to argue that the Spirit establishes the bond of peace in the church by spreading charity in Christian hearts. For this reason, the forgiveness of sins which charity works can be given only within Catholic unity.[21]

Through these reflections on charity as the bond of unity and cause of forgiveness, Augustine was prepared to expand and develop Cyprian's interpretation of Christ's dual giving of the Spirit and the power of forgiveness, first to Peter and then to the disciples. That power, Cyprian believed, had been given to and was commonly held by the college of bishops, though it was exercised by each in his own community.[22] Instead of following Cyprian, Augustine affirmed that the Lord gave the power of forgiveness to Peter as a symbol of that unity which the canticle calls the perfect dove.[23] He then argued that evil ministers within the church as well as heretics and schismatics outside it would be excluded from the unity, that dove. They would neither share nor exercise the power to forgive. He then posed his own hypothesis in the form of a question: might one conclude that when a person comes to receive baptism with a heart open to the peace of Catholic unity, the sacrament is conferred and sins are forgiven through the prayers of the holy and spiritual persons who constitute that unity? If so, then a person baptized without accepting that unity, either inside or outside the church, would receive the sacrament itself but not the irrevocable remission of sins which comes through the prayers of the saints.[24]

Turning then to the Lord's second giving of the power to forgive sins, to the assembled disciples, in John 20, Augustine suggested that these disciples were likewise symbolic of the church. The peace of the church, therefore, forgives sins, and alienation from that peace binds in sin. This peace of unity can be found only among the good, whose prayers forgive the sins of those joined to them.[25]

Augustine then distinguished true Christians from false on the basis of their persistence in charity, the mutual love which Christ commands. The enemies of this love, whether they be within the visible communion of the church or in schism from it, are separated from that invisible body established by charity.[26] This extended analysis brings together the earlier developments into a new hypothesis which would account for the relation between Christ and the Spirit in baptism. Each element in the theory can be related to a scriptural text. According to Romans 5.5, the unity of the saints is established by the charity which is the gift of the Holy Spirit. The text of John 20.21-23 associates the gift of the Spirit with the power to forgive sins. The quotation from 1 Peter 4.8 states that charity covers a multitude of sins. Thus Augustine proposed that the charity which unites the saints is the power to forgive sins. Further, he asked whether the saints might exercise this power to forgive sins through their prayer, which the charity of unity makes effective. As we shall see, the efficacy of the charity which unites and works through the saints becomes a permanent part of his theory; the prayers of the saints as the means of its operation does not.

Although he did not affirm its truth, Augustine exploited Cyprian's opinion that Catholic unity might gain the Lord's favour for those he considered unbaptized. By using the notion of charity as a key, he linked together the gift of the Spirit, the unity of the church, the efficacy of intercessory prayer, and the power to forgive sins. On that base he constructed a new hypothesis which would allow Christ to baptize without the sanctifying effects of the Holy Spirit. Christ baptizes through the minister; the Spirit forgives sins through the saints.

Still, Augustine did not abandon the alternate explanation according to which Christ baptizes even schismatics and the unconverted within the church with the Holy Spirit and momentarily forgives their sins. He did, however, distinguish that forgiveness from the irrevocable remission given through the saints.[27]

We return to a survey of the later books of *On Baptism.* At the beginning of book five of the treatise, Augustine extended his use of the principle that charity covers a multitude of sins to interpret Cyprian's claim that the unity of the church would win forgiveness for the allegedly unbaptized. In Cyprian's time, he recalled, bishops acting within the unity of the church followed different opinions and practices regarding the baptism of heretics and schismatics. If schismatic baptism was true, then Cyprian and his party violated it when they rebaptized. If schismatic baptism was false, those who disagreed with Cyprian denied to converts the baptism which Christ had commanded them to give. One set of bishops was certainly wrong in both theory and practice. That error, however, was covered by the charity of the unity to which they all held. Thus Augustine argued that, in fidelity to Cyprian's theory and practice, the Donatist must grant that either he or his Catholic colleagues who refused to rebaptize would be covered and pardoned through the efficacy which Cyprian recognized in the charity of unity.[28] In this analysis, Augustine extended the forgiving power of charity into the life of the Christian after baptism and initiation into the church.[29]

Later in book five, in discussing a passage from the conciliar letter of the autumn of 255 AD, Augustine explained that God gives baptism even through evil ministers, but the grace of the sacrament is given either through himself or through his saints. Similarly, the forgiveness of sins is accomplished either through God himself or through the members of the dove to whom had been given the power to bind and loose.[30] The two hypotheses for the sanctifying operation of the Spirit stand side by side. We note, however, that Augustine did not mention the prayers of the saints as a means or medium of forgiveness.

Finally, in a summary of his interpretation of the writings of Cyprian which precedes the review of the opinions of the African bishops assembled in Carthage in 256 AD, Augustine repeated his teaching. Charity is the gift of the Holy Spirit through which the saints are joined together; sins are loosed or bound by union or division from this peace.[31]

We may summarize our findings. In the treatise *On Baptism,* Augustine reviewed the Cyprianic literature to which the Donatists had made their appeal. First he asserted that neither the Catholic nor the schismatic minister but only Christ baptizes with the Holy Spirit and forgives sins. As the commentary proceeded, he exploited Cyprian's concession of a saving power to the unity of the church. Through this, he was then able to advance a new and radically different interpretation of the subject of the power to forgive sins. The right to baptize might be given to bishops by ordination; Christ himself acts through their ministry. The power to bind and loose, however, is the presence of the Holy Spirit, the charity, which Christ gave to the saints. Charity establishes the union of peace within the church. Those joined into the unity of the saints receive an irrevocable forgiveness of sins; separation from their unity and peace, through either schism from the church's communion or an evil life within it, rejects charity and prevents its effect either from occurring or from enduring. The second element in the original hypothesis, the efficacy of the prayers of the saints, as a medium of forgiveness was not developed or continued.

In the other treatises of the Donatist controversy, Augustine focussed on the arguments of his particular adversary. He continued to insist on the connection between unity, charity, and sanctification.[32] He routinely identified the forgiveness of sins as the effect of charity.

In the second book of his reply to Cresconius, moreover, he linked the society of saints to the city of God. The invisible gift of the Holy Spirit, symbolized by water, flows only within the city of God. Those who share in this charity partake of heavenly peace and holy unity, as fellow citizens of the angels. The society of saints, united by the gift of the Holy Spirit, becomes the city of God, built upon this same principle.[33]

The limitations of the controversy and the focus of Cyprian's theory on the bishop as recipient and transmitter of the Holy Spirit effectively prevented Augustine from further exploiting his identification of charity as the gift of the Spirit through which the saints are empowered to forgive sins. In the sixth book of *On Baptism,* he extended the power of charity to the failures of Christians who exercise love toward others: by pardoning one wins God's pardon.[34] Nowhere in the controversy, however, did he develop the statements on mutual forgiveness in Matthew 18.15-20, whose final sentence had served as a basis for the short-lived hypothesis of the efficacy of the prayers of the saints. Only in his letter to Boniface on the baptism of infants did he signal the role of the society of saints, joined by charity, in presenting the child and communicating the Holy Spirit.[35]

We should also note that although he exploited Cyprian's opinion that the unity of the church would win forgiveness of sins even for the unbaptized, Augustine never affirmed its truth.[36] Neither, however, did he attempt to demonstrate any intrinsic connection between the consecration Christ confers in baptism and either forgiveness or eternal life. Yet the necessity of baptism played a central role in supporting, if not developing, his doctrine of inherited guilt and divine election or predestination.

NOTES

1. I would take this to be the meaning of the reflection on the humility of the incarnate Word and on Victorinus's making a public confession of faith. *Conf.* 7.18.24, 8.2.3.

2. *Bapt.* 5.9.10, *Ep. cath.* 22.62, *Con. Cres.* 2.13.16. He did allow for the substitution of faith on the part of the thief in *Bapt.*, 4.22.29 which he later corrected: *Ret.*, 2.18. In *Con. Cres.* 2.9.11 he remarked on the power of conversion to make one innocent, but did not mention the absence of baptism.

3. *Bapt.* 4.21.28, 4.24.31-4.25.32.

4. *De lapsis* 17-19, *Ep.* 18, 55.18.

5. I take this to be the implication of his statements in *Ep.* 55.11, 65, 67.6, 72.2. The Donatist applied this to the baptism conferred by a bishop dead in sin.

6. See, among other discussions, *Ep.* 69.10-11, 73.7, 25, 74.4-6,11, 75.9-16, 25. *De unitate ecc. cath.* 11.

7. *Bapt.* 5.12.14-5.15.18; *Con. litt. Pet.* 2.37.87-88.

8. *Con. ep. Parm.* 2.10.22; *Con. litt. Pet.* 1.9.10, 2.7.15-16.

9. *Con. ep. Parm.* 2.6.11; *Bapt.* 2.11.24, 3.14.19-3.15-20, 4.11.17, 6.25.47, 7.47.12; *Con. litt. Pet.* 2.5.11, 2.6.13, 2.51.118.

10. *Con. ep. Parm.* 2.11.23-24. The parallel is the Spirit's speaking through the disciples during trials.

11. The Donatists were relying on Cyprian; see the texts cited in note 6 above.

12. *Bapt.* 1.11.15-1.12.20. Cyprian used his parable to a similar effect in *De oratione dominica* 23.

13. Cyprian's *Epistula* 69,17 offers foundation for Augustine's interpretation.

14. Ibid., 2.6.7-9, 2.10.15. Augustine argues that if communion with known sinners corrupts the sanctity of the church and renders its ministry ineffective, the church perished in the time of Cyprian through his communion with these former schismatics and heretics whose sins the Donatists would judge unforgiven because they had never been truly and properly baptized.

15. Ibid., 2.11.16. See Cyprian's *Epistula* 73.23.

16. Ibid., 2.13.18-2.14.19.

17. Ibid., 2.13.18-2.14.19. Note that Augustine does not assert his interpretation of Cyprian's letter to Jubian as true, but uses it as an argument against the Donatists. In *Bapt.* 1.12.18 he asserts, in passing, that conversion to unity cannot cleanse without baptism.

18. Cyprian made such an argument for the efficacy of prayer offered in unity: *Epistula* 11.3, *De unitate ecc. cath.* 12; *De oratione dominica* 8.

19. Ibid., 3.4.6. The discussion continues through 5.17.23.

20. Ibid., 3.13.18. In the following section, Augustine discussed the obstacle to salvation posed by heretical faith, inside or outside the visible Catholic church. Again he concluded that once this error is corrected, the bond of peace and the excellence of charity make baptism and all other gifts salvific.

21. Ibid., 3.16.21.

22. See especially *De unitate ecc. cath.* 4-5. In *Epistula* 68 one sees the common responsibility for the church as work.

23. Canticle 6.8.

24. Ibid., 3.17.22.

25. Ibid., 3.18.23. This point is made again in 3.19.26.

26. Ibid., 3.19.26.

27. Irrevocable remission of sins can be attained only through baptism within the unity of the church. Ibid., 5.8.9.

28. Ibid., 5.2.2-5.4.4.

29. Later in the treatise he asserted that charity covers the sins of those in the unity of the church who fail to keep all of the commandments, Ibid., 6.24.45.

30. Ibid., 5.21.29.

31. Ibid., 6.3.5-6.5.7.

32. See, for example, *De unico baptismo,* 13.22, 15.26 and *Epistula* 93, 10.36.40.

33. *Con. Cres.* 2.12.15-2.15.18.

34. *Bapt.* 6.24.45. He used Luke 6.37 and Matthew 6.14-15.

35. *Epistula* 98, 5.

36. The reference recurs in *Con. Cresc.* 2.33.41, 2.35.45.

AUGUSTINE'S ECCLESIOLOGY REVISITED

MICHAEL A. FAHEY, S.J.

In 1954 on the occasion of the 1600th anniversary of Augustine of Hippo's birth, Ernest Benz, Marburg professor of ecclesiastical history, addressed the learned *Akademie der Wissenschaft und der Literatur* to expatiate on Augustine's theory of Church.[1] Likewise, hardly any Oxford Patristic Congress goes by without some communication on Augustine's ecclesiology. Hence at this Sedecentennial celebration commemorating Augustine's Christian initiation it is not surprising that someone would want to propose a modest overview about how most recent scholars are assessing his doctrine of Church. And doubtless in 2030, as those who will follow us gather to hail the 1600th anniversary of his death, there will be scheduled a report on this same matter. Whether Augustine himself would have been all that sympathetic to such analyses is not self-evident since, as with other theologians up to Thomas Aquinas and beyond, separate theological treatises *de natura ecclesiae sanctae* were not envisaged.

In preparing this overview I have noted some 36 publications (not that I have read them all with the same level of attentiveness) stretching from the years 1861 to 1979. I think I have learned as much about our collective shortcomings, our flawed methodologies, and shifting horizons as I have about Augustine's views of Church. But these insights have hermeneutical significance and serve as cautionary signals to our investigations of Augustine's thought.

The earliest studies, such as those published by H. Schmidt (1861), H. Reuter (1887), Thomas Specht (1892), and Pierre Battifol (1920) betray notable confessional prejudices and appear more as apologetical treatises that would have Augustine say what we would like him to have said in support of our confessional allegiances.[2] The earliest works in this time-frame are far from ecumenical documents and betray the worst of isolationist theologizing. Historical-critical method, which had already impacted Scriptural studies, had scarcely touched this patristic research. Also notably lacking in these first assessments is the kind of philological analysis such as developed by the Nijmegen school of Christine Mohrman. Perhaps following the example of F.C. Baur and Adolph von Harnack persons gave more attention to their philosophical and doctrinal theses than to the mass of Augustine's texts themselves.

In 1933 two Roman Catholic studies treating Augustine's ecclesiology appeared: one reflected familiar weaknesses, another became a harbinger of new sensitivities. The Louvain Jesuit theologian, Emile Mersch, in what would become, at least in Catholic circles, an influential study, *Le corps mystique du Christ: Etudes de théologie historique* (1933), cited a number of Augustine's texts to show the interdependence of Christology and ecclesiology.[3] His weakness was his proclivity for blurring categories from Scripture, patristics, and modern Catholicism, especially in not differentiating *verum corpus Christi* from *corpus Christi mysticum.* (Later, another francophone theologian, Henri de Lubac, corrected his somewhat hasty conclusions, all the while recognizing and appreciating Mersch's importance in having reintroduced "body-of-Christ" ecclesiology). Mersch's work, for all its faults, helped to diminish the importance among Catholics of the Counter-Reformation ecclesiology dominated by Robert Bellarmine, and his book prepared for new emphases to be picked up ten years later in the encyclical *Mystici corporis Christi* written for Pius XII by Sebastian Tromp. The year 1933 also saw a more nuanced study by Fritz Hofmann, one of Karl Adam's protégés, entitled *Der Kirchenbegriff des hl. Augustinus in seinen Grundlagen und in seiner Entwicklung.*[4] Hofmann outlined Augustine's ecclesiology in relationship to his spiritual odyssey. He identified various stages in its articulation: first, a movement by the platonizing rhetorician in search of wisdom and theory to a choice for Christian faith; second, especially in his struggle against Manichaeism, Augustine's recognition of the need for dogmatic authority "Ego vero Evangelio non crederem ..."; thirdly, not only because of his struggle with Donatists, Hofmann argues, but more basically because of his growing spiritual maturity and the demands of preaching, there emerged a deeper appreciation for the inter-relatedness of the Holy Spirit and divine grace to the Church. More and more the Church became the *catholica,* a visible society with a sacramental function; Augustine, wrote Hofmann, came to recognize the insufficiency of local councils to settle highly involved disciplinary and doctrinal issues, and so he concluded that confirmatory support from the apostolic Church of Rome was appropriate. Later in Augustine's anti-Pelagian struggles he refined his understanding of tradition and the relationship between Christ's sovereign grace and the Church (the need to belong to the Body of Christ in order to live in the Spirit of Christ). Finally, toward the end of his life he reflected more explicitly on the relationship of Church and State.

The work of Frederik van der Meer, *Augustine de zielzorger* (1949), which stressed the importance of Augustine's homilies and sermons corrected what had been an exaggerated stress on the *City of God* and the *Confessions* and gave centrality to research on his episcopal ministry.[5] Without van der Meer's work, later important studies such as those of Lamirande and Borgomeo might never have been conceived.

In 1954 at the University of Munich, under the direction of Professor G. Soehngen and with supporting encouragement from Professor Romano Guardini, there appeared an "oeuvre de jeunesse," a doctoral dissertation by a Bavarian priest named Joseph Ratzinger.[6] Though it was not seen as blazing totally new frontiers it at first received generally favourable reception by Catholic scholars such as Henri Rondet and Yves Congar as further proof that old-style liberal Protestant assessments such as those of Reuter and Harnack were now a thing of the past. Ratzinger focussed his analysis of Augustine's ecclesiology around two biblical concepts: "People of God" and "House of God," which, although themselves not the central categories for Augustine's exposition, are nonetheless useful focal points for unifying what he had to say about the Church as the Body of Christ. Ratzinger continued the work of Hofmann and further stressed the unity of the two orders or, more precisely, the unity of the two levels of reality: *sensibilis* and *intelligibilis, homo exterior,* and *homo interior.* But in 1970 Ratzinger's work was criticized rather strongly in a doctoral dissertation prepared at the Jesuit theological faculty of St. Georgen, Frankfurt, by Walter Simonis on *Ecclesia Visibilis et Invisibilis* in the ecclesiology and sacramental theology of African theology from Cyprian to Augustine.[7] Simonis perceived the originality and independence of Augustine vis-à-vis his African predecessors quite differently from Ratzinger; he was also skeptical about the presumed centrality of Platonic or Neo-platonic thought forms on Augustine's understanding of the visibility and invisibility of the Church.

Two florilegia of Augustine's texts on the Church appeared in the mid-fifties, Hans Urs von Balthasar's *Augustinus: Das Antlitz der Kirche* (1955) followed in short order by its French edition sponsored by Congar, *Le visage de l'Eglise.*[8] While not systematic or synthetic in its presentation, von Balthasar's collection did make possible broader familiarity with the complexity and variety of Augustine's attitudes toward the Church. An expatriate Hungarian, Stanislaus Grabowski published *The Church: An Introduction to the Theology of Augustine* (1957) which contains many snippets from Augustine's writings but which is more a synopsis of Grabowski's own personal theology than an exposé of Augustine.[9]

It is particularly satisfying in the context of this Canada-based symposium to note the singular achievements of the Ottawa historical theologian, Emilien Lamirande, whose 1963 work *L'Eglise céleste selon saint Augustin,* soon to be followed in 1969 and 1973 by companion volumes as well as a comprehensive critical bibliography covering a century and a half of studies on Augustine's ecclesiology, from 1809 to 1954.[10] Lamirande stated categorically that Augustine's ecclesiology is far from being a perfectly unified synthesis and noted that its very pluralism and complexity are what give it its appeal. He stressed four guiding principles in Augustine's ecclesiology: (1) the Church in its present reality is formed essentially of two zones, one pertaining to the earth, the other to heaven; one composed of human beings, the other of angels; (2) in its final and total eschatological state the two zones of the Church now separated will be unified in a common *consortium aeternitatis;* (3) one part of the Church is the angelic Church now in glory; (4) another part of the Church is made up of the pilgrim people. All this implies that the Reign of God has not only a future not-yet-realized dimension, but enjoys even now a present embodiment in the Church. Lamirande helped my generation to appreciate Augustine's eagerness (to us at first somewhat disconcerting) to speak of *ecclesia ab Abraham* and even *ecclesia ab Abel.* Just at the time when New Testament studies were stressing more and more the differentiation of the kingdom of God and the Church we were seeing in Augustine that they were distinct but not separate.

After Lamirande's volume on the heavenly Church it was not surprising that by 1972 it would be complemented by a study of *ecclesia quae nunc est* or *ecclesia hujus temporis.* The Italian patristic scholar Pasquale Borgomeo, writing in French, does that in his volume *L'Eglise de ce temps dans la prédication de saint Augustin.*[11] He restricts himself exclusively (and given the value of Augustine's letters one might say regrettably) to the sermons of the Bishop of Hippo. The investigation is not of the "earthly Church" but of a Church existing in time, already heavenly on earth, of a kingdom of heaven in its present condition of Church confronted with the ambivalence of the present where time and eternity combine to produce history. For Augustine, the whole Church is heavenly because of its origin, because of a number of its citizens (the angels), and because of its ultimate goal. Part of this heavenly Church is on pilgrimage, and it is impossible to speak of the heavenly Church without considering the earthly part. In my judgement I would award this volume the highest marks amid all those written on Augustine's ecclesiology in the last forty years. No one researching Augustine's ecclesiology should go without consulting his index (p. 422) which lists Augustine's various metaphors and adjectives used to describe the Church. There are numerous insights into matters such as the relationship of the Church of this time with both Israel (as distinguished from the Jews) and with the Gentiles (as distinguished from the pagans). The Church is an expression of the mystery of hope; the virtue of *patientia* is seen as adherence to belief in the not-yet-realized eschatological form of the Church. Catholicity, Borgomeo writes, is the obvious sign of the Church's victory; although catholicity is seen as a geographical note (*tota terrarum orbe diffus*) and a polemical one (*non in Africa sola*) it is nowhere at home as befits the pilgrim. The secret of the Church's unity is rooted in its oneness with the Body of Christ. Hence one must reflect on the relationship between Head and Body, on the Church as bride (*sponsa,* but also *coniux* and even *matrona*) and on the demands of true love (*caritas/unitas*). Of course the Church of this time is also *corpus Christi mixtum in area.* The Church is a *permixtio,* with saints and sinners in its midst, as is supported by the evangelical parables of the fish net and the mixture of the wheat and the tares. There is also a useful discussion in this connection on the important distinction about how one can be *in ecclesia* without ultimately being *ecclesia in.* Church can denote, therefore, the empirical, universal society with its ordained clergy, its sacraments, its celebrations, the total field of wheat and tares, or it can denote the small number of persons in the society who are in truth being made holy by God (the wheat alone), wheat that is growing but sure of its forthcoming harvesting. Lamirande's generally favourable review of this book notes that it is not Borgomeo's fault if themes such as institution and spirit, liberty and authority, even the role of the Holy Spirit (except in the context of Christology) are not emphasized. But Lamirande criticizes Borgomeo's book for not sufficiently showing Augustine's conviction that the Church of this time must be concerned about its mission, about the dignity and duties of its members as *uncti, christi,* and about its institutions, in sum, what we might describe today as concern for orthopraxis.

The book by Borgomeo has begun to have wider impact, as is witnessed by its creative application in the article by Louvain professor T. J. van Bavel, translated into English as: "What Kind of Church Do You Want? The Breadth of Augustine's Ecclesiology."[12]

In 1978 the first of several projected volumes on Augustine's ecclesiology was published by Attilio Giacobbi, professor of the history of Canon Law at the Lateran University in Rome.[13] The author, a canonist *in utroque jure,* is neither a patristic scholar nor an expert in Augustinian studies. But he is part of that increasing number of scholars who are asking new questions of ancient texts, persons such as philologists, philosophers, archaeologists, liturgists, biblicists, historians. Giacobbi plans a second volume which will describe the structures of that communion and a third volume that will treat of the doctrine and praxis needed to safeguard that communion. Thus, his volume one is an unfinished work. While it is laudable that Giacobbi has tried to read Augustine to see what he might have to say in terms of modern interest in a theology of *communio,* still there does seem to be reversion to an earlier trait of using Augustine to consecrate one's contemporary confessional preoccupations. Perhaps we shall have to wait for the completion of the final two volumes before drawing a firm conclusion.

What is encouraging, however, is that among the most recent short works I was able to track down by the Spaniard Victorino Capanaga and the Yugoslavian Djuro Puskaric, the focus is on the trinitarian, mystery dimension of Augustine's view of the Church rather than on any apologetic, institutional preoccupation.[14]

CONCLUSION

The more we look at Augustine's understanding of *ecclesia* or *catholica* the more we realize the complex and complementary views that existed side by side. For him Church was not only an institution but it was the Christ-event; not only a sociological datum, but the Body of Christ; not only the Church in time and space, but was part of the Reign of God in heaven; it was the Church on earth but the City of God; the Church of the here and now but the Church of the eschatological community; Church pure and holy, but Church imperfect and sinful.[15] As van Bavel has noted, the phrase "to be in the Church" is for Augustine a multi-layered reality. His firm conviction that the reality called Church was not something restricted to a little part of Africa but was in fact *ecclesia toto orbe diffusa.* For him *catholica* meant *universa,* and *ecclesia* meant *catholica.* At the same time Augustine distinguished between *ecclesia qualis nunc est* and *ecclesia quae futura est.* The church that corresponds to Eph 5.27 ("ut exhiberet ipse [Christus] gloriosam ecclesiam non habentem maculam aut rugam aut aliquid eiusmodi sed ut sit sancta et inmaculata"). The term *ecclesia* in Augustine's thought is closer to our words *communio, communitas, populus, genus, societas.*

Augustine's interest is predominantly in the worldwide Church taken as a unified entity. In my own research on the perception of the notion "sister churches" (*ecclesiae sorores*) in pre-Nicene Christianity, a notion that enhances the role and dignity of the local church with relative autocephaly, a characteristic that I found very alive in Cyprian's Church, I have not had much success yet in finding this notion strongly affirmed in Augustine. I am interested in pursuing the lines of research begun by Ludwig von Hertling in connection with the first three centuries in which he traces the notion of *communio.* There are here and there hints at this perspective in Augustine, as when he writes in Letters 87.5 and 43.9.25 about the need for a local church to remain in *communicatio* or in *communio* with apostolic churches (and not simply the apostolic church of Rome) if it wishes to remain the Church of Christ. What has occurred to me in the course of this symposium is that perhaps we have to see it embodied less in what Augustine says about the local independent Catholic Church (which would give him difficulty in dealing with the Donatists) but rather in the African conciliar legislation formulated in the eleven councils that took place between AD 393 and 407 to which he and his African colleagues deferred in resolving disciplinary and doctrinal tensions.

It is my hope that as the Christian churches try to resolve their present differences and mutual mistrust of their doctrines and practices, we shall be better able to read the multivalent ecclesiological texts of Augustine, not as confirmation of what we are doing as particular embodiments of Church, but rather as invitations to become what we have not yet realized in our own particular *ecclesia hujus temporis.*

NOTES

1. Ernst Benz, "Augustinus Lehre von der Kirche. Zum 1600 jährigen Geburtstag Augustins am 13. November 1954," *Akademie der Wissenschaft und der Literatur,* 1954, 17-63.

2. H. Schmidt, "Des Augustinus Lehre von der Kirche," *Jahrbücher für deutsche Theologie* 6 (1861), 197-255; H. Reuter, *Augustinische Studien* (Gotha: 1887, reprinted Aalen: 1966); Thomas Specht, *Die Lehre von der Kirche nach dem hl. Augustinus* (Paderborn: F. Schönongh, 1892).

3. Emile Mersch, *Le corps mystique du Christ: Etudes de théologie historique* 2 vols. (Louvain: Museum Lessianum, 1933). English translation: *The Whole Christ: The Historical Development of the Doctrine of the Mystical Body* (Milwaukee: Bruce, 1938).

4. Fritz Hofmann, *Der Kirchenbegriff des hl. Augustinus in seinen Grundlagen und in seiner Entwicklung* (Munich: Kaiser, 1933).

5. Frederik van der Meer, *Augustine de zielzorger,* 1949. English translation: *Augustine the Bishop: The Life and Work of a Father of the Church* (New York: Sheed and Ward, 1962).

6. Joseph Ratzinger, *Volk und Haus Gottes in Augustins Lehre von der Kirche* (Munich: Zink, 1954). See also his "Die Kirche in der Frömmigkeit des heiligen Augustinus," in *Sentire Ecclesiam: Festschrift für Hugo Rahner* (Freiburg: Herder, 1961), 152-74, reprinted in Ratzinger's *Das Neue Volk Gottes* (Düsseldorf: Patmos, 1969, 24-48).

7. Walter Simonis, *Ecclesia visibilis et invisibilis: Untersuchungen zur Ekklesiologie und Sakramentenlehre in der afrikanischen Tradition von Cyprian bis Augustinus* (Frankfurt: J. Knecht, 1970).

8. Hans Urs von Balthasar, *Augustinus: Das Antlitz der Kirche: Auswahl und Uebertragung* (Einsiedeln: Benziger, 1955). French translation: *Le visage de l'Eglise: textes choisis et présentés.* Unam Sanctam no. 31 (Paris: Cerf, 1958).

9. Stanislaus Grabowski, *The Church: An Introduction to the Theology of Augustine* (St. Louis: B. Herder, 1957).

10. Emilien Lamirande, *L'Eglise céleste selon Saint Augustin* (Paris: *Etudes augustiniennes,* 1963). See also his *Etudes sur l'ecclésiologie de saint Augustin* (Ottawa: Editions universitaires, 1969), and *La situation ecclésiologique des Donastistes d'après saint Augustin. Contribution à l'histoire doctrinale de l'oecuménisme* (Ottawa: Editions universitaires, 1972).

11. Pasquale Borgomeo, *L'Eglise de ce temps dans la prédication de saint Augustin* (Paris: Etudes Augustiniennes, 1972). See on this book the reviews by Lamirande in *Augustinian Studies* 5 (1974), 237-48; and by D. Olivier in *Revue des études augustiniennes* 19 (1973), 389.

12. Tarsicius J. van Bavel, "What Kind of Church Do You Want? The Breadth of Augustine's Ecclesiology?" *Louvain Studies* 7 (1979), 147-71. The Dutch original appeared in *Tijdschrift voor Theologie* 16 (1976), 355-75.

13. Attilio Giacobbi, *La chiesa in S. Agostino*, vol. 1: *Mistero de communione* (Rome: Citta Nuova Editrice, 1978).

14. Victorino Capanaga, "El misterio de la Iglesia: Textos y comentarios agustinanos," *Augustinus* 23 (1978), 249-58; Djuro Puskaris, "La Chiesa e il mistero trinitario nella predicazione de s. Agostino," *Augustinianum* 19 (1979), 487-506.

15. A number of other important studies on Augustine's ecclesiology appeared during the period covered in this essay but which I have not been able to discuss. The titles are given here in chronological order: Gavino Spanedda, *Il mistero della Chiesa nel pensiero di Sant'Agostino* (Sassari: La Casa, 1944); Gérard Philips, "L'Influence du Christ-chef sur son corps mystique suivant saint Augustin," *Augustinus Magister* (Paris: Etudes Augustiniennes, 1954), 805-15; Denis Faul, "Sinners in the Holy Church: A Problem in the Ecclesiology of St. Augustine," (Oxford Patristic Congress, 1963), *Studia Patristica* vol. 9, = *Texte und Untersuchungen* vol. 94; Remi Crespin, *Ministère et sainteté: Pastorale du clergé et solution de la crise donatiste dans la vie et la doctrine de saint Augustin* (Paris: Cerf, 1965); Hugo Rahner, *Symbole der Kirche: Die Ekklesiologie der Vater* (Salzburg: Müller, 1964); Michel Réveillaud, "Le Christ-Homme, tête de l'Eglise: Etude d'ecclésiologie selon les Enarrationes in Psalmos d'Augustin," *Recherches augustiniennes* 5 (1968), 67-84; Salvador Vergés, *La Iglesia esposa de Christo: La incarnación del Verbo y la Iglesia en san Augustin* (Barcelona: Balnes, 1969); Yves Congar, *L'Eglise de saint Augustin à l'époque moderne* (Paris: Cerf, 1970), 11-24; Rafael Palmero Ramos, *"Ecclesia Mater" en san Augustin: teología de la imagen en los escritos antidonatistas* (Madrid: Ediciones Cristianidad, 1970); Jeremy D. Adams, *The Populus of Augustine and Jerome: A Study in the Patristic Sense of Community* (New Haven: Yale University, 1971); Robert F. Evans, *One and Holy: The Church in Latin Patristic Thought* (London: SPCK, 1972); Michele Pellegrino, "La Chiesa in S. Agostino, istitutione o misterio?" in: *Chiesa e salvezza: Atti della Settimana Agostiniana Parese, 5, Pavia, 29 aprile – 6 maggio 1973* (Pavia: P.P. Agostiniana, 1975); Segundo Folgado Flórez, *Dinamismo catolico de la Iglesia en San Augustin* (Madrid: Monasterio de El Escorial, 1977); Andrés Manrique, "La Iglesia como comunión. Breve florilegio patrístico," *La Ciudad de Dios* 190 (1977), 3-25.

THE STUDY OF AUGUSTINE'S CHRISTOLOGY IN THE TWENTIETH CENTURY

JOANNE MCWILLIAM

The study of Augustine has so mushroomed in the twentieth century that Isidore's dictum must be extended: No one can now safely say that she or he has read all that has been written about even one aspect of Augustine's thought. But such a claim (which I do not make) would be more plausible in the area of Augustine's christology than in almost any other; examination of Augustine's understanding of Christ has been relatively neglected.[1]

There are, in my view, three principle reasons for this, two originating with Augustine himself, and the third with the contexts of Augustinian studies until recently. The Jesus of the synoptic gospels was not the focus either of Augustine's various controversial writings or of his non-polemical treatises.[2] To say that Augustine devoted no particular work to christology is not to say that Christ was unimportant to him, but that his writing on Christ was occasional or episodic – a mosaic composed over at least a quarter of a century – and consequently harder to control than other aspects of his thought. Anyone who talks of "the Christ" of Augustine does not do justice to the shifts evidenced in the texts – there are in fact several Christs in Augustine's writings. He used many christological models, and even in his later years, when a more or less fixed model appeared, incoherencies remained.

Those sensitive to these many faces of Augustine's Christ have tended to steer clear of a vexed and non-compelling question. "Non-compelling" because patristic christological research in general has been largely centred on Chalcedon, its preliminaries and aftermath. Augustine rarely discussed in a sustained manner the questions which gave urgency to the controversies preceding Chalcedon, and so he contributed only indirectly to their settlement. In the vast field of patristic christology there have been more promising furrows to plough. Not only was the examination of Augustine's understanding of Christ apparently unrewarding, it was – in some circles at least – a vexed question. The modernist battles of the first decades of this century and the *assumptus homo* controversy, which to some degree overlapped them, alerted those concerned with the maintenance of the Cyrillian or neochalcedonian tradition to the deviations from that tradition in some of the Augustinian christological models. The resultant nervousness tended to restrict such earlier studies as there were to (frequently polemical) defences of Augustine's christological orthodoxy, with orthodoxy interpreted in a neochalcedonian sense. About 1954 (the date cannot be too firmly set) a broadening to examinations (often pious in tone) of other christological themes can be observed. In recent years the prevailing trend has been away from the defensive and the pious, but traces of these older approaches still linger.

This essay will follow interpretations of Augustine's christology from the early part of the century to the 1980s. I have selected what I considered to be typical writings on certain themes considered – in the past at least – to be the most significant. Only a few will be examined; their choice was personal and made somewhat arbitrarily by the limitations of space. Others might have chosen differently. I shall not – with one or two exceptions – treat general works on Augustine which include chapters on his understanding of Christ. An extensive (but not exhaustive) bibliography is appended.

REVISION AND REACTION

The vitality and correctness of Augustine's understanding of Christ was challenged as early as 1873 by Dorner in his influential *History of the Development of the Doctrine of the Person of Christ.*[3] Probably the most serious of his specific accusations were those of implicit doceticism – that Augustine's refusal to attribute *concupiscientia* of any kind to Christ necessarily led to the denial of the freedom of his human will and the reality of his human development – and the claim that for Augustine the significance of Christ's death was as a ransom paid to the devil. Dorner was followed by Harnack in 1889, Loofs in 1897, and Scheel in 1901,[4] who among them made the following points concerning Augustine's christology: (1) The *Confessions* could not be taken as an historically accurate account of Augustine's conversion. Contrary to his testimony there, his attitude to Christ prior to 386 had not been a religious one; he had been converted first to Neoplatonism, then to the church, and only after that to Christ. (2) In his early years as a Christian Augustine had been at one point a modalist, at another a subordinationist, and his Photinianism had lasted longer than he had admitted. (3) His interest was in the cosmological role of Christ, not the historical, and his understanding of salvation was so intellectual that Christ's death was relatively unimportant to him. (4) Harnack and Scheel in particular said that Augustine had so sharply distinguished the human and the divine in Christ that there was no real communication of idioms, and that his notion of the christological union was not the Cyrillian hypostatic union, but a union by grace.

The revisionists succeeded in setting the agenda, and their points were taken up systematically by the defenders of the traditional reading of Augustine's christology. Of these, the writings of Portalie and van Crombrugghe were not only typical and important but set the pattern for decades.[5]

Portalie insisted that Christ was central to Augustine's theology, religion, and understanding of history. Rejecting the charge of continuing Photinianism, he maintained that by the time the first book of *De libero arbitrio* was written (388) Augustine had "L'idée la plus catholique de Fils de Dieu engendré égal à son Peré."[6] He accused "les critiques protestants" of attempting "arracher [Augustin] à l'orthodoxie et le rejeter tantôt dans le docetisme, tantot dans le nestorianisme."[7] Portalie insisted that "Augustin affirme la réalité de la nature humaine du Christ"[8] and taught "l'union du Verbe et de l'humanité ... en parfaite harmonie avec saint Cyrille d'Alexandrie."[9] The person of Christ "est celle de Verbe ... en se l' [Christ] appropriant par une communication de sa personalité."[10] Christ's mediatorial role, in Augustine's eyes, has two aspects – to appease God and to convert humankind; the first a divine work, the second a human. The revisionists, Portalie continued, themselves denied the divinity of Christ and so understood his salvific role as only moral and exemplary. "[L]es nouveaux nestoriens ... ont osé attribuer à Augustin leur conception rationaliste."[11] "Tous les théologiens catholiques, au contraire, ayant reconnu dans ses ecrits le veritable Homme-Dieu, y trouvent également ... l'*expiation* de nos peches sur la croix par *une victime* innocente *substituée* à l'humanite coupable."[12] This expiation of sin is a deliverance from the devil. "[Augustin] affirme que le sang du Christ a été le prix de notre rachat; il parle de piège tendu au démon sur la croix.... Mais si l'on examine le sens de ces images, il est absolument évident que cette mise en scène n'est qu'une façon de dramatiser la défaite du démon et notre déliverance."[13] Portalie's article dealt with virtually every aspect of Augustine's christology and remained the definitive word for the "traditionalists" for a least half a century.

Van Crombrugghe began with the reality of Augustine's conversion to Christianity in 386. He agreed that for Augustine, as for many others, Neoplatonism was the "vestibule" to Christianity, but he repudiated as "unacceptable" the resultant effects that Harnack et al. saw in Augustine's christology – that he "réduit l'humanité du Christ à la fonction de forme révélatrice du Verbe" and, even after repudiating Manichaeism, maintained "l'identification du *cosmos noetos* avec le Verbe."[14] Augustine was not, as Scheel and others claimed, a docetist. "[P]our le saint Docteur, le Verbe s'est uni une nature humaine réelle et ... les restrictions du docetisme étaient loin de sa pensée."[15] Nor was Augustine a precursor of Nestorius ("[O]n aurait mauvaise grace à insister sur quelques expressions plus ou moins heureuses, propres à cette epoque, où le langage théologique était encore en voie de formation").[16] On the basis of *De Trinitate* 2.10, van Crombrugghe argued, it is clear that Augustine understood Christ to be "un être avec le Verbe."[17] Van Crombrugghe was equally firm in his assertion (against Dorner and Harnack) that, despite the ontological union, Christ retained the freedom of his human will.

While Augustine shared with Athanasius and others the realistic-mystical understanding of salvation in which "l'oeuvre rédemptrice est une grande partie accomplie par le fait historique de l'Incarnation même,"[18] he shifted the weight of Christ's redemptive work to his death. " 'Christus mortalis mortales morte, morte mortuos liberavit' ... est devenue predominante au point d'influencer toute la sotériologie augustinienne."[19] With Portalie, van Crombrugghe insisted that Augustine understood Christ's death as a substitutionary and expiatory sacrifice. The material for Anselm's theology is to be found in Augustine. Van Crombrugghe was more ready than others to admit that some of Augustine's writings seemed to recognize certain rights of the devil, but this phraseology was used "uniquement pour signifier que la servitude du genre humain ne constitue pas une injustice à l'égard de celui-ci."[20]

THE PERSON OF CHRIST

Many of the debated areas of Augustine's christology were those which had been at issue in the modernist controversy generally.[21] Among these was the character – the "mechanics," as it were – of the christological union. The "*assumptus homo*" debate of the 1920s and 1930s brought Augustine's terminology to general attention, and it was acknowledged that, while "*assumptus homo*" or "*susceptus homo*" were not the only terms he used to refer to Christ, they were, in the early years particularly, the most common.[22] The question was – and is – what understanding lay behind Augustine's use of the term. Portalie, it will be recalled, had insisted that it was Cyrillian,[23] and his position was adopted by many.

In 1954 Van Bavel brought out the first book on Augustine's christology since Scheel's.[24] Although its focus was the psychology of Christ (this aspect will be discussed later), Van Bavel undertook to answer the points raised by Scheel and the other revisionists of the early part of the century. He dealt with Augustine's understanding of the christological union chronologically and in the contexts of the controversies which absorbed so much of his attention. Taking the texts in four states: 386-391, 394-397, 397-400, after 400, Van Bavel recalled the absence of the fixed terminology of the mid-fifth century, but said that in the earliest period Augustine had arrived at the notion that "La Sagesse, immuable et consubstantielle au Père, a pris une nature humain complète" and that "[L]a susception de cette homme par Dieu est tout à fait différente de celle des autres saints et sages."[25]

Looking at the texts of the second period, Van Bavel turned his attention to Augustine's use of the world *persona* and found "... neque praepotentia et singularitate susceptionis ad habendam naturaliter et agendam personam sapientiai, sicut ipse mediator unum ipsua suscipiente sapientia."[26] Other texts from the same period supported Van Bavel's conclusion that "saint Augustin était fortement convaincu de l'unité de sujet dans le Christ."[27] In the period 397-400, Van Bavel found convincing the sentence in *De agone christiano,* "Aliud est enim sapientem tantum fieri per sapientiam Dei, et aliud personam sustinere sapientiae Dei."[28] Recognizing the fluidity of Augustine's use of "person" before 400, he examined the many metaphors Augustine used to describe the christological union and recognized that ultimately he saw it as a union by grace. Nevertheless Van Bavel termed Augustine's understanding of the christological union "hypostatic," although he nowhere claimed that it was

Cyrillian. He adamantly rejected Scheel's charges of Augustinian Nestorianism and adoptionism and gave several instances of Augustine's use of the communication of idioms.

Not all agreed that the correct questions were being put to Augustine's writings. Babcock (in a preliminary overview in his 1972 study of Augustine's christology) remarked that "To approach Augustine through the concepts of *natura* and *persona* is not irrelevant to his doctrine.... [But] it inevitably tends to give more weight to these terms than Augustine did himself, to reduce the study of his Christology to the study of intimations of Chalcedon in his writings."[29] Augustine, in Babcock's eyes, was less interested in "adequately defining the union of Godhead and manhood in one person than ... [in understanding] Christ as God acting in our situation and for our redemption."[30] To deal with the tension of divine and human "Augustine modifies ... the expressions of weakness and suffering, either by qualifying the sense in which they are to be applied to God or by qualifying their meaning as applied to God."[31] Unlike the others, Augustine did not safeguard Christ's divinity by separating it from his human experience, but "by modifying the meaning of that experience."[32]

Geerlings (1978) undertook to lay the dogmatic groundwork for his study of Augustine's use of *Christum exemplum.* He, like Van Bavel, took issue with Scheel and the other revisionists, drawing attention to the use Augustine made of the tradition of "Logos speculation" and the analogy of human speech. "Mit Hilfe dieser Wortanalogie kann Augustin nun die stoische Logos-spekulation für die Christologie fruchtbar machen."[33] Geerlings rejected O'Connell's Antiochene reading of the early Augustine, attaching importance to Augustine's frequent comparison of the christological union to that of the human soul and body, a unity in which each constituent retains its identity. He argued not only that by 405 Augustine was preaching Chalcedonian christology, without its terminology, but that "vor ihm innerhalb der lateinischen Kirche niemand die Deutung der hypostatisschen Union vom anthropologischen Zwei-Natura-Schema her vorgenommen hat."[34]

Drobner in a recent (1986) book has put Augustine's use of the word *persona* under close scrutiny.[35] As early as 392, when he began his *Enarrationes in Psalmos,* Augustine had to decide who was the subject of predication, and this exercise was a factor – an important factor in Drobner's eyes – in the development of the dogmatic formula, *una persona.* Like

Theodore of Mopsuestia ("Das Beispiel Theodors zeigt aber gut, dass derselbe Weg auch im Osten unabhangig gegangen wurde"[36]), Augustine went from the grammatical and exegetical consideration of person to the metaphysical and theological, and this terminological development and precision Drobner judged to have been Augustine's most important contribution to christology.

AUGUSTINE, PHOTINIAN?

The question of the relation between Augustine's Neoplatonism and his Christianity was brought to a boil again by the publication in 1918 of Alfaric's *L'evolution intellectuelle de saint Augustin.*[37] Alfaric's contention was that Augustine's conversion in 386 had indeed been to Neoplatonism and that his Christianity was adapted to fit that philosophy. Much was written on both sides of the general question, but I shall refer to the discussion only as it touched on Augustine's christology. Alfaric's argument was that Augustine's adherence to Christ followed that to Neoplatonism and that, consequently, he was unable, for several years at least, to believe in the Incarnation. One reaction was that of Boyer, who found Augustine's admission of Photinianism (*Conf.* 7.19,25) surprising and surmised that, despite Monica and Ambrose, he had not been properly taught, that he interpreted the Johannine and credal phrases "selon l'idée qu'il se faisait de l'Incarnation et qu'il regardait comme la seule possible."[38]

Courcelle, in a series of writings, took another tack. The admission of Photinianism comes in the *Confessions* in the context of reading the Neoplatonic books and the key lies there. Courcelle's thesis was that Augustine was convinced by Porphyry's *Philosophy of Oracles* and "pour ... déloger [Augustin] de sa position 'photinienne' ... Simplicien lui enseigne longuement la doctrine catholique du Dieu incarné."[39] Simplician's correction was before Augustine's baptism, before even his months at Cassiciacum – Augustine was therefore never simultaneously a Christian and a Photinian.

Marrou's interpretation of the *Confessions* passage was more open to the possibility of the Photinianism surviving longer, of Augustine being somewhat slower than he indicated to work out the identity of Christ and the Word of God: "Augustin semble bien plutôt donner son adhésion à l'Incarnation ... tout en refusant a l'expliquer."[40] Polman (1961) described the gradual changes in Augustine's thinking from the

"Incarnation as precept and example" to "a philosophical interpretation of the Word" and finally to "a more scriptural interpretation, in which the Word was considered as the revelation of the Father." He located the turning point between the second and third stages in 397.[41] Solignac, in 1962, accepted Augustine's timing, questioning, however, whether he did indeed owe his Photinian views to Porphyry. Solignac pointed out that Porphyry would not have attributed "the excellence of Christ's humanity to his virginal birth" (*Conf.* 7.19), and that Augustine in fact repudiated this position in 396 (*De agone christiano* 22.22).[42]

O'Connell, in 1967, took the opposite position. He suggested that, far from Augustine's error being cleared up by Simplician in Milan, it took him "some years to come to a better (though imperfect) settlement of the issue," that in fact his Photinianism became more accented after his conversion, was at its peak ca. 390 and condemned for the first time in the *Confessions.*[43] In a book published the following year, O'Connell reiterated his position, suggesting that Augustine's "submission of faith" could have been to an erroneous christology. If "in AD 386 a man of Alypius' intelligence and seriousness could be confused about what orthodox Catholic Christology was [*Conf.* 7.25]," it is possible that the instruction he and Augustine were receiving was not the best.[44] O'Connell saw Augustine's Photinianism as a variant of Antiochene "Word-man" christology, and, following Van Bavel, interpreted Augustine's christology as moving between 386 and 400 from emphasis on the distinction of the divine and human to the unity of the Word incarnate.

The answer to the question rests mainly on whether or not one accepts as accurate Augustine's recollections in the *Confessions* of his attitude to Christ in 386-387. Madec, particularly resistant to the allegation of continuing Photinianism and seeing in the Antiochene Christ O'Connell discovered in the writings of the 390s a figure no more than human, insisted that Augustine had abandoned Photinianism by November 386.[45] Madec has become the chief champion in recent years of Augustine's factual accuracy in the *Confessions,* reacting negatively (and somewhat polemically – O'Connell's "garants" are Turmel, Scheel, and Alfaric[46]) to the continuing importance O'Connell gives Neoplatonism in Augustine's thought generally and (the interest here) in his christology. In a recent (1986) article defending the historicity of the Cassiciacum dialogues, Madec made the same point somewhat differently: the thanksgiving offered to Christ by Licentius on his conversion to philosophy at Cassiciacum (*De ordine* 1.8.21) reveals that he had been instructed by Augustine "de l'identité de la Sagesse et du Christ."[47] Augustine, in turn, Madec maintained, following Courcelle, had learned this from Simplician in Milan.

CHRIST'S KNOWLEDGE AND EMOTIONS

Another topic much discussed in the first half of the century was that of the psychology of Christ. Portalie and van Crombrugghe had also addressed this point, stating that Augustine had refused to recognize any ignorance in Christ, understanding him to participate in the knowledge of the Word.[48] This theme was pursued by Richard, in 1916, in an article on Christ's intuitive vision of the Word.[49] In 1924 Jouassard turned his attention to the question of Christ's emotions, especially the cry of dereliction on the cross, seeking the reason for Augustine's refusal to see those words as referring to Christ himself, thus apparently denying him human feelings.[50] Augustine understood the cry rather as the voice of the "old [sinful] man" (whom Christ had taken on), refusing to turn his back on earthly life and embrace eternal life. Why, asked Jouassard, had Augustine adopted this tradition rather than, for instance, that of most of the Greek theologians that abandonment referred not to divine desertion but to Christ's deliverance into the hands of his enemies? The reason, he concluded, was that Augustine was too much imbued with the Stoic ideal of impassibility to attribute psychological suffering to Christ, and his interpretation prevailed in the West even when its philosophic underpinnings were forgotten. Augustine's influence "poussait les Latins à denier à Jesus ce par quoi il est la plus notre frère."[51]

Van Bavel (1954), admitting that Augustine seemed to play down the role of Christ's humanity in matters concerning his will and even more his knowledge, also asked "why?" Part – but not all – of the reason was Augustine's conviction of the penetration of the humanity by the divinity. But Augustine, Van Bavel pointed out, was too well aware of the distinction of predication for this to be the complete answer. Although Van Bavel concluded that Augustine did not in fact work this problem out, his discussion of Augustine's treatment of Christ's temptations and cry of dereliction is particularly interesting. He rejects Jouassard's theory of Stoic influence and puts forward a less simple explanation. In each case – temptation and human emotions – he argues that, on the one hand, Augustine saw Christ as taking on temptation, fear, and despair on behalf of humankind; on the other, that these psychological sufferings were real for him. The cry of dereliction could not have come from an ontological or moral separation of God from Christ, nor would Christ have complained at falling into the hands of his enemies. "Augustin refuse donc de mettre cette plainte dans la bouche du Christ au nom de sa propre personne.... Les souffrances éprouvées par le Christ sont les nôtres, qu'il a voulu transposer dans la ressemblance de la chair de péché, sans qu'aucune cause interne ne l'y forcé. Mais cela ne veut point dire qu'il n'a pas souffert personnellement. L'introduction du principe du Christ-Corps mystique n'exclut pas un réalisme dans le sens indiqué."[52]

Babcock agreed, although for different reasons than either Jouassard or Van Bavel, with the conclusion that Augustine denied human feelings to Christ. Accounting for his general interpretation that "Augustine presents a Christ whose humanity is ... 'made radically subordinate to the divine nature,'"[53] Babcock writes: "[I]t seems clear that Augustine would not have found the Christ of the gospels a palatable figure without some notion that he governed rather than merely suffered his historical career," and "[A] vivid portrayal of the emotional instabilities and mental uncertainties of a man would simply be proof that the man is not God."[54]

CHRIST'S SAVING WORK

Alfaric in 1918 and Turmel in 1922 again raised the issue of Augustine's understanding of the value of Christ's death. For Alfaric the strong Neoplatonic cast of Augustine's theology led him to deny "que l'Incarnation était destinée à racheter l'humanité déchue en payant la dette du péché," but rather, "C'est en nous montrant le chemin du salut qu'il a reparé la faute originelle et qu'il nous a reconcilié avec Dieu."[55] Joseph Turmel (writing under one of his many pseudonyms, Hippolyte Gallerand) renewed the claims that Augustine saw the devil as having rights and that the death of Christ was a ransom paid to redeem those rights.[56]

The two charges – that Augustine did not understand the death of Christ to have been expiatory and that he saw that death as a payment to the devil – elicited and continue to elicit the attention of students of Augustine. J. Rivière, in a series of articles throughout the 1920s, vigorously repudiated Turmel's claim, not only on Augustine's behalf but more generally on behalf of patristic and medieval soteriology.[57]

Rivière's work was a close analysis of all aspects of the question, ending with that of "sacrifice." The interior bowing to the Father's will (which Turmel saw as the real sacrifice) would have had no import without the cross. The death on the cross was an expiatory sacrifice and efficacious precisely because it was not owed: "Mais cet abandon à la volonté du Père ... n'a jamais de sens et de réalité qu'en vue de la croix qui en est le terme definitif.... [L]e sacrifice d'une victime pure par le Christ pur était la condition *sine qua non.*"[58]

No subsequent writer has examined the question in more depth than Rivière, but several of the same themes have been pursued in the intervening fifty years. In 1954 Lecuyer argued that the truest meaning of Augustine's notion of sacrifice was to be found in *De civitate Dei* 10.6: "verum sacrificium est omne opus, quo agitur, ut sancta societate inhaereamus Deo." This, Lecuyer maintained, is the primordial idea of sacrifice and implies reconciliation, and – in Augustine's eyes – that Christ alone can accomplish what true sacrifice must because his actions alone fulfill the necessary conditions.[59] The Augustinian idea of Christ as the one true priest and sacrifice was discussed again in 1957 by La Bonnardière and in 1962 by Quinot, both in reference to the Epistle to the Hebrews.[60] Eborowicz in 1966, examining the *Confessions,* saw the notion of penal substitution as the key to Augustine's soteriology.[61] In a different vein, Rondet in 1951 studied the symbolism of the cross in Augustine's writings, concluding that prior to 400 he understood it as an allegory of the Christian life and later as a symbol of the mystery of grace.[62]

While Augustine's understanding of Christ's death as sacrifice continues to attract interest (in a recent [1985] article I attempted to show how Augustine came to that position through a changing anthropology[63]), it is generally recognized that Augustine's soteriology is extraordinarily rich and attention has, on the whole, shifted to other aspects of it. A relatively early (1938) and fruitful addition came in Burnaby's book, *Amor Dei.*[64] Replying to Rashdall's contention that "Augustine has no characteristic doctrine [of redemption] of his own,[65] Burnaby maintained that Augustine understood the revelation of God's love to be redemptive. "If Augustine had represented the work of redemption as nothing more than the showing forth in time of an eternal truth, he would have been not only more Platonist than Christian, but more Pelagian than Augustinian. But it is not so.... Redemption is in the fullest sense a new creation, restoring in sinful man the love toward God which he had lost. And how is that restoration accomplished?.... The humility of Jesus is redemptive *because* it is the humility of Mediator, the God-Man, and therefore has the divine potency of creation."[66]

Ladner (1954) pointed out that Augustine did not see the reconciliation of humankind to God as a return to the state of Adam, but to something different and better. On the one hand, we are not renewed to Adam's body, but – through Christ's death – raised to a spiritual body. On the other, the restored image of God is not marked by the free will of Adam, but by the gift of perseverance.[67] This theme of the restoration of the divine image has received a good deal of attention. Berrouard (1969) described the Augustinian insistence on the constant human need to be reformed and purified until perfected by the vision of God,[68] and the noetic content of that purification and vision has been explored. Holte, in an extensive study (1962), wrote that "La conception du christianisme, telle qu'Augustin l'exprimée dans ses premiers écrits, s'accorde parfaitement, dans ses lignes essentielles, avec la gnose d'Alexandrie."[69] The beatitude which Augustine envisioned was a participatory knowledge of God, and that psychological ascent, involving different functions of the soul, entailed for him a corresponding hierarchy of being.[70] Geerlings tied the divine image to Augustine's notion of the person of Christ: "Christus ist Sohn Gottes auf Grund seiner Natur, der Mensch dank der Gnade.... Hier ist Christus Bild des Vaters auf Grund des gemeinsamen gottlichen Wesens, der Mensch Bild Gottes auf Grund der Schopfung."[71] He went on to say that Christ as *exemplum* in this and other respects is more than what is usually understood by "exemplary." "Wie der in diesem Zussammenhang gebrauchte Terminus prototypus verrat, erhalt hier das exemplum eine über die rein pädagogische Funktion hinausgehende Dignitat."[72]

"Christus Mercator" was the topic of an article in 1960 by Poque. Commenting on the dramatic impact of that image in North Africa, where caravans from across the Sahara came with exotic wares, she directed her attention to the frequent Augustinian examples of "commercia" ("acceptit mortem de nostro ut daret nobis vitam").[73] The most extensive examination of this theme has been by Babcock. Asking which soteriological strand, of the many introduced, has priority in Augustine's writings, Babcock opts for that of "exchange" in the overall descent-ascent scheme of the return of the human person to God. It is not the same, he points out, as the Greek "realistic-mystic" doctrine; rather, "we have in the pattern of exchange a view of man's redemption ... which is intimately bound up with an understanding of who Christ is and how he acts for our sake.... Christ himself, as the one in whom God descends to us, sets the form and movement of our ascent to God: he descended to us *so that* we might ascend to him."[74] The total hegemony of the Word as subject, which Babcock sees in Augustine's christology, "supplies the Christological basis for the Augustinian version of the pattern of exchange as a whole.... [It] requires a real ascription of Christ's human experience to the Word himself. All the rich imagery of the exchange depends upon this point."[75]

Agaesse (1969) stressed the importance for Augustine of the mediatorial role of Christ as man: his authority illumines the intellect, his grace delivers from sin and heals.[76] O'Connell maintained that at Cassiciacum Augustine saw "Christ's soteriological function ... in terms of the Plotinian fall and return of the soul."[77] The theme of Christ "unique juste pour nous" is, suggested Studer in 1980, among the abundance of salvific themes, the most precise way of describing Augustinian soteriology. In death Christ's justice overcame the devil, and that justice is communicated to humankind in the power of the resurrection. Studer pointed out that, in Augustine's eyes, Christ's justice was not received (as is the case with saints), but resulted from the christological union: "[I]l a été tellement uni au Fils de Dieu qu'il a été radicalement juste et que donc il a été même incapable de pécher."[78]

No theme is more prominent or important in Augustine's christology than that of "totus Christus" and it has, of course, earned considerable attention. Philips, in a paper given at the 1954 Augustine conference and printed in *Augustinus Magister,* examined how Augustine understood Christ, as Head, to influence his body, the church. The western tradition of salvation has not been the divinizing transformation common in eastern theology and so, Philips noted, the strength of the "whole Christ" theme in Augustine is surprising. Philips made it clear that the humanity of Christ, which always plays the mediatorial role in the salvific exchange, is not the instrument of grace to humankind. Christ as Head has many functions; he redeems humankind by his obedience, he guides and teaches, but – except in the case of the resurrection – he is the source of grace only in the sense of his temporal priority. The philosophical reason that kept Augustine from attributing this role to Christ, Philips explained, is his Neoplatonism, which sees matter – even the humanity of Christ – as resistant to the Spirit. The theological reason is that grace in Augustine's understanding is not only an aid to moral living, but an assimilation to uncreated Wisdom. It is adoptive filiation, "une transformation ontologique,"[79] and such a transformation is the work of the divine Son. Augustine, said Philips, was "tout près du réalism mystique ... [mais] au moment crucial, une prudence tenace le fait reculer."[80] His conclusion was reinforced in Philips's mind by the near occasionalism he found in Augustine's sacramental theology: the Spirit works not "par la chair du Christ, par l'Eglise and par les sacrements," but "en raison du Christ, dans l'Eglise et à l'occasion des sacrements."[81]

Bernard in 1965 undertook to argue (against W. Boublik) that Augustine's idea of predestination was the same as Paul's and that that predestination was of the "total Christ." "[L]e Christ qui nous predestine comme Dieu et lui-même, comme Verbe incarné, predestine très gratuitement par la Sainte Trinité: et il est prédestiné come 'Christ total' ... l'église des prédestinés qui constitue la Cité de Dieu definitive du ciel."[82]

An interesting pattern was discerned in 1970 by Desjardins, examining the language Augustine used to describe both the christological union and the union of Christ with Christians. The first union is personal, the second is not, but both deal with an "in-corporation." "Quand Augustin veut signifier les deux aspects de l'incarnation, les distinguer sans jamais les disjoindre, quel genre d'aide lui apportent les mots?"[83] Desjardins's answer is that there is in Augustine's writings a "coherence of words" working on different levels. Examining a number of Augustine's verbal usages, Desjardins concludes that the image of anointing "est la plus coherente de l'incarnation du Verbe dans le Christ et dans l'Eglise."[84] "Le nom de Christ vient de l'onction ... en latin, unctus. Mais il donne l'onction a son corps entier" (Augustine, *En. Ps.* 103.3.13). Desjardins began by speaking of a "jeu des mots" and he concluded his article with the question: does the speaker play with words, or words with the speaker? Is he or she the producer of the product of his or her discourse? Desjardins concluded that Augustine "s'est finalement servi du mot."[85]

CONCLUSION

It is not easy to draw conclusions from a survey necessarily as brief and selective as this one has been, but I will venture a few. Although Augustine remains the teacher of the patristic age whom Anglicans, Protestants, and Roman Catholics alike share, he is no longer *the* teacher of the Western church. Christianity has become more explicitly polyvalent. This change in status frees Augustine's writings from doctrinal and polemical concerns, and this attitudinal freedom is matched by different approaches and methods. The old questions that have been so amply explored will continue to be studied, but new (or in the past less prominent) questions will also be examined. Both will surely benefit from the increasing attention to literary genre and to the social and political contexts.

All this is true of Augustine's writings generally, and specifically of his christology. Here, I think, there is a particular lacuna to be filled, and no one book or article will do it. It seems to me obvious that Augustine's christology changed markedly over the forty-three odd years of his writing life. Perhaps less obvious is that christology did not lead the way but changed in response to other changes in his thinking. There is a need to delineate these changes and to account for them more thoroughly than has yet been done. The notion of a steady progress towards something resembling the Chalcedonian definition, brought about simply by an increased reading and better interpretation of Scripture, must be discarded. The answer to the question *why* the christological changes came about will be less straightforward and much less self-contained. It will also, I am convinced, make Augustine's christology more interesting.

NOTES

1. See Wm A. Babcock, *The Christ of the Exchange: A Study in the Christology of Augustine's "Enarrationes in Psalmos"* (Ann Arbor: University Microfilms, 1972), 2: "Patristic studies ... have shown a singular lack of interest in Augustine's Christology."

2. I am intentionally distinguishing (without implying thereby separation), as did Augustine, between the gospel Figure and the "second Person" of the Trinity, the object of a good deal of his explicit attention. Those trinitarian writings have been extensively studied.

3. J.A. Dorner, *Entwickelungsgeschichte der Lehre von der Person Christi* (Berlin, 1845-1853). E.T. *The Doctrine of the Person of Christ* (Edinburgh: T. and T. Clark, 1880), vol. I.ii.1, 77-79.

4. A. von Harnack, *The "Confessions" of Saint Augustine* E.T. (London: Williams and Norgate, 1902).

———, *Lehrbuch der Dogmengeschichte,* vol. 1 (Freiburg, 1888). E.T. *History of Dogma* (New York, [1961]), 125-34; F. Loofs, *Leitfaden zum Studien des Dogmengeschichte* (Halle:

M. Niemeyer, 1901); O. Scheel, *Die Auschauung Augustins über Christi Person und Werk* (Leipzig: H. Laupp, 1901).

5. E. Portalie, "Augustin (saint)," *Dictionnaire de Théologie Catholique* I(2) (Paris: Letouzey et Ane, 1931; the imprimatur for this volume is, however, 1902), 2268-2472. E.T. *A Guide to the Thought of St Augustine* (Chicago: Henry Regnery, 1960). C. van Crombrugghe, "La doctrine christologique et sotériologique de saint Augustin," *Revue d'Histoire Ecclésiastique* 5 (1904), 237-57, 477-504.

6. Portalie, 2322.

7. Ibid., 2362.

8. Ibid., 2362.

9. Ibid., 2363.

10. Ibid., 2364.

11. Ibid., 2366.

12. Ibid., 2366 (emphasis Portalie's).

13. Ibid., 2371.

14. van Crombrugghe, 241.

15. Ibid., 247.

16. Ibid., 250.

17. Ibid., 246.

18. Ibid., 481.

19. Ibid., 482.

20. Ibid., 489.

21. See the relevant sections of *Lamentabili* and *Pascendi,* and J.E. McWilliam (Dewart), "Patristic Scholarship in the Aftermath of the Modernist Crisis," *Anglican Theological Review* 68 (1986), 25-42.

22. See J. Rivière, " 'Assumptus homo,' " *De Fide et Symbolo; Enchiridion* (Paris, 1947), note complémentaire #22. For a different view, H.-M. Diepen, "L''assumptus homo' patristique," *Revue Thomiste* 71 (1963), 225-45, 363-88, 72 (1964), 32-52.

23. Portalie, 2362.

24. T. Van Bavel, *Recherches sur la christologie de saint Augustin* (Fribourge: Editions Universitaires, 1954).

25. Ibid., 11, 12.

26. *Exp. ep. Gal.* 27, quoted Van Bavel, 14.

27. Van Bavel, 15.

28. *Agon.* 22, quoted Van Bavel, 17.

29. Babcock, 13.

30. Ibid., 15.

31. Ibid., 331.

32. Ibid., 337.

33. W. Geerlings, *Christum Exemplum: Studien zur Christologie und Christuskundigung Augustins* (Mainz: Matthias-Grunewald Verlag, 1978), 100.

34. Ibid., 104.

35. H.R. Drobner, *Person-Exegese und Christologie bei Augustinus: zur Herkunft der Formel "una persona"* (Leiden: E.J. Brill, 1986).

36. Ibid., 273.

37. P. Alfaric, *L'evolution intellectuelle de saint Augustin: du manichéisme au néoplatonisme* (Paris: E. Noury, 1918).

38. C. Boyer, *Christianisme et Néoplatonisme dans la formation de saint Augustin* (Paris: Beauchesne, 1920), 122.

39. P. Courcelle, "Saint Augustin 'Photinien' a Milan," *Richerche di Storia Religiosa* 1 (1954), 63-71.

40. H.-I. Marrou, "Les sources platoniciennes de l'augustinisme,"*Augustinus Magister* III (Paris, 1954), 99.

41. A.D.R. Polman, *The Word of God According to Saint Augustine.* E.T. (London: Hodder and Stoughton, 1961), 13, 22.

42. A. Solignac, "La christologie d'Augustin au temps de sa conversion," *Conf.* [*BA* 13] (Paris, 1962), 693-98.

43. R.J. O'Connell, "Alypius' 'apollinarianism' at Milan," *Revue des Etudes Augustiniennes* (13), 1967, 209-210.

44. R.J. O'Connell, *Saint Augustine's Early Theory of Man, 386-391* (Cambridge, Mass.: Belknap Press of Harvard University Press, 1968), 67.

45. G. Madec, "Une lecture de Confessions VII.9.13-11.27: Notes critiques à propos d'une thèse de R.J. O'Connell," *Revue des Etudes Augustiniennes* 16 (1970), 79-137.

46. Ibid., 125.

47. G. Madec, "L'historicité des Dialogues de Cassiciacum," *Revue des Etudes Augustiniennes* 32 (1986), 207-31.

48. See Portalie, 2363 and van Crombrugghe, 255.

49. L. Richard, "Un texte de saint Augustin sur la vision intuitive du Christ," *Recherches de Science Religieuse* 39 (1951-52) [=Mélanges Lebreton I], 472-77.

50. G. Jouassard, "L'abandon du Christ d'après saint Augustin," *Revue des Sciences Théologiques et Philosophiques* 13 (1924), 310-26. See also his "L'abandon du Christ en croix dans la tradition grecque des IVe et Ve siècles," *Revue des Sciences Religieuses* 5 (1925), 609-33.

51. Jouassard, 325.

52. Van Bavel, 142, 145.

53. Babcock, 333.

54. Ibid., 337-38.

55. Alfaric, 525.

56. Hippolyte Gallerand [=J. Turmel], "La rédemption dans saint Augustin," *Revue d'Historie et Littérature Religieuse* 8 (1922), 38-77.

57. The articles, originally published in *Recherches de Science Religieuse,* were gathered into a book, *La dogme de la rédemption chez saint Augustin,* 3rd edition (Paris: J. Gabalda,

1933). See also his " 'Muscipula diabole': origine et sens d'une image augustinienne," *Revue de Théologie Ancienne et Medievale* 1 (1929), 484-96, and "Economie de la redemption," in *De Fide et Symbolo; Enchiridion* (Paris, 1947), note complémentaire #27, 369-71.

58. *La dogme*, 207.

59. J. Lecuyer, "Le sacrifice selon saint Augustin," *Augustinus Magister* II (Paris, 1954), 905-14.

60. A.-M. La Bonnardière, "L'épître aux Hebreux dans l'oeuvre de saint Augustin," *Revue des Etudes Augustiniennes* 3 (1957), 137-62; B. Quinot, "L'influence de l'Epître aux Hebreux dans la notion augustinienne du vrai sacrifice," *Revue des Etudes Augustiniennes* 8 (1962), 129-69.

61. W. Eborowicz, "Les approches du mystère sotériologique dans les 'Confessions' de Saint Augustin," *Studia Patristica* IX [=Texte und Untersuchungen] (Berlin: Akademie-Verlag, 1966), 393-403.

62. H. Rondet, "Notes d'exégèse augustinienne," *Recherches de Science Religieuse* 39 (1951-52), 472-77.

63. J.E. McWilliam, "Augustine's Developing Understanding of the Cross, 386-400," *Augustinian Studies* 17 (1985) 15-33.

64. J. Burnaby, *Amor Dei. A Study of the Religion of St. Augustine* (London: Hodder and Stoughton, 1938).

65. H. Rashdall, *The Idea of the Atonement in Christian Theology* (London: Macmillan, 1920).

66. Burnaby, 170-71.

67. G.G. Ladner, "St Augustine's Conception of the Reformation of Man to the Image of God," *Augustinus Magister* II (Paris: Etudes Augustiniennes, 1954), 867-78.

68. M.-F. Berrouard, *Homelies sur l'Evangile de Saint Jean* [*BA* #71], 2 vols. (Paris. 1969).

69. R. Holte, *Béatitude et Sagesse. Saint Augustin et le problème de la fin de l'homme dans la philosophie ancienne* (Paris: Etudes Augustiniennes, 1962), 187.

70. Ibid., 189, 216ff.

71. Geerlings, 233-44.

72. Ibid., 205.

73. S. Poque, "Christus Mercator," *Recherches de Science Religieuse* 48 (1960), 564-77.

74. Babcock, 30.

75. Ibid., 341.

76. P. Agaesse, "L'humanité du Christ d'après Saint Augustin," *Dictionnaire de Spiritualité* 7 (Paris: Beauchesne, 1969), 1049-53.

77. R.J. O'Connell, "Augustine's Rejection of the Fall of the Soul," *Augustinian Studies* 4 (1973), 1-32.

78. B. Studer, "Le Christ, notre justice, selon saint Augustin," *Recherches Augustiniennes* 15 (1980), 99-143, 137.

79. G. Philips, "L'influence du Christ-Chef sur son corps mystique suivant saint Augustin," *Augustinus Magister* II (Paris: Etudes Augustiniennes, 1954), 805-15, 810.

80. Ibid., 813.

81. Ibid., 813.

82. R. Bernard, "Le prédestination du Christ total selon saint Augustin," *Recherches Augustiniennes* 3 (1965), 1-58.

83. R. Desjardins, "Une structuration de mots chez saint Augustin: le thème de l'incarnation," *Bulletin de Littérature Ecclésiastique* 71 (1970), 161-73. See also his "Le Christ 'sponsus' et l'Eglise 'sponsa' chez saint Augustin," *Bulletin de Littérature Ecclésiastique* 67 (1966), 241-56.

84. "Structuration....," 171.

85. Ibid., 173.

BIBLIOGRAPHY

Agaesse, Paul. "L'humanité du Christ d'après Saint Augustin." *Dictionnaire de Spiritualité* 7 (1969). Paris: Beauchesne, 1969, cols. 1049-1053.

Alfaric, P. *L'évolution intellectuelle de saint Augustin: du manichéisme au neoplatonisme.* Paris: Etudes Augustiniennes, 1918.

Arbesmann, R. "Christ, the 'medicus humilis' in Saint Augustine," *Augustinus Magister* II. Paris, 1954, 623-29.

Babcock, Wm. A. *The Christ of the Exchange: A Study in the Christology of Augustine's 'Enarrationes in Psalmos.'* Ann Arbor, Mich.: University Microfilms International, 1972.

Bailleux, E. "La sotériologie de saint Augustin dans le 'De Trinitate.' " *Mélanges de Science Religieuse* 23 (1966), 149-73.

Bavard, G. "Un thème augustinien: le mystère de l'Incarnation à la lumière de la distinction entre le Verbe intérieur et le Verbe proferé." *Revue des Etudes Augustiniennes* 9 (1963), 95-101.

Bavel, T. van. *Recherches sur la christologie de saint Augustin.* Fribourg: Editions Universitaires, 1954.

———. "L'humanité du Christ comme *lac parvulorum* et comme *via* dans la spiritualité de saint Augustin." *Augustiniana* 7 (1957), 245-81.

———. "Die Einheit des 'totus Christus' bei Augustinus." *Scientia Augustiniana* [=Festschrift für Adolar Zumkeller]. Wurzburg: Augustinus-Verlag, 1975, 43-75.

Bernard, René. "La prédestination du Christ total selon saint Augustin." *Recherches Augustiniennes* 3 (1965), 1-58.

Berrouard, M.-F. *Homelies sur l'Evangile de Saint Jean.* 2 vols. *BA* #71 and 72. Paris: Desclée de Brouwer, 1969.

Bonnardière, A.-M. La. "L'Epître aux Hebreux dans l'oeuvre de saint Augustin." *Revue des Etudes Augustiniennes* 3 (1957), 137-62.

Bonner, G. "Christ, God and Man in the Thoughts of St Augustine." In *God's Decree and Man's Destiny: Studies in the Thought of Augustine of Hippo.* London: Variorum Press, 1987, 268-94.

Boyer, C. *Christianisme et néoplatonisme dans la formation de saint Augustin.* Paris: Beauchesne, 1920; 2nd edition.

Brabant, O. *Le Christ, centre et source de la vie morale chez saint Augustin.* Gembloux: J. Duclot, 1971.

Burnaby, J. *Amor Dei. A Study of the Religion of St. Augustine.* London: Hodder and Stoughton, 1938.

Clarke, T.E. "St Augustine and the Cosmic Redemption." *Theological Studies 19* (1958), 133-64.

Comeau, Marie. "Le Christ, chemin et terme de l'ascension spirituelle d'après saint Augustin." *Recherches de Science Religieuse* 40 (1951-52), 80-89.

Courcelle, P. "Litiges sur la lecture des 'libri Platonicorum' par saint Augustin." *Augustiniana* 4 (1954), 9-23.

———. "Les premières Confessions de Saint Augustin." *Revue des Etudes Latines* 21-23 (1943-45), 155-74.

———. *Recherches sur les Confessions de Saint Augustin.* Paris, 1950; 2nd edition, 1968.

———. "Saint Augustin 'Photinien' à Milan." *Ricerche di Storia Religiosa* 1 (1945), 63-71.

Crombrugghe, C. van. "La doctrine christologique et sotériologique de saint Augustin." *Revue d'Histoire Ecclésiastique* 5 (1904), 237-57, 477-504.

Desjardins, René. "Le Christ 'sponsus' et l'Eglise 'sponsa' chez saint Augustin." *Bulletin de Littérature Ecclésiastique* 67 (1966), 241-56.

———. "Une structuration de mots chez saint Augustin: le theme de l'incarnation." *Bulletin de Littérature Ecclésiastique* 71 (1970), 161-73.

Demmer, K. *Ius caritatis. Zur christologishchen Grundlagen der augustinischen Naturrechtslehre.* Rome: Libreria Editrice dell'Universita Gregoriana, 1961.

Dorner, J.A. *The Doctrine of the Person of Christ.* E.T. Edinburgh: T. and T. Clark, 1880. Vol. I.ii.1.

Drobner, H.R. *Person Exegese und Christologie bei Augustinus.* Leiden: E.J. Brill, 1986.

———. "Exegesis grammatical y cristologia en san Agustin." J. Oroz Reta, ed., *Augustinus* 31 (1986) [=San Agustin en Oxford], 95-112.

Dubarle, A.-M. "La connaissance humaine du Christ d'après saint Augustin." *Ephemerides Théologicae de Lovanienses* 18 (1941), 5-25.

———. "La science humaine du Christ selon S. Augustin." *Revue des Sciences Philosophiques et Théologiques* 29 (1940), 244-63.

DuRoy, O. *L'intelligence de la foi en la Trinité selon S. Augustin: Génèse de sa théologie trinitaire jusqu'en 391.* Paris: Etudes Augustiniennes, 1966.

Eborowicz, W. "Les approches du mystère sotériologique dans les 'Confessions' de saint Augustin." *Studia Patristica* IX [=Texte und Untersuchungen 94]. Berlin, 1966, 393-403.

Eijkenboom, P. "Christus Redemptor in the Sermons of St Augustin." *Mélanges offerts à Mademoiselle Christina Mohrmann.* Utrecht-Anvers, 1963, 233-39.

Ferrari, L.C. "Surprising Omissions from Augustine's *City of God.*" *Augustiniana* 20 (1970), 336-46.

———. "*Christus Via* in Augustine's 'Confessions'." *Augustinian Studies* 7 (1976), 47-59.

Gallerand, Hippolyte. "La rédemption dans saint Augustin." *Revue d'Histoire et de Littérature Religieuse* 8 (1922), 38-77.

Geerlings. W. *Christum Exemplum: Studien zür Christologie und Christusverkündigung Augustins.* Mainz: Matthias-Grunewald, 1978.

Gilson, E. *Philosophie et Incarnation selon saint Augustin.* Montréal: Institut d'études mediévales, 1969.

Gottschick, J. "Augustinus Anschauung von den Erlöserwirkungen Christi." *Zeitschrift für Theologie und Kurche* 11 (1901), 97-213.

Harnack, A. *The "Confessions" of Saint Augustine.* E.T. London: Williams and Norgate, 1902.

———. *History of Dogma,* vol. 5. New York, [1961].

Holte, R. *Béatitude et Sagesse. Saint Augustin et le problème de la fin de l'homme dans la philosophie ancienne.* Paris: Etudes Augustiniennes, 1962.

Jordan, M.D. "Words and Word: Incarnation and Signification in Augustine's *De Doctrina Christiana.*" *Augustinian Studies* 11 (1980), 177-96.

Joussard, G. "L'abandon du Christ d'après saint Augustin." *Revue des Sciences Théologiques et Philosophiques* 13 (1924), 310-26.

———. "L'abandon du Christ en croix dans la tradition grecque des IVe et Ve siècles," *Revue des Sciences Religieuses* 5 (1925), 609-33.

Kondoleon, T. "Divine Exemplarism in Augustine." *Augustinian Studies* 1 (1970), 181-95.

Ladner, G.G. "St Augustine's Conception of the Reformation of Man to the Image of God." *Augustinus Magister* II. Paris: Etudes Augustiniennes, 1954, 867-78.

Lambot, C. "Le sermon 126 de saint Augustin sur le thème foi et intelligence et sur la vision du Verbe." *Revue Benedictine* 49 (1959), 177-90.

Lange, D. "Zum Verhaltnis von Geschichtsbild und Christologie in Augustins *De Civitate Dei.*" *Evangelische Quartalschrift* [Münster] 28 (1968), 430-41.

Lauras, Antoine. "Deux images du Christ et l'Eglise dans la prédication augustinienne." *Augustinus Magister* II, 667-75.

Laurentin, A. "Jean 17.5 et la prédestination du Christ à la gloire chez saint Augustin et ses prédécesseurs." *L'Évangile de Jesus* [=Recherches bibliques III]. Bruges: Desclée de Brouwer, 1958, 225-48.

Lecuyer, J. "Le sacrifice selon saint Augustin." *Augustinus Magister* II. Paris: Etudes Augustiniennes, 1954, 905-14.

Lods, Marc. "La personne du Christ dans la 'conversion' de saint Augustin." *Recherches Augustiniennes* 11 (1976), 3-34.

McCallin, J.A. "The Christological Unity of Saint Augustine's 'De Civitate Dei.'" *Revue des Etudes Augustiniennes* 12 (1966), 85-109.

McWilliam, J.E. "La Autobiografia de Casiciaco." *Augustinus* 31 [=San Augustin en Oxford]. 1986, 41-78.

———. "Augustine's Developing Understanding of the Cross, 386-400." *Augustinian Studies* 17 (1986), 15-33.

———. "The Christology of the Pelagian Controversy." *Studia Patristica* XVIII. E.A. Livingstone, ed., London: Pergamon Press, 1982, 1221-44.

———. "The Influence of Theodore of Mopsuestia on Augustine's *Letter* 187." *Augustinian Studies* 10 (1979), 111-32.

———. "Patristic Scholarship in the Aftermath of the Modernist Crisis." *Anglican Theological Review* 68 (1986), 25-42.

Madec, Goulen. "Une lecture de *Confessions* VII.9.13-11.27: Notes critiques à propos d'une thèse de R.J. O'Connell." *Revue des Etudes Augustiniennes* 16 (1970), 79-137.

———. "Christus, scientia et sapientia nostra, le principe de cohérence de la doctrine augustinienne." *Recherches Augustiniennes* 10 (1974), 77-85.

———. "Analyse du *De Magistro*." *Revue des Etudes Augustiniennes* 21 (1975), 63-71.

———. "L'historicité des *Dialogues* de Cassiciacum." *Revue des Etudes Augustiniennes* 32 (1986), 207-31.

Mallard, W. "The Incarnation in Augustine's Conversion." *Recherches Augustiniennes* 15 (1980), 80-98.

Marrevee, W. *The Ascension of Christ in the Works of St Augustine.* Ottawa: St. Paul's University Press, 1967.

Marrou, H.-I. in "Les sources platoniciennes de l'augustinisme." Report by A. Pincherle, followed by discussion. *Augustinus Magister* III. Paris: Etudes Augustiniennes, 1954, 71-102.

Miles, Margaret. *Augustine on the Body.* Missoula, Mont.: Scholars Press, 1979.

Newton, J.T. *Neoplatonism and Augustine's Doctrine of the Person and Work of Christ: A Study of the Philosophical Structure underlying Augustine's Christology.* Ann Arbor: University Microfilms International, 1969.

O'Connell, R.J. "The Plotinian Fall of the Soul." *Traditio* 19 (1963), 1-35.

———. "Alypius' 'Apollinarianism' at Milan (*Conf.* 7.25)," *Revue des Etudes Augustiniennes* 13 (1967), 209-210.

———. *St Augustine's Early Theory of Man.* Cambridge, Mass.: Belknap Press of Harvard University Press, 1968.

———. "Augustine's Rejection of the Fall of the Soul." *Augustinian Studies* 4 (1973), 1-32.

O'Meara, J.J. "The Historicity of the Early Dialogues of Saint Augustine." *Vigiliae Christianae* 5 (1951), 150-78.

———. "Augustine and Neo-platonism." *Recherches Augustiniennes* 1 (1958), 91-111.

Outler, A.C. "The Person and Work of Christ." In *A Companion to the Study of St. Augustine.* New York: Oxford, 1955, 343-70.

Philips, G. "L'influence du Christ-Chef sur son corps mystique suivant saint Augustin." *Augustinus Magister* II. Paris: Etudes Augustiniennes, 1954, 805-15.

———. "Le mystère du Christ." *Augustinus Magister* III. Paris: Etudes Augustiniennes, 1954, 213-29.

Piolanti, A. "Il mistero del 'Cristo totale' in s. Agostino." *Augustinus Magister* III. Paris: Etudes Augustiniennes, 1954, 453-70.

Plagnieux, J. "Influence de la lutte antipélagienne sur *De Trinitate,* ou: christocentrisme de saint Augustin." *Augustinus Magister* II. Paris: Etudes Augustiniennes, 1954, 817-26.

Poque, Suzanne. "Christus Mercator." *Recherches de Science Religieuse* 48 (1960), 564-77.

Portalie, E. "Augustin (saint)." *Dictionnaire de Théologie Catholique* I(2). Paris: Letouzey et Ane, 1931, cols. 2268-2472. E.T. *A Guide to the Thought of St Augustine.* Chicago, 1960.

Quinot, B. "L'influence de l'Epître aux Hebreux dans la notion augustinienne du vrai sacrifice." *Revue des Etudes Augustiniennes* 8 (1962), 129-69.

Reveillard, M. "Le Christ-Homme, Tête de l'Eglise. Etude d'écclésiologie selon les Ennarationes in Psalmos d'Augustin." *Recherches Augustiniennes* 5 (1968), 67-69.

Richard, L. "Un texte de saint Augustin sur la vision intuitive du Christ." *Recherches de Science Religieuse* 39 (1951/52), 472-77.

Rivière, J. " 'Muscipula diaboli': origine et sens d'une image augustinienne." *Revue de Theologie Ancienne et Medievale* 1 (1929), 484-96.

———. *La dogme de la rédemption chez saint Augustin.* 3rd ed. Paris: J. Gabalda, 1933.

———. " 'Assumptus homo,'" *De fide et symbolo; Enchiridion. BA* 9. Paris: Desclée de Brouwer, 1947, note complémentaire #22, 359-62.

———. "Economie de la rédemption," ibid., note complémentaire #27, 369-71.

Rondet, Henri. "Le Christ nouvel Adam dans la théologie de saint Augustin." *Etudes Mariales* II (1955), 28-41.

———. "Notes d'exégèse augustinienne." *Recherches de Science Religieuse* 39 (1951/52), 472-77.

Sage, A. "De la grace du Christ, modele et principe de la grace." *Revue des Etudes Augustiniennes* 7 (1961), 17-34.

Scheel, O. *Die Anschaung Augustins über Christi Person und Werk.* Tubingen/Leipsig: H. Laupp, 1901.

Schlitz, E. "Aux sources de la théologie du mystère de l'Incarnation: La christologie du Saint Augustin." *Nouvelle Revue Théologique* 7 (1936), 669-713.

Schlitz, E. "Si Christus humanam naturam quam assumpsit deponeret...." *Divus Thomas* 42 (1939), 3-16.

Solignac, A. "La christologie d'Augustin au temps de sa conversion." *Les Confessions. BA* 13. Paris: Desclée de Brouwer, 1962, note complémentaire #27, 693-98.

Studer, B. " 'Sacramentum et exemplum' chez s. Augustin." *Recherches Augustiniennes* 10 (1974), 87-141.

———. "Le Christ, notre justice, selon saint Augustin." *Recherches Augustiniennes* 15 (1980), 99-143.

———. "La foie de Nicée selon saint Augustin." *Revue des Etudes Augustiniennes* 19 (1984), 133-54.

Verheer, Jacques. "Heiliges Geist und Inkarnation in der Theologie des Augustins von Hippo." *Revue des Etudes Augustiniennes* 22 (1976), 234-53.

AUGUSTINE IN TRANSLATION: ACHIEVEMENTS AND FURTHER GOALS

THOMAS HALTON

Since one of the announced themes of this sedecentennial celebration is Augustine in twentieth-century scholarship, an overall view of translations into modern languages of Augustine may be both opportune and pedagogically useful. In a survey of such magnitude there will be time for few value judgements, but some reviews of various works are noted in parentheses.

SERIES

Nicene and Post-Nicene Fathers (NPNF)

The Nicene and Post-Nicene Fathers series came into existence a hundred years ago as an American updating of the series, A Library of the Fathers, begun in 1837 by the three leaders of the Anglo-Catholic movement of Oxford, Drs Pusey, Newman, and Keble. The preface to NPNF by Philip Schaff of Union Theological Seminary, New York, dated October 1886, notes that the three Oxford leaders were aided by a number of able classical and ecclesiastical scholars. It goes on: "Dr. Pusey, the chief editor and proprietor, and Dr. Keble died in the communion of the church of their fathers to which they were loyally attached; Dr. Newman alone remains, though no more an Anglican, but a Cardinal of the Church of Rome. His connection with the enterprise ceased with his secession (1845)." (It was a classic case of gone, but not forgotten, and forgotten but not gone!)

NPNF, series 1, devoted volumes one through eight to Augustine, and these volumes were reprinted by Eerdman, Grand Rapids, Michigan, in 1979.

NPNF I.

Confessions, 27-207. *Epistles* (269), 209-593.

NPNF II.

City of God, 1-511. *On Christian Doctrine*, 519-97.

NPNF III. 1. Doctrinal Treatises

On the Holy Trinity, 1-228. *Enchiridion*, 237-76. *On the Catechising of the Uninstructed*, 282-314. *On Faith and the Creed*, 321-33. *Faith in Things Not Seen*, 337-43. *On the Profit of Believing*, 347-66. *On the Creed: A Sermon to Catechumens*, 369-75.

NPNF III. 2. Moral Treatises

Of Continence, 379-93. *On the Good of Marriage*, 397-413. *Of Holy Virginity*, 417-38. *On the Good of Widowhood*, 441-54. *On Lying*, 457-79. *Against Lying. To Consentius*, 481-500. *Of the Work of Monks*, 503-24. *On Patience*, 527-36. *On Care to be had for the Dead*, 539-51.

NPNF IV. 1. Anti-Manichaean Writings

On the Morals of the Catholic Church, 41-63. *On the Morals of the Manichaeans*, 69-89. *On Two Souls, against the Manichaeans*, 95-107. *Acts* or *Disputation against Fortunatus*, 113-24. *Against the Epistle of a Manichaean*, 129-50. *Against Faustus the Manichaean*, 155-345. *On the Nature of the Good, against the Manicheaeans*, 351-65.

NPNF IV. 2. Anti-Donatist Writings

On Baptism, against the Donatists, 411-514. *Against the Letters of Petilianus*, 519-628. *On the Correction of the Donatists*, or *Epistle 185*, 633-51.

NPNF V. Anti-Pelagian Works

On the Merits and Remission of Sins, and on the Baptism of Infants, 12-78. *On the Spirit and the Letter*, 80-114. *On Nature and Grace*, 116-51. *On Man's Perfection in Righteousness*, 155-76. *On the Proceedings of Pelagius*, 176-212. *On the Grace of Christ and on Original Sin*, 214-55. *On Marriage and Concupiscence*, 258-308. *On the Soul and its Origin*, 310-71. *Against Two Letters of the Pelagians*, 376-434. *On Grace and Free-Will*, 436-65. *On Rebuke and Grace*, 468-91. *On the Predestination of the Saints*, 495-519. *On the Gift of Perseverance*, 521-552.

NPNF VI. Exegetical and homiletical writings on the Gospel

The Lord's Sermon on the Mount, 1-63. *On the Harmony of the Gospels*, 65-236. *Sermons (97) on Selected Lessons of the New Testament* (LI-CXLVII, Benedictine ed.), 237-545.

NPNF VII.

Homilies on the Gospel of John, 7-452. *Homilies on the First Epistle of John*, 459-560. *Soliloquia*, 537-60.

NPNF VIII.

Enarrationes in Psalmos, 1-683

The Fathers of The Church (FOTC)

In 1946 appeared the first of a projected seventy-two-volume series (vol. 76 appeared in 1987) called The Fathers of the Church, edited by Ludwig Schopp. In his Preface to volume one Schopp tells us: "The translations, although done by American Catholic scholars, are destined neither for scholars only, or exclusively for Catholics but for the entire English-speaking world." As present editorial director of the Fathers of the Church series of translations may I take the liberty of chronicling the achievements of FOTC before those of ACW, which Quasten and Plumpe launched also in 1946?

FOTC 2 (1947)
Christian Instruction, tr. J.J. Gavigan. *Admonition and Grace,* tr. J.C. Murray. *The Christian Combat,* tr. R.P. Russell. *Faith, Hope and Charity,* tr. B.M. Peeble.

FOTC 4 (1947)
Immortality of the Soul, tr. L. Schopp. *Magnitude of the Soul,* tr. J.J. McMahon. *On Music,* tr. R.C. Taliaferro. *Advantage of Believing,* tr. Sr. L. Meagher. *On Faith in Things Unseen,* tr. R. Deferrari and Sr. M.F. McDonald.

FOTC 5 (1948)
The Happy Life, tr. L. Schopp. *Answer to Skeptics* (= *Contra Academicos*), tr. D.J. Kavanagh. *Divine Providence and the Problem of Evil* (= *De ordine*), tr. R.P. Russell. *Soliloquies,* tr. T.P. Gilligan.

The next undertaking was a three-volume *City of God.*

FOTC 8 (1950). *St. Augustine, The City of God,* Bks. 1-7, tr. G.G. Walsh, D.B. Zema, intro. E. Gilson

FOTC 14 (1952). *St. Augustine, The City of God,* Bks. 8-16, tr. G.G. Walsh and G. Monahan

FOTC 24 (1954). *St. Augustine, The City of God,* Bks. 17-22, tr. G.G. Walsh and D.J. Honan

Meantime,

FOTC 11 (1951). *St. Augustine, Commentary on the Sermon on the Mount and 17 related Sermons,* tr. D.J. Kavanagh.

Between 1951 and 1956 the Letters appeared in 5 volumes; the translator was Sr. W. Parsons.

FOTC 12 (1951). *St. Augustine, Letters, 1* (Letters 1-82)
FOTC 18 (1953). *St. Augustine, Letters, 2* (Letters 83-130)
FOTC 20 (1953). *St. Augustine, Letters, 3* (Letters 131-64)
FOTC 30 (1955). *St. Augustine, Letters, 4* (Letters 165-203)
FOTC 32 (1956). *St. Augustine, Letters, 5* (Letters 204-70)

Meantime, there appeared:

FOTC 16 (1952). *St. Augustine, Treatises on Various Subjects*
The Christian Life, On Lying, The Works of Monks, and *The Usefulness of Fasting,* tr. Sr. M.S. Muldowney. *Against Lying,* tr. H.B. Jaffee. *On Continence,* tr. Sr. M.F. McDonald. *On Patience,* tr. Sr. L. Meagher. *The Excellence of Widowhood,* tr. C. Eagen. *The Eight Questions of Dulcitius,* tr. M. DeFerrari.
FOTC 27 (1955). *St. Augustine, Treatises on Marriage and Other Subjects*
The Good of Marriage, tr. C.T. Wilcox. *On Adulterous Marriages,* tr. C.T. Huegelmeyer. *On Holy Virginity,* tr. J. McQuade. *On Faith and Works, The Creed,* and *In Answer to the Jews,* tr. Sr. M.L. Ewald. *Faith and the Creed,* tr. R.P. Russell. *The Care to be Taken of the Dead,* tr. J.A. Lacy. *The Divination of Demons,* tr. R.W. Brown.
FOTC 35 (1957). *St. Augustine, Against Julian,* tr. M.A. Schumacher
FOTC 38 (1959). *St. Augustine, Sermons on the Liturgical Seasons,* tr. Sr. M.S. Muldowney

Volume 40 was issued in the series in 1959 and of these forty volumes, seven had been devoted to Augustine, including such major undertakings as *The City of God* and the *Letters.*

The 1960s were less productive, vols. 41 to 69 including only four Augustine volumes:

FOTC 45 (1963). *St. Augustine, The Trinity,* tr. S. McKenna
FOTC 56 (1966). *St. Augustine, The Catholic and Manichaean Ways of Life,* tr. Donald A. and Idella J. Gallagher
FOTC 59 (1968). *St. Augustine. The Teacher, The Free Choice of the Will,* and *Grace and Free Will,* tr. R.P. Russell
FOTC 60 (1968). *St. Augustine, Retractations,* tr. Sr. M.I. Bogan.

The 1970s was a lean decade for FOTC, mainly due to irreconcilable differences between publishers and editors, and of the five volumes issued none was assigned to Augustine.

So far in the 1980s one volume of Augustine has been added:

FOTC 70 (1982). *St. Augustine, Eighty-Three Different Questions* by D. L. Mosher.

Several others are planned:

The Newly Discovered Letters, tr. R. Eno
Tractates on the Gospel of St. John, tr. J.W. Rettig
The Gift of Perseverance, On Nature and Grace, and *The Acts of Pelagius,* tr. J.A. Mourant
On Heresies, and *On Diverse Questions,* tr. L. Muller
On the Agreement of the Gospels, tr. J.J. Dillon.

Ancient Christian Writers (ACW)

Volume 1 of ACW has a Foreword by Quasten and Plumpe, dated Feast of St. Athanasius, 1946, saying among other things: "That there is need of such a new collection of translations should be evident. On the Catholic side we have been entirely without one for much too long."

Like FOTC, ACW devoted three of its first five volumes to Augustine.

ACW 2 (1946). *St. Augustine, The First Catechetical Instruction,* tr. J.P. Christopher
ACW 3 (1947). *St. Augustine, Faith, Hope and Charity,* tr. L. Arand. [*CW* 44 (1950) 25 Peebles]
ACW 5 (1948). *St. Augustine, The Lord's Sermon on the Mount,* tr. J.J. Jepson.

The 1950s added 4 volumes:

ACW 9 (1950). *St. Augustine. The Greatness of the Soul* and *The Teacher,* tr. J.M. Colleran
ACW 12 (1950). *St. Augustine, Against the Academics,* tr. J.J. O'Meara
ACW 15 (1952). *St. Augustine, Sermons for Christmas and Epiphany,* tr. T.C. Lawler
ACW 22 (1955). *St. Augustine, The Problem of Free Choice,* tr. Dom M. Pontifex.

In the 1960s only two Augustine volumes were issued:

ACW 29, 30 (1960, 1961). *St. Augustine, On the Psalms,* tr. Dame S. Hebgin and Dame F. Corrigan

And finally, after a 20-year hiatus on Augustine:

ACW 41, 42 (1982). *St. Augustine, The Literal Meaning of Genesis,* tr. J.H. Taylor.

The report for ACW, 1983-1987, to the 1987 Oxford Patristic Conference announced as forthcoming:

St. Augustine, On Faith and Works, tr. G. Lombardo, OCSC.

Patristic Studies (PSt)

A less well-known series from The Catholic University of America is Patristic Studies, a series of about one hundred volumes, for the most part doctoral dissertations in my own department of Greek and Latin, issued between 1922 and 1966.

The following should be noted:

PSt VIII. *S. Aurelii Augustini Liber de catechizandis Rudibus.* A translation with a commentary, J.P. Christopher

PSt XXIII. *S. Aurelii Augustini De Doctrina Christiana Liber IV.* A Commentary with a revised text, introduction and translation, Sr. T. Sullivan, 1930

PSt LXXII. *S. Aurelii Augustini De beata vita.* A translation with an introduction and commentary, R.A. Brown, 1944

PSt LXXXIV. *Saint Augustine's De Fide Rerum Quae Non Videntur.* A critical text and translation with introduction and commentary, Sr. M.R. McDonald, 1950

PSt LXXXV. *Sancti Aureli Augustini, De Utilitate Ieiunii.* A text with a translation, introduction, and commentary, Bro. S.D. Ruegg, 1951

PSt LXXXVIII. *The Natura Boni of Saint Augustine.* A translation with an introduction and commentary, Bro. A.A. Moon 1955

PSt LXXXIX. *Sancti Aurelii Augustini De Excidio Urbis Romae Sermo.* A critical text and translation with introduction and commentary, Sr. M.V. O'Reilly, 1955

PSt XC. *The De Haeresibus of Saint Augustine.* A translation with an introduction and commentary, L.G. Muller, 1956

PSt XCI. *The Dono Perseverantiae of Saint Augustine.* A translation with an introduction and commentary, Sr. M.A. Lesousky, 1956.

Here should be added:

Frances O'Brien, *De Patientia*, Ann Arbor, Microfilm, 1980

Library of Christian Classics (LCC)

Three volumes of Augustine have been issued by this series:

LCC 6 (1953). *Earlier Writings*, tr. J.H.S. Burleigh
The Soliloquies. The Teacher. On Free Will. On True Religion. The Usefulness of Belief. The Nature of the Good. Faith and the Creed. To Simplician on Various Questions.

LCC 7 (1955). *Augustine: Confessions and Enchiridion*, tr. Albert Cook Outler, 1955

LCC 8 (1955). *Later Works*, tr. J. Burnaby
The Trinity, Books VIII-XV. *The Spirit and the Letter. Ten Homilies on the First Epistle of John.*

Classics in Western Spirituality (CIWS)

Mary T. Clarke, *Augustine of Hippo. Selected Writings*, Paulist Press, 1984. *Confessions*, Books 7, 8, 9, 10; *The Happy Life; Homilies on the Psalms*, 119-122; *Homilies on the Gospel of St. John*, 1 and 12; *Homily 7 on the First Epistle of St. John; On the Trinity*, Books 8 and 14; *On Seeing God* and *On the Presence of God* [= Letters 147 and 148]; *The City of God; The Rule of St. Augustine.*

SBL Texts and Translations, Early Christian Literature Series (SBL)

Paula Fredriksen Landes, *Augustine on Romans: Propositions from the Epistle to the Romans. An Unfinished Commentary on the Epistle to the Romans*, Chico, CA., 1982.

Bibliothèque Augustinienne (BA)

'Oeuvres de saint Augustin' is one of the ongoing projects of l'Institut des Etudes Augustiniennes in Paris. At the 1975 Oxford Congress it reported seventy-two treatises of Augustine already issued. For the present status I refer to the recently issued G. Madec, "Table de la Bibliothèque Augustinienne", dans H. Rochais, *Tables de la Revue des Etudes Augustiniennes, tomes 1(1955)-30 (1984)*, Paris, 1986.

This edition, in Latin and French, of Augustine's works was splendidly planned in ten series and is a standing reproach to all English counterparts:

Première série: Opuscules

BA 1. Introduction générale, F. Cayré et F. Van Steenberghen. La morale chrétienne, tr. B. Roland-Gosselin.
De moribus ecclesiae catholicae et De moribus Manichaeorum. De agone christiano. De natura boni.

BA 2. Problèmes moraux, tr. G. Combès.
De bono coniugali. De coniugiis adulterinis. De mendacio. Contra mendacium. De cura gerenda pro moruis. De patientia. De utilitate ieiunii.

BA 3. L'Ascétisme chrétien, tr. J. Saint-Martin, 1948
De continentia. De sancta virginitate. De bono viduitatis. De opere monachorum.

BA 4. Dialogues philosophiques, Problèmes Fondamentaux. tr. R. Jolivet
Contra Academicos. De beata vita [BA 4 / 1: ed. J. Doignon, 1986]. *De ordine.*

BA 5. Dialogues philosophiques, 2. Dieu et l'Ame, tr. P. de Labriolle.
Soliloquies. De immortalitate animae. De quantitate animae.

BA 6. Dialogues philosophiques, 3. De l'Ame à Dieu, tr. F.-J. Thonnard.
De magistro. De libero arbitrio.

BA 7. Dialogues philosophiques, 4. La Musique, tr. G. Finaert, F.-J. Thonnard.
De musica.

BA 8. La Foi Chrétienne, tr. J. Pegon. Intro., trad., notes par J. Pegon, mise à jour par G. Madec, 1982.
De vera religione. De utilitate credendi. De fide rerum quae non videntur. De fide et operibus.

BA 9. Exposés Généraux de la Foi, tr. J. Rivière
De fide et symbolo. Enchiridion.

BA 10. Mélanges Doctrinaux, 1952, G. Bardy, J.A. Bechaert, J. Boulet
Quaestiones LXXXIII. Quaestiones VII ad Simplicianum. Quaestiones VIII Dulcitii. De Divinatione Daemonum.

BA 11. Le Magistère Chrétien
De catechizandis rudibus. De doctrina christiana.

BA 12. Les Revisions, 1950, G. Bardy
Retractationes.

Deuxième série: Dieu et son oeuvre 1960,
A. Solignac, E. Trehorel, G. Bouissou

BA 13. *Les Confessiones* (Livres I-VII)

BA 14. *Les Confessiones (Livres VIII-XIII)*

BA 15. *La Trinité. I. Le mystère (Livres I-VII).* Intro E. Hendrikx, tr. et notes, M. Mellet et Th. Camelot

BA 16. *La Trinité. II. Les images (Livres VIII-XV).* Tr. P. Agaësse; notes avec J. Moingt

BA 17. Six Traités Anti-Manichéens, R. Jolivet, M. Jourjon
De duabus animabus. Contra Fortunatum. Contra Adimantum. Contra epistulam fundamenti. Contra Secundinum. Contra Felicem manichaeum.

Troisième série: La Grâce

BA 21. La Crise Pélagienne, 1, 1966, tr. G. de Plinval et J. de La Tullaye
Epistula ad Hilarium Syracusanum. De perfectione iustitiae hominis. De natura et gratia. De gestis Pelagii.

BA 22. La Crise Pélagienne, 2, 1975, tr. J. Plagnieux et F.-J. Thonnard
De gratia Christi et de peccato originali. De anima et eius origine

BA 23. Les Premières polémiques contre Julien, tr. J. Chéné et J. Pintard
De Nuptiis et concupiscentia. Contra duas epistolas Pelagianorum.

BA 24. Aux Moines d'Adrumete et de Provence
De gratia et libero arbitrio. De correptione et gratia. De praedestinatione sanctorum. De dono perseverantiae.

Quatrième série: Traités anti-donatistes

BA 28. Traités anti-Donatistes I. Text: R. Anastasi et M. Petshenig; introduction et notes, Y. Congar; tr. G. Finaert et G. Bouisso
Psalmus contra partem Donati. Contra epistulam Parmeniani libri tres. Epistula ad catholicos de secta donatistarum.

BA 29. Traités anti-Donatistes II. Intro et notes, G. Bavaud; tr. G. Finaert
De baptismo libri VII

BA 30. Traités anti-Donatistes III
Contra litteras Petiliani libri tres

BA 31. Traités anti-Donatistes IV
Contra Cresconium libri quattuor. Liber de unico baptismo.

BA 32. Traités anti-Donatistes V
Breviculus collationis cum Donatistis. Ad Donatistas post collationem. Sermo ad Caesariensis ecclesiae plebem. Gesta cum Emerito Donatistarum episcopo. Contra Gaudentium Donatistarum episcopum libri 2 tr. M. Petschenig, G. Finaert, E. Lamirande.

Cinquième série: La Cité de Dieu

BA 33. *De Civitate Dei Libres I-V.* Texte de la 4 ed., B. Dombard et A. Kalb; Introduction et notes, G. Bardy; Trad., G. Combès

BA 34. *De Civitate Dei Livres VI-X.* Dombard et Kalb, Bardy, Combès

BA 35. *De Civitate Dei Livres XI-XIV.* Dombard et Kalb, Bardy, Combès

BA 36. *De Civitate Dei Livres XV-XVIII.* Dombard et Kalb, Bardy, Combès

BA 37. *De Civitate Dei Libres XIX-XXII.* Dombard et Kalb, Bardy, Combès

Septième série: Exégèse

BA 48. *De Genesi ad litteram, 1-7,* 1972. P. Agaësse, A. Solignac

BA 49. *De Genesi ad litteram, 8-12,* 1972.

Neuvième série: Homélies sur l'Evangile de saint Jean

BA 71. *Homélies sur l'Evangile de saint Jean I-XV.* tr., introduction et notes par M.-F. Berrouard, 1969

BA 72. *Homélies sur l'Evangile de saint Jean, XVII-XXXIII.* 1982.

Biblioteca de Autores Christiano (BAC)

As reported by Dr. José Oroz Reta, O.S.A. to the 1983 Oxford Patristic Congress [*ThSt* 45 (1984), 289]: "Despite the fact that its productivity in patristics is little known outside Spain and Latin America ... most impressive is BAC's effort to publish in a bilingual edition the works of Augustine. Thus far 22 volumes have appeared" and "it is now preparing, in agreement with the Federacion de Agostinos Espanoles, the rest of his corpus in 22 more volumes, the whole Augustine project to be completed by 1992.

BAC 1 (10) 1946: 2 ed., 1951; 5th ed., 1979: tr. A.C. Vega General. Introduction, bibliography
Possidius, Vita. Soliloquia. De ordine. De beata vita.

BAC 2 (11) 1946, 6 ed., 1974: tr. A.C. Vega
Confessiones

BAC 3 (21) 1947; 5th ed., 1983: tr. V. Capanaga / E. Seijas / E. Cuevas / M. Martinez / M. Lanseros
Contra Academicos. De libero arbitrio. De quantitate animae. De magistro. De anima et eius origine. De natura boni.

BAC 4 (30) 1948; 3rd ed., 1976: tr. V. Capanaga / T. Prieto / A. Centeno / S. Santamarta / H. Rodriguez
De vera religione. De moribus ecclesiae catholicae. Enchiridion. De unitate ecclesiae. De fide rerum quae non videntur. De utilitate credendi.

BAC 5 (39) 1948; 3rd ed., 1969: tr. L. Arias
De Trinitate

BAC 6 (50) 1949; 3rd ed., 1971: tr. V. Capanaga / A. Centeno / G.E. De Vega / E. Lopez / T. De Castro
De spiritu et littera. De natura et gratia. De gratia Jesu Christi et de peccato originali. De gratia et libero arbitrio. De correptione et gratia. De praedestinatione sanctorum. De dono perseverantiae.

BAC 7 (53) 1950; 3rd ed., 1964: ed. P. Amador del Fueyo
Sermones, 1 (Serm. 1-50)

BAC 8 (69) 1951; 3rd ed., 1967: tr. L. Cilleruelo
Epistolae (epp. 1-140)

BAC 9 (79) 1952; 3rd ed., 1974, tr. V. Capanaga / G. Erce
De diversis quaestionibus ad Simplicianum. De peccatorum meritis et remissione. Contra duas epistulas Pelagianorum. De gestis Pelagii.

BAC 10 (95) 1952; 2nd ed., 1965: tr. A. Del Fueyo
Sermones, 2 (Serm. 51-117)

BAC 11 (99) 1953; 2nd ed., 1971: tr. l. Cilleruelo
Epistolae, 2 (epp. 141-187)

BAC 11b *Epistolae,* 3 (epp. 188-270)

BAC 12 (121) 1954; 2nd ed., 1973. *Tradados morales:* tr. F. Garcia, L. Cilleruelo, R. Floréz
De bono coniugali. De sancta virginitate. De bono viduitatis. De continentia. De coniugiis adulterinis. De patientia. De agone christiano. De mendacio. Contra mendacium. De opere monachorum. De sermone Domini in monte.

BAC 13 (139) 1955; 2nd ed., 1969: ed. Teofilo Prieto
Tractatus in Evangelium Iohannis, 1, s. 1-35

BAC 14 (165) 1957; 2nd ed., 1965; ed. Vicente Rabanal
Tractatus in Evangelium Iohannis, 2, s. 36-124

BAC 15 (168) 1957; 2nd ed., 1965; *Tradados escrituristicos.*
De doctrina christiana. De Genesi contra Manichaeos. De Genesi ad Litteram liber imperfectus. De Genesi ad Litteram.

BAC 16, 17 (171, 172) 1958; 3rd ed., 1977, *De civitate Dei,* tr. S. Santamarta del Rio, M. Fuertes Lanero

BAC 18 (187) 1959; tr. B. Martin Pérez; Escritos bibliocos, 2.
Expositio propositionum ex Epistula ad Romanos. Epistolae ad Romanos inchoata expositio. Expositio Epistolae ad Galantas. Tractatus in epistolam Ioannis ad Parthos.

BAC 19 (235) 1964; ed. Balbino Marti Pérez
Enarrationes in psalmos, 1

BAC 20 (246) 1965; ed. B.M. Pérez
Enarrationes in psalmos, 2

BAC 21 (255) 1966; ed. B.M. Pérez
Enarrationes in psalmos, 3

BAC 22 (264) 1967; ed. B.M. Pérez
Enarrationes in psalmos, 4

The seven-year plan (1983-1992) for completing the series was outlined as follows:

BAC 23-26. Sermones, 3-6
BAC 27-29. Escritos biblicos, 1-3
BAC 30-32. Controversia donatista, 1-3
BAC 33-34. Controversia maniquea, 1-2
BAC 35. Escritos antiarrianos y otros
BAC 36-38. Controversia pelagiana, 1-3
BAC 39-41. Escritos varios, 1-3
BAC 42-43. Indices generales

This numeration was not adhered to, however, in subsequent volumes. BAC 23, *Sermones, 3* (s. 117-83) appeared in 1983. The edition of the sermons is now complete (see below) and the following have recently appeared:

BAC 35.
De perfectione iustitiae hominis. De nuptiis et concupiscentia, 1984. *Contra secundam Iuliani responsionem.*

BAC 36.
Contra Julianum, I-III, tr. L. Arias

BAC 37.
Contra Iulianum, IV-VI, 1985.

Nuova Biblioteca Agostin (NBA)

The NBA series, Latin / Italian, began in 1965 with: e Parte III: Discorsi,

XXV: *Le Confessioni,* based on Skutela's text, revised by M. Pellegrino., tr. C. Carena.

The second volume, XXVI: *Enarrationes in Psalmos* appeared in 1967, tr. R. Minuti. This undertaking was completed, XXVI, 2. XXVI, 3 (Ps. 86-120), tr. T. Mariucci, V. Tarulli, 1976. XXVI, 4 (Ps 121-150), tr. V. Tarulli, indici, F. Monteverde, 1977.

The third, in 1968, was the *Tractatus in Joannem* (124) and *In epistolam Joannis ad Parthos,* tr. E. Gandolfo and J. Madurini / M. Mascolini.

Two volumes of *Letters* followed in 1969, with a lengthy (pp. VII-CIII) and notable introduction by Cardinal Pellegrino, tr. T. Alimonti (epp. 31-184).

De Trinitate was issued in 1973.

Pt. III, Dialoghi, vol. I, appeared in 1970.

Contra Academicos. De beata vita. De ordine. Soliloquia. De immortalitate animae.

Dialoghi, II, 1976

De quantitate animae. De libero arbitrio. De musica. De magistro.

Parte 1 Libri: XVII / 1: Natura e Grazia, 1, 1981, tr. I. Volpi

De peccatorum meritis et remissione et *de baptismo parvulorum. De spiritu et littera. De natura et gratia. De perfectione iustitiae hominis.*

NBA 7 / 1: Matrimonio e Verginita, 1978, tr. M. Palmieri, V. Tarulli, N. Cipriani

De bono coniugali. De sancta virginitate. De bono viduitatis. De adulterinis coniugiis. De continentia. De nuptiis et concupiscentia.

NBA 7 / 2. Libri XVII / 2:

Natura e Grazia, 2, 1981, tr. I. Volpi. *De gestis Pelagii. De gratia Christi. De anima et eius origine;* In appendice Frammenti riuniti de opere pelagiane.

Parte III: Discorsi, 1979-1983

1. *Sermons 1-50,* Sul Vecchio Testamento, 1979, tr. P. Bellini, F. Cruciani, V. Tartulli; indici di F. Monteverde. 11 / 1 Sermons 51-81, Sul Novo Testamento, tr. L. Carrozzi, 1981. 11 / 2 Sermons 82-116, tr. L. Carrozzi, indici di F. Monteverde, 1983.

Piccola Biblioteca Agostiniana (PBA)

PBA 1. *Sant'Agostino. La verginita consacrata,* tr. A. Trapè, 1982

PBA 2. *Sant'Agostino. La dignita del matrimonio,* tr. A. Trapè, 1982

PBA 3. *Mia madre,* ed. A. Trapè, 1983

PBA 4. *La reconciliazione cristiana; prassi, ministero, tensione,* ed. V. Grossi, 1983.

Sources Chretiennes (SC)

SC has wisely decided to avoid duplication of effort with BA and so there is not too much to report:

SC 75, 1961, 1966: (reimpression). *S. Augustin Commentaire de la première Epître de Jean,* P. Agaësse.
SC 116, 1966: *Augustin d'Hippone, Sermons pour la Pâque,* S. Poque.

INDIVIDUAL WORKS

Most of the information on translations provided below in capsule form is already available in the splendid treatment by Trapè in what I will call Quasten 4 [=Augustinian Patristic Institute, Rome, *Patrology,* ed. by A. Di Berardino, with an introduction by Johannes Quasten, Volume IV, *The Golden Age of Latin Patristic Literature.* Translated into English by Rev. Placid Solari, O.S.B., Westminster, Md., 1986, c. VI Saint Augustine by Agostino Trapè, pp. 342-401].

Hereinafter I will be following Trapè's subdivisions, based on Augustine's own tripartite division into books, letters, and treatises, with books subdivided into eight further sections.

Books: 1. Autobiographical

Confessiones

NPNF I. FOTC. LCC VII. LCL, 7 vols., 1957-1972. Clark, CIWS, contains Bks. 6, 8, 9, 10. BA 13, 14. BAC 2 (11), 6th ed., 1974. NBA III, v. 25.

This work continues to challenge new translators:

Augustin. Confessions. Trad. par L. Mondadon, pres. par A. Mandouze, Coll. points, série Sagesse, 31, Paris, 1982.
Bornemann, W. *Augustinus Bekentnisse.* In neuer Ubersetzung und mit einer Einleitung. Repr. Ann Arbor Microfils, 1982.
Blaiklock, *The Confessions of Saint Augustine,* Nashville, Tennessee, 1983 (Bks. 1-X).

Deserving notice is the attractive new Lectio Augustini series from Palermo: *Le Confessioni di Agostino d'Hippona, Le Confessioni,* Libri I-II,

L.F. Pizzolato, G. Ceriotti, F. Di Capitani; Libri III-V, J. Ries, A. Rigobello, A. Mandouze; Libri VI-IX, J.M. Rodriguez, M.G. Mara, P. Siniscalco; Libri X-XIII, J. Pepin, A. Solignac, L. Corsini, A. Di Giovanni.

Retractationes

For text see now CCL 57 (1985), ed. A. Mutzenbecher. FOTC 60 (1968). BA 12. 275-447. *Die Retractationen in zwei Buchern,* C.J. Perl, Paderborn, 1977.

Books: 2. Philosophical

1. *Contra Academicos.*
2. *De beata vita*
3. *De ordine*
4. *Soliloquiorum libri II*
5. *De immortalitate animae.* Text, translation and commentary by C.W. Wolfskeel, Amsterdam, 1977.
6. *Disciplinarum libri* (lost)
7. *De quantitate animae*
8. *De libero arbitrio.* CCL in preparation, ed. G. Vecchi.
9. *De musica.* Zum erstenmahl in deutscher Sprache von C.J. Perl, 3 Aufl., Paderborn, 1962. Also *Agostino Aurelio De Musica,* a cura di Giovanni Firenze, 1969, 687 p.
10. *De magistro*

ACW 12:1; ACW 9: 7, 10; ACW 22: 8. FOTC 4: 5, 7, 9; 5: 1, 2, 3, 4. 59: 10. Clark, CIWS: 2. LCC 6: 4, 8, 10. BA 4: 1, 2, 3; BA 5: 4, 5, 7. BA 6: 8, 10; BA 7: 9. BAC 1 (10): 2, 3, 4; BAC 3 (21): 1, 7, 8, 10.

For 4 see *San Agustin. Soliloquis,* tr. J. Pegueroles, Barcelona, 1982. For 1, 2, 3, 4, 5, see NBA III / 1; for 7, 8, 9, 10, see NBA III / 2 (1976). For 9 see *Augustinus. De musica sacra libri sex.* For 1, see 2, 3, Voss et al, in Bibliothek der Alten Welt series, 1972. See also C.J. Perl, *Aurelius Augustinus, Der Lehrer,* Liber 1, Paderborn, 1959.

Books: 3. Apologetics

1. *De vera religione*
2. *De utilitate credendi*
3. *De fide rerum quae non videntur*
4. *De divinatione daemonum*
5. *Quaestiones expositae contra paganos VI* = ep. 102 [FOTC 18. 149-177]

FOTC 4: 2, 3; FOTC 27: 4. LCC 6: 1, 2. BA 8: 1, 2, 3; BA 10: 4. BAC 4 (30): 1, 2, 3. C.J. Perl, *Nutzen des Glaubens,* 1966.

6. *De civitate Dei*
   BAC 16, 17 (171, 172). FOTC 8, 14, 24 (1950-54). The Loeb Classical Library begun in G.E. McCracken, *St. Augustine, The City of God against the pagans, Vol. I Books I-III,* London, Cambridge, Mass., 1957, is now complete. Vom Gottesstaat, I (Bk. I-X), II (XI-XXII). W. Thimme, Die Bibliothek der Alten Welt, Zurich, 1978.

Books: 4. Dogmatic

1. *De fide et symbolo*
2. *De diversis quaestionibus octoginta tribus liber I.*
   Mosher, FOTC 70 (1982), because of delay in publishing, was unable to utilize CCL 44A (1975) by Mutzenbecher.
3. *De diversis quaestionibus ad Simplicianum libri II.*
   For new critical text see A. Mutzenbecher, CCL 44, 1970.
4. *Ad inquisitionem Ianuarii libri II* (= ep. 54-55)
5. *De fide et operibus liber I*
6. *De videndo Deo liber I* (= ep. 147)
7. *De praesentia Dei liber I* (= ep. 187).
   For 6 and 7 in English, see M.T. Clark, CIWS.
8. *Enchiridion ad Laurentium, or De fide, spe et caritate liber I.*
   In German, P. Simon, *Augustinus, Das Handbuchlein, De Fie, spe et caritate,* Paderborn, 1963. Also J. Barbel, *Aurelius Augustinus. Enchiridion.* Text und Ubersetz., Dusseldorf, 1960.
9. *De cura pro mortuis gerenda liber I*
10. *De octo Dulcitii quaestionibus liber I.*
    For text see Mutzenbecher, CCL 44A, 1975.
11. *De Trinitate libri XV*
    For text, W.J. Mountain / F. Glorie, CCL 50, 1968, 2v.

NPNF 3: 1, 8. LCC 6: 3. LCC 8: 11. FOTC 27: 1. FOTC 70: 2. BA 2: 9; 8: 5; 9: 1, 8; BA 10: 2, 3, 10.

Books: 5. Moral and Pastoral

1. *De mendacio*
2. *Contra mendacium*
3. *De agone christiano*

4. *De catechizandis rudibus*
5. *De bono coniugali*
6. *De sancta virginitate*
7. *De bono viduitatis liber I*
8. *De continentia*
9. *De patientia*
10. *De coniugiis adulterinis*
11. *Contra Hilarium* (lost)

NPNF, 3: 1, 2, 4, 5, 6, 7, 8, 9. FOTC 16: 1, 2, 3, 7, 8, 9. FOTC 27: 5, 6, 10. FOTC 2: 3. ACW 2: 4. PSt VIII: 4. BA 1: 3; BA 2: 1, 2, 5, 9, 10; BA 3: 6, 7, 8. BA 11: 4. BAC 12 (121): 1, 2, 3, 5, 6, 7, 8, 9.

For 4 see *Aurelius Augustinus, Vom ersten katechesischen Unterricht,* hrsg., W. Steinmann, O. Wermelinger, N. Brox, Munchen, 1985. Also, *Agostino d'Ippona La catechesi dei principianti,* tr. Anna Maria Villi, Torino, 1984.

Books: 6. Monastic

1. *Regula ad servos Dei*
   L. Verheijen, *La Règle de Saint Augustin: I. Tradition manuscrite; II Recherches historiques.* Paris 1967. See also "La Règle de saint Augustin: l'état actuel des questions," *Augustiniana* 35 (1985), 193-263 and 36 (1986), 297-303. See now *The Rule of St. Augustine,* tr. R. Canning, introduction T.J. van Bavel, London, 1984. Also Clark, CIWS.
2. *De opere monachorum* liber I
   NPNF 3 and FOTC 16 (Muldowney). BAC 12 (121). R. Arbesmann, *Die Handarbeit der Monche,* 1977.

Books: 7. Exegetical

1. *De doctrina christiana libri IV (O.T.)*
2. *De Genesi adversus Manichaeos libri II*
3. *De Genesi ad litteram liber imperfectus*
4. *De Genesi ad litteram libri XII*

NPNF 2: 1. PSt XXIII: 1. FOTC 2:1. BA 11: 1. BAC 15 (168): 1, 2, 3, 4. BA 48, 49: 4. ACW 41, 42 (1982): 4. M.M. Gorman, CCL edition, of 4, in preparation. German: C.J. Perl, tr., 2v., 1961, 1964: 4.

5. *Locutionum in Heptateuchum libri VII* and *Quaestionum in Heptateuchum libri VII*

6. *Adnotationes in Iob liber I*
7. *De octo quaestionibus ex Veteri Testamento*

For text of 5 and 7 see CCL 33 (1958). Text of 2, CCL in prep., ed. H. Mayr (N.T.)

8. *De sermone Domini in monte libri II*
   For text, CCL 35, 1967, ed. A. Mutzenbecher.
9. *Expositio quarumdam propositionum ex epistola ad Romanos; Expositio epistolae ad Galantas; Epistolae ad Romanos inchoata expositio*
   Paula Fredericksen Landes, *Augustine on Romans*, Chico, CA, 1982. For the *Expos. Ep. ad Galatas* see BAC 18 (187) (1959) 105-191.
10. *Quaestiones Evangeliorum libri II*
11. *De consensu Evangelistarum libri IV*
12. *Expositio epistolae Iacobi ad duodecim tribus* (lost)
13. *Speculum de Scriptura sancta*
14. *Quaestionum septemdecim in Evangelium secundum Matthaeum*

NDNF 6: 8, 11.

Books: 8. Polemical. a. Against the Manichaeans

1. *De moribus Ecclesiae catholicae et de moribus Manichaeorum libri II*
   A critical text by J.K. Coyle for CCL is in preparation. Note also: CSEL 90, *Augustinus, De moribus ecclesiae catholicae,* Rec. Iohannes Bauer
2. *De duabus animabus liber I*
3. *Acta contra Fortunatum Manichaeum*
4. *Contra Adimantum Manichaei discipulum liber I*
5. *Contra epistolam Manichaei quam vocant fundamenti liber I*
6. *Contra Faustum Manichaeum libri XXXIII*
7. *De actis cum Felice Manichaeo libri II*
8. *De natura boni liber I*
9. *Contra Secundinum Manichaeum liber I*

BA 1: 1, 8; BA 4: 1. BA 17: 2, 3, 4, 5, 7, 9. BAC 4: 1; BAC 3: 8. NPNF 3: 1, 2, 3, 5, 6, 8. FOTC 56 (1966): 1. PSt 88:8.

Books: 8. Polemical. b. Against the Donatists

1. *Psalmus contra partem Donati*
2. *Contra epistolam Parmeniani libri III*

3. *De baptismo libri VII*
4. *De unitate Ecclesiae* or *Epistola ad catholicos de secta Donatistarum*
5. *Contra litteras Petiliani libri III.*
   Text for CCL in preparation by J. Van der Speeten.
6. *Contra Cresconium grammaticum partis Donati*
7. *De unico baptismo contra Petilianum liber I*
8. *Breviculus collationis cum Donatistis libri III.*
   [See also SC 194, 195, 224, Actes de la Conference de Carthage en 411, ed. S. Lancel.]
9. *Post collationem contra Donatistas liber I*
10. *De correptione donatistarum liber I* (= ep. 185)
11. *Gesta cum Emerito donatista liber I*
12. *Sermo ad Caesariensis ecclesiae plebem*
13. *Contra Gaudentium donatistarum episcopum libri II*

NPNF 4:10. BA devotes 5 volumes to Traités Anti-Donatistes: BA 28: 1, 2, and 4, BA 29 (1964): 3, BA 30: 5, BA 31: 6, 7, BA 32: 8, 9, 11, 12, and 13.

Books: 8. Polemical. c. Against the Pelagians:
i. Pelagianism in General

1. *De peccatorum meritis et remissione et de baptismo parvulorum ad Marcellinum libri III*
2. *De gratia Novi Testamenti ad Honoratum liber I* (= ep. 140)
3. *De spiritu et lettera ad Marcellinum liber I.* See E. Perl, *Augustinus, Geist und Buchstabe,* (Lat. / Deutsch), Paderborn, 1968.
4. *De natura et gratia liber I*
5. *De perfectione iustitiae hominis epistola sive liber*
6. *Ad Hieronymum presbyterum libri II*
7. *De gestis Pelagii liber I*
8. *De gratia Christi et de peccato originali libri II*
9. *De anima et eius origine libri IV*

NPNF 5: 1, 2, 3, 4, 5, 7, 8, 9. BA 21: 4, 5, 7 (as well as *Epistula ad Hilarium Syracusanum,* that is, ep. 157 = FOTC 20, 319-354). BA 22 (1975): 8, 9; BA 28: 1. FOTC 20, 58-136: 2; FOTC, projected: 4, 7. LCC 8: 3. BAC 6: 3, 4, 8; BAC 9: 1, 7; BAC 35: 5. NBA XVII / 1: 1, 3, 4, 5; XVII / 2 (1981): 7, 8, 9. FOTC 20: 2 (pp. 58-136, 37 chpts.). *Aur. Augustinus. Schriften gegen die Peagianer,* ed. A. Zumkeller, 1, 1971: 1, 3, 4; 3, 1977: 9, 10, 11

Books: 8. Polemical. c. Against the Pelagians:
ii. Against Julian of Eclanum

10. *Contra duas epistolas pelagianorum libri IV*
11. *De nuptiis et concupiscentia libri II*
12. *Contra Iulianum libri VI*
13. *Contra secundam Iuliani responsionem opus imperfectum*

FOTC 35: 12. LCC 8: 12. BA 23: 10, 11. BAC 9 (79): 10; BAC 35 (?): 11, 13. BAC 36 (?), 1985: 12 (Books I-III);. BAC 37 (?): 12 (Books IV-VI). Note also that CSEL has announced as in preparation: *Augustinus, Opus imperfectum contra Iulianum, libri IV-VI,* Rec. Michaela Zelzeh.

Books: 8. Polemical. c. Against the Pelagians:
iii. To the Monks of Hadrumetum and Marseilles

14. *De gratia et libero arbitrio liber I*
15. *De correptione et gratia liber I*
16. *De praedestinatione sanctorum* and *De dono perseverantiae*

FOTC 59: 15. NPNF 5: 14, 15, 16. BA 24: 14, 15, 16. BAC 6 (150): 14, 15, 16. NBA XVII. For 14 and 15 a new CSEL text is in preparation by Werner Heyseller and Peter Schilling; and for 16, one by Gerhard May.

Books: 8. Polemical. d. Against Arianism

1. *Contra sermonem Arianorum liber I*
2. *Collatio cum Maximino Arianorum episcopo*
3. *Contra Maximinum arianum libri II*

For 1, 2, and 3, CCL texts in preparation, ed. H. Oosthout.

Books: 8. Polemical. e. Against the Priscillianists, the Marcionites, and the Jews

1. *Ad Orosium contra Priscillianistas et Origenistas liber I*
2. *Contra adversarium legis et prophetarum libri II*
3. *Tractatus adversus Iudaeos*

For text of 1 and 2 see now CCL 49 (1985), ed. K.D. Daur. For 2 see Ciccarese, MAL 25, 3 (1981) 283-425. FOTC 27:3.

Books: 8. Polemical. f. Against Heresies in General

1. *De haeresibus*

The PST 90 (1965) text of one has been incorporated into CCL 46 (1969).

Letters

NPNF I: 160 letters. FOTC 12, 18, 20, 30, 32 (1951-1956). LCL, ed. Baxter: 62 letters. New discovered: CSEL 88 (1981), ed. J. Divjak. FOTC, projected: tr. Eno. NBA XXII / 2 (1971): ep. 124-184. NBA XXIII / 3 (1974): ep. 185-270. BAC 8 (69), 1-140, 11 (99), 188-270.

Note that a CCL text of the letters is in preparation, ed. K.D. Daur.

Treatises: 1. Commentaries on St. John

1. *Tractatus in evangelium Ioannis*
   NPNF VII: p. 7-452. FOTC, tr. J. Rettig, forthcoming. BA 71 (1969): Homs. I-XV. BA 72 (1982): Homs. XVII-XXXIII. BAC 14 (165), *Tratados sobre el Evangelio de San Juan* (1-35), ed. P. Fr. Teofilo Prieto. CCL text in prep., ed. D.F. Wright.
2. *Tractatus in epistolam Ioannis ad Parthos*
   NPNF VII: 2 (pp. 459-560). LCC 8: 2 (10 homilies). BAC 18 (187), ed. P. Fr. Balbino Martin Pérez. CCL text in preparation, ed. W.J. Mountain.

See also *Saint Augustin commente la Première Lettre de saint Jean.* Intro. par I. de la Potterie et A.G. Hamman, trad. par les Soeurs Carmelites de Mazille, Coll.: Les Pères dans la foi, Desclee de Brouwer, Paris.

Treatises: 2. Homilies on the Psalms

Enarrationes in Psalmos

NPNF 8. ACW 29 (Ps. 1-29), 30 (Ps. 30-37). BA 72, 73. NBA XXV-XXVIII, 1967-1977. BAC 19 (235): Ps. 1-40; 20 (246): 41-75. BAC 21 (255): 76-117; 22 (264): 118-150.

Treatises: 3. Sermones

A complete translation of the Sermons in English is probably our remaining greatest need. The necessary starting point is, of course, Pierre-Patrick Verbraken, *Etudes critiques sur les Sermons authentiques de saint Augustin,* Stenbrugge, 1976. As a complementary study to the present, I am preparing a list of available translations in English of the numbered items in his Fichier Signaletique. I solicit aid in this project because I presume there may be many of them translated in MA dissertations that I may not be aware of. I am also happy to announce that I am in discussion with Villanova University about publishing in FOTC the first fruits of such a project, Sermons, 1-50, based on NBA, 1967.

NPNF 6 contains sermons 51-147 (Benedictine edition), "Sermons on Selected New Testament Lessons."

BAC has recently completed a six-volume edition of the Sermons:

1. BAC 7 (53), 1981, 4th ed., *De veteri testamento,* A. del Fueyo
2. BAC 10 (441), 2nd ed., 1983, *De novo testamento* (Synoptic Gospels), (s. 51-116) [*REAug* 30 (1984) 327 Madec]
3. BAC 23 (443), 1981, *De novo testamento* (John, Acts, Epistles, s. 117-183)
4. BAC 24, s. 184-272B
5. BAC 25 (448) *Sermones sobre los martires* 1984, Pio de Luis, s. 273-338
6. BAC, 1985, Pio de Luis, includes indices, biblical, liturgical and thematic [See review, *Estudio Agostiniano* 20 (1985) 573]

Likewise NBA has produced 29, 30, 1979-1983: *Discorsi* I (1-50), II / 1 (51-81), II / 2 (82-116), tr. P. Bellini, F. Cruciani, V. Tarulli [v. I], L. Carozzi [v. II / 1-2]. There is a lengthy introduction by Cardinal Michele Pellegrino.

The popular French selection, G. Humeau, *Les plus belles sermons de saint Augustin,* published originally 1932-1934, in three vols., has been re-issued, Paris, Etudes Augustiniennes, 1986, and contains 99 of the 363 sermons deemed authentic in the Maurist edition.

CCL is planning, as a successor to C. Lambot, *Sermones de Veteri Testamento* (CCL 41, 1961), a volume of sermons, edd. P. Verbraken and R. Cemeulenaere.

Treatises: 4. Dubia

1. *Sermo de urbis excidio*
2. *Sermo ad catechumenos de symbolo*
3. *Sermo de disciplina christiana*
4. *Sermo de utilitate ieiunii*

All four are contained in CCL 46, 1969, edited respectively by Sr. M.V. O'Reilly, R. Vander Plaetse (2 and 3), and Sr. D. Ruegg.

Dubia

1. *De grammatica*

2. *Principia dialecticae*
3. *Principia rhetorices*
4. *Oratio s. Augustini in librum de trinitate*
5. *Versus de s. Nabore*
6. *Capita or Breviculi*

For 2 above, see B. Darrell Jackson & J. Pinborg (Boston, 1975).

INDEX